D1479525

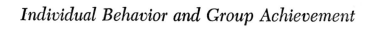

*Individual Behavior and Group Achievement*

# INDIVIDUAL BEHAVIOR AND
# GROUP
# ACHIEVEMENT

## A THEORY

*The Experimental Evidence*

## RALPH M. STOGDILL

*New York* OXFORD UNIVERSITY PRESS 1959

© 1959 by Oxford University Press, Inc.
Library of Congress Catalogue Card Number: 59-5363

Printed in the United States of America

IT IS the purpose of this book to develop a theory of organization achievement. The theory is based on the assumption that the structure and operations of a group can be described in terms of the behaviors of its members in interaction. It is further assumed that the different aspects of group achievement represent transformations of member behavior into forms of value which differ from the input behaviors of the individuals who comprise the membership of the group. The reasonableness of these assumptions is subjected to careful consideration and analysis. The ability of the theory to account for research findings is examined in reference to a large body of experimental literature.

I was forced to undertake the task of theory building because of demands imposed by the research I am doing. Although the struggle for understanding in the sciences that study human social behavior is progressing at a very rapid rate, much of the work tends to be fragmented, dealing with small subsets of problems rather than with integrative theories. At the opposite extreme, the work on large theoretical systems is often defined in such broad terms as to make it immune to experimental test. There is a need for middle range theory that can be tested both in detail and as a total system. Such theory is essential to the design of integrated programs of research.

The proposed theory represents a system that is limited in scope. Although groups are influenced by the larger physical and social environments in which they operate, the theory attempts to explain only what happens inside the group. It represents a

v

segment of theory that exists on the boundaries between psychology and sociology. It is sociological in that it attempts to explain how member roles emerge in the social group. It is psychological in that it seeks to explain respects in which the behavior of the members exerts effects upon the group. It represents a study in social psychology in that it attempts to relate and integrate the two approaches. In doing so, it also attempts to integrate certain theoretical areas in the fields of business organization and management.

The theory is founded on the insights and experimental work of a host of predecessors and contemporaries. Yet there are many respects in which it differs from any theory which attempts to accomplish a similar purpose. It differs first in the strong effort made to define a set of input variables capable of generating all the effects which such a theoretical system seeks to explain. It differs second in the outcomes generated by the system. Group achievement is found to consist of a greater number of factors than is generally believed.

This book is concerned, not with the human drama provided by the interactions between flesh and blood beings, but with the interplay among the concepts of a theoretical system. The concepts, however, refer to measurable aspects of human behavior.

In an attempt to present a complex subject matter as clearly and simply as possible, the discussion has been limited to the development of the general structure and operations of the theory. As a result, a number of subjects usually encountered in an analysis of group functioning receive rather scant attention. The businessman may feel that the group member as a human being concerned with practical problems has been lost in a maze of abstractions. The scientist may feel that a complicated subject has been oversimplified and that important considerations such as leadership, decision making, and communication have been accorded less attention than they deserve. Although these factors are important in a theory of group organization, they represent specific subsets of problems within the larger theoretical system. Any extensive discussion of these subsets would tend to obscure the outlines of the larger system. The complexities of the leadership role alone are so great as to require a book the size of the present one to do justice to the subject.

I am aware that many of my colleagues fear the premature structuring of theories in the social science field. A theory, if overly accepted, can close the door to further inquiry. In answer to this objection, it may be said that the proposed theory uncovers a number of problems which will require years, if not decades, of research in order to provide satisfactory solutions. Also, I believe that a theory should be regarded as a challenge, and that it can be considered useful only if it enables us to go about the task of acquiring new knowledge in a more systematic and effective manner than we could do without it. Therefore, the point of view developed in this book is presented, not as an answer, but as a challenge to continued search.

It is a pleasure to acknowledge my indebtedness to a number of professional colleagues. Foremost among these are Dr. Carroll L. Shartle, who encouraged the undertaking, and Dr. Viva Boothe, who provided valuable support throughout the writing of the book. Valuable criticisms and suggestions relative to single chapters were contributed by Doctors Alvin E. Coons, Paul G. Craig, Donald R. Meyer, Melvin Seeman, Emily L. Stogdill, and Delos D. Wickens. Dr. Mary Alice Price read each of the several versions of the manuscript and suggested revisions chapter by chapter.

I am much indebted to Dr. Jack R. Gibb for his critical reading of the manuscript and for his insightful and helpful contribution to the organization of the book. Mr. Paul O. Whitfield, of Oxford University Press, provided technical assistance, as well as encouragement and support, which I value highly.

It is especially pleasant to acknowledge the assistance of several staff members of the Ohio State University Bureau of Business Research in the processing of the manuscript. Mrs. Martha A. Mounts, Mrs. Esther E. Edgar, Mrs. Mary P. Martin, and Miss Grace Hull proofread the manuscript. Mrs. Sharon Kamada typed and checked the references. Mrs. Mary Dontas, and Misses Bessie Gardikes, Jeanne Deffet, Sherlene Keefer, and Claudette Tinstman typed various sections of the manuscript.

RALPH M. STOGDILL

*Columbus, Ohio*
*November, 1958*

# Contents

*Individual Behavior and Group Achievement*

1

# Introduction

As MAN's knowledge of the physical universe increasingly out-
strips his knowledge of his own nature, he is becoming
more keenly conscious of the importance of group organization
for his own survival. This is particularly true in the United
States, where the selection of leaders and the management of
government has been a responsible concern of citizens throughout the history of the nation. The fact that an individual's
chances of attaining leadership are not circumscribed by law,
custom, or status at birth acts further to sensitize the citizenry
to the factors that operate in organizations of all sizes and kinds.
Thus, it is not surprising, as Myrdal [511] has pointed out, that
a concern with leadership is a distinctly American phenomenon.
Nor is it surprising that group organization as a subject for scientific inquiry is an associated preoccupation.

## Starting Points in Group Theory

Philosophers, from ancient times, have been interested in the
theory of the state. Several have ventured to outline the conditions necessary for the development of utopian societies. However, the accounts of travelers who visited foreign lands and re-
turned with descriptions of the customs and institutions of various peoples caused critical students to question the general applicability of armchair theories. As a distinct science of sociology

emerged, the scientists began the task of classifying various kinds of social groupings, seeking concepts for analyzing and describing them, and studying their structure and action.

Although attempts have been made to explain groups in terms of the concepts used to describe the behavior of individuals, these attempts have generally been regarded as inadequate. Tarde [700], for example, regarded the social order as a summative effect of the behaviors and mental processes of individuals activated by desire and belief. The patterning of behavior and the transmission of patterned behavior from individual to individual was explained by the "law of imitation." Tarde appears to have been struggling to develop a theory with concepts which resemble in some respects those employed in modern theories of learning. Durkheim [186], on the contrary, suggested that although the individual and the social system of which he is a part are mutually interdependent, separate sets of principles are required to account for individual behavior and group behavior. Although sensation and perceptual representation are basic to the transmission of cultural patterns from individual to individual, the social system consists of something more than a sum of individual sensations and representations and is not explainable in terms of similarity and imitation. Rather, solidarity and common purpose in social orders are dependent upon individual differences and the division of labor. It is not similarity but differentiation which is basic to organization.

Cooley's [155] view that the individual does not exist independently of society, nor society independently of the individual, and his conception of the "primary group" as fundamental in shaping the social nature and ideals of the individual led him to analyze society in terms of organization and process.

Mead [478] developed a still more modern conception of sociology. He analyzed social life in terms of the "social act," in which the action of one individual serves as a stimulus to reaction from another. An individual derives his perception of himself from the reactions of others toward him and from his reactions to his own behavior. He acquires the behaviors, symbols, and attitudes of his culture through the process of "taking the role of the other." The internalization of role perceptions and the anticipation of the behaviors and expectations of other persons constitute the essential nature of the socialization process.

Simmel and Weber rank high among the many social theorists whose original contributions have influenced present-day American research and theory. Simmel [644] regarded a group as an interaction system, and he analyzed the interactions of dyads (two-person groups) and triads (three-person groups) in great detail. His concern with the form rather than with the content of social interaction anticipated the recent sociometric methods for the study of groups. Weber [750] developed equally valuable concepts and methods for the study of formal authority structures in large organizations, institutions, and societies.

Among contemporary sociologists, Pareto [524] and Parsons [525] have originated major theories using a small number of input variables or basic concepts for the generation of integrated theories. The theories of Weber [750] and Parsons [525] contain greater potentialities for stimulating research than have as yet been realized because of the difficulties inherent in the design of experiments for large, complex organizations. The theories of Simmel [644], Cooley [155], Mead [478], Moreno [502], and Lewin [415] have exerted a marked influence on contemporary research because of their ready applicability to the study of small groups.

The brief comments presented above are not offered as a survey of sociological theory. They serve to acknowledge several trends of thought which have been influential in shaping the author's own thinking. The history of the theory of groups and of organizations has been summarized by Wilson [771] and Znaniecki [793]. Lundberg [443] discusses the difficulties encountered in the classification and measurement of groups.

Until within the past three decades, research on groups and organizations was concerned primarily with an enumeration or frequency count of the characteristics of the individuals who comprise a group, and with the characteristics of groups as entities. Groups have generally been defined as collections of individuals who, by one criterion or another, must be thought of as belonging together. Smith [653] made a distinct theoretical advance in defining a social group in terms of the mutual perception among the members of their identity and of their ability to operate in a unitary manner upon the environment. Krech and Crutchfield [398] have stated two criteria for determining whether a given set of individuals constitutes a group. The members must be in interaction and must perceive each other as constituting a group. Whereas previous definitions provided merely a basis for counting or describing the numbers and kinds of bodies that make up a group, the new definitions specify operations for determining whether or not a given collectivity may be regarded as a group.

In recent decades, sociological theory has made rapid progress in the direction of developing concepts and definitions which suggest research operations. As a result, theory and research exhibit a rapidly converging parallelism.

## Beginnings in Organization Theory

Urwick [736] has outlined the training, professional careers, and achievements of 70 men whom he regards as the founders of the theory of business organization and modern management practice. Only seven of these men were academicians, but 15 of them held academic posts at one time or another. Several were engaged in military affairs or politics. The remainder were business owners, managers, and consulting engineers.

Beginning about 1900, or a little before, the businessman became conscious of the fact that, with the introduction of powered machines, the skilled craftsman had been replaced in industry by the semiskilled worker. Factories were rapidly increasing in size and complexity. New types of organizations were being created and new methods of management instituted without any established body of theory or standardized method of procedure available to guide the executive.

The businessmen who devoted themselves to the task of writing down their insights and deliberations proved themselves to be highly literate, systematic in the development of principles, and essentially humane in their outlook. They were probably influenced to a very high degree by philosophers, sociologists, engineers, and students of military organization, but few bothered to record the sources of their ideas. However, both Taylor [701] and Diemer [179] cautioned in 1910 against introducing the military type of organization into the industrial situation. Taylor's advocacy of a "functional" type of organization, in which various aspects of a worker's task were supervised by different technical specialists, appears to have stimulated an intense interest in organization theory.

Among the books cited by Urwick [736], the earliest to attempt a theory of organization was that of Lewis [418], published in 1896. Urwick states that this book presented the first known examples in Britain of a monthly profit and loss account, a flow chart, and an organization chart. The first chapter of the book considered problems of organization, division of labor, personnel qualifications of officers, selection of staff, encouragement, contentment of staff, promotions, discipline, staff procedures, manufacturing operations, and the like. Separate chapters were devoted to the duties and management principles that apply to the directors, manager, secretary, accountant, works manager, foreman, and others. These topics sound quite modern in tone.

Taylor [702] and Gilbreth and Gilbreth [250] developed time and motion study as methods of increasing worker efficiency. Kimball [392] in 1913, and Church [139] in 1914, clearly enunciated the principle of specialization of function. Church regarded the functions of design, equipment, operation, comparison, and control as aspects of the organization process. Kimball, however, discussed function as an aspect of managerial responsibility. Kimball's point of view is the one held by contemporary students of organization, as represented by Barnard [35] and Davis [175]. Anderson and Schwenning [10] present a comprehensive historical review of the various points of view that have been advanced by different students of organization. Recent controversy has been concerned, not so much with matters of fact as with points of emphasis. The invaluable technical papers edited by Gulick and Urwick [282] deal largely with problems of organization effectiveness and the specialization of function. In contrast to the latter two authors, Simon [645] emphasizes the importance of interpersonal problems involved in the vertical differentiation of responsibility and authority. The two points of view relative to vertical and horizontal specialization are admirably reconciled in the *Industrial Sociology* of Miller and Form [490].

The scholarly and informed writings of Barnard [35] have influenced the behavior scientist to a far greater extent than those of any other businessman who has dealt with problems of organization theory. The original contributions of Mooney [498], in showing the relationships between vertical and horizontal structure, have received less attention than they deserve. The classical papers edited by Gulick and Urwick [282] provide the foundation for modern organization theory.

The organization theorist has shown individual performance, the differentiation of function, the vertical differentiation of responsibility and authority, and organization effectiveness to be important concepts for a theory of organization.

## Justifications for a New Theory

Since World War II, the concept *interaction* has been relied upon heavily in the development of theories of group functioning. The concepts *role, status,* and *structure* are also used frequently as input variables. A theory of groups developed on the basis of interaction alone fails to account for such factors as group purpose, norms, and integration. A theory that is developed on the basis of concepts such as role and status, the behavioral components of which are unspecified, is better designed to explain group structure than group function, operations, and achievement.

Much of the research which studies the emergence and structuring of member roles seeks to explain different patterns of role enactment not only in terms of interaction, but also by the process of equating interaction with performance. The practice of defining interaction as performance throws a greater explanatory burden on the concept of interaction than it is capable of handling, in terms of any reasonable definition of the concept. This practice also results in the overloading of concepts and incapacitates the resultant theory as a systematizing and explanatory system. Neither performance nor interaction is capable of accounting for the development of group norms and group purpose.

The concept of the role system as a structure of mutual expectations has been largely disregarded as a subject of research. This neglect is in accord with those theories which define the group in terms of interaction alone. Research reports on experimentation with small groups are making increased reference to expectation as an undefined term. However, the concept is seldom introduced as an input variable, but it is called upon after the fact to explain otherwise ambiguous findings.

The deficiencies of existing theories of group organization are most clearly revealed in their inability to account for the findings on group achievement. Morale, conceived as an intervening variable between performance and productivity, is found more often than not in research reports to bear a relationship with productivity which is contrary to that hypothesized. Morale is generally defined as a combination of member satisfaction, group loyalty, and enthusiastic effort. However, it is found under some circumstances that satisfaction and enthusiastic effort are unrelated, which suggests that one or the other cannot be regarded as a measure of morale.

An attempt to develop a new theory would appear to be justified if the theory can suggest the resolution of discrepancies such as those discussed above. Since inadequacies in theory have the effect of slowing progress both in research and in practice, and since troublesome inconsistencies have been apparent in the theoretical literature for some time, there appears to be a need for an adequate theory of group achievement.

## Basic Concepts for a Theory

There are many possible ways of building a theory of groups. What is achieved as an end product is determined to a very large degree by the concepts that are put into the theory at the beginning. The choice of a set of basic concepts is dictated by the scientist's perception of the level of synthesis that can be generated by the input elements. Fortunately, it is not necessary to invent the basic concepts needed for a theory of groups. Attempts have been made to explain group behavior in terms of two well-established bodies of theory. These are learning theory and interaction theory. Of these learning theory is the older and more thoroughly developed.

Learning theorists seek to account for the various factors involved in the patterning and habituation of responses. However, no theory of groups thus far constructed in terms of learning theories has been able to account satisfactorily for the development of group structures. Nevertheless, these theories suggest that the concept of *response* is a useful one for the description of behavior in groups.

Interaction theory, the basic details of which were elaborated by Simmel [644], has been shown by Moreno [502], Bales [28], and many others to provide essential concepts and methodologies for the study of group structure. The concept of *interaction* is also derived from an established body of theory. However, group theories that have been developed on the basis of interaction, or of action and interaction in combination, appear unable to account for a variety of empirical findings relating to group achievement, most of which are contrary to the hypothesized relationships.

Expectation theory has been developed as a branch of learning theory. It represents an alternative solution of the same problems with which learning theories are concerned. Mead [478] and others, however, have shown it to be a useful concept in studying the behavior of groups. The author believes that the use of the concept of *expectancy* in a theory of groups adds a degree of systematizing and reconciling power which has not been achieved by any other solution thus far proposed. It must be recognized, however, that it is not possible to justify in advance the assumptions in terms of which a theoretical system is developed. Such justification can only come from the operation of the system as a totality.

In order to identify the sources of concepts which will be employed in the system being developed, reference has been made to three different bodies of theory. It will be assumed in the following discussion that *performances, interactions,* and *expectations* represent aspects of behavior that are necessary for a description of group behavior. It is not assumed that these three aspects of behavior represent all the factors that need to be taken into account in a complete description of a group's status and its operations in the community. It is obvious that a group's physical resources, its land, buildings, equipment, financial reserve, and the like if it owns such things, represent important factors in its description and identification. But many groups possess few if any physical facilities. They do not operate upon physical values but upon ideational or recreational values. Educational and religious bodies, although they may possess buildings, do not produce, or operate upon, physical values as a primary objective. The values they create are social, cultural, and ideational.

The elements *performance, interaction,* and *expectation* proposed by the writer resemble in many respects those employed by Parsons [525] and later by Homans [331]. Parsons, whose system is concerned with the social order in general, includes actions, interactions, and sentiments among the basic elements of his theory. Since the writer is interested in the development of a theoretical subsystem which is confined to the internal structure and operations of groups, his terms are more narrowly defined than those employed by Parsons and Homans.

Each of the three concepts (performance, interaction, and expectation) must be regarded as representing a complex aspect of behavior. In other words, none of the three characteristics of individual or group behavior described by the elements can be measured in terms of a single scale. The physical scientist uses the term *atom* to represent a basic concept used in building a theoretical system. However, the atom is not considered to be irreducible. Rather, it is regarded as being very complex in structure. Similarly, in developing a theory of groups, the term element will be used to refer to three complex structural concepts which represent aspects of behavior. These concepts were selected by processes of observation, trial and error, and estimates of their utility for the end to be achieved. Each is grounded in an existing body of theory.

## Underlying Assumptions

In beginning any theoretical discussion, it is necessary to make one or more assumptions which can be taken for granted. The argument presented in this book is based on the assumption that a social group can be described in terms of the performances, interactions, and expectations of its members. Many other factors are taken for granted. It is assumed that human beings act, sense, perceive, feel, and learn, and that these experiences determine to some extent their behavior in relation to other persons. It is assumed that a social order exists, and that the nature of the social order determines to some extent the behaviors of individuals as well as the kinds of groups that are formed in a given culture. It is recognized that the nature of a group will be determined by the kinds of people who make up its membership as well as by the social environment of which it is a part. The theory does not seek to systematize or explain these assumptions. However, it is obvious that the theory can be sound only insofar as the assumptions on which it is based are valid.

No attempt will be made to explain the behavior of man in general. That is the task of the science of psychology. Nor will it attempt to explain the nature of human society in general. That is the task of the science of sociology. The proposed theoretical system is concerned only with the group and what happens inside it. It is concerned with the individuals who make up the group membership, their relationships to each other, and their joint action as an entity. It seeks to isolate and define basic dimensions of group organization as a foundation for the development of a theory of group achievement and to show how these variables operate to generate group structure and achievement.

## Structure of the Theoretical System

An organized group may be regarded as an input-output system in unstable balance. Since a group is an open system (i.e. exchanges members and values with its environment), it is difficult to substantiate the assumption of absolute input-output equality. However, a high degree of equivalence may be assumed. In order to increase output above a standard level, it appears necessary to increase input energy or values.

More than one irreducible input variable is needed to generate a theoretical system. The choice of a set of input variables is justified only by the system which it generates. The input variables selected for the present system are performances, interactions, and expectations. Performances and expectations are aspects of individual behavior. Interactions are aspects of interpersonal behavior. It is assumed that these three aspects of member behavior are sufficient to generate a theory of organization achievement.

The structure of the theoretical system is shown in Figure 1.

Figure 1. Structure of a Theory of Organization Achievement

| MEMBER INPUTS | MEDIATING VARIABLES | | GROUP OUTPUTS |
|---|---|---|---|
| *Behaviors* | *Formal Structure* | *Role Structure* | *Achievement* |
| Performances | Function | Responsibility | Productivity |
| Interactions | Status | Authority | Morale |
| Expectations | (Purpose, Norms) | (Operations) | Integration |
| | GROUP STRUCTURE AND OPERATIONS | | EFFECTS |

Performances, interactions, and expectations are shown as behavior inputs. These variables are attributes of individuals, singly and in interaction. The effects of these behavior variables in combination are exhibited in the form of role differentiation and role performance, or in group structure and operations. Role structure and group operations are properties of groups and result from the interrelated performances, interactions, and expectations of the members. The end effects of these personal and interpersonal behaviors, mediated through group structure and operations, are exhibited in the form of group achievement. The different aspects of achievement are productivity, morale, and integration.

The dominant direction of effects between the four sets of variables represented in Figure 1 is conceived as moving from left to right. However, feed-back effects are exerted by the different sets of variables, and the variables in each of the four segments not only interact with each other but also exert forward and backward effects upon the variables in each of the other segments in the chart. The variables listed under Role Structure and Formal Structure may be conceived as representing merely the structuring and patterning of the input performances, interactions, and expectations which bring about group achievement. Furthermore, if the group is not operating upon physical values of any sort, the group achievement represents merely a modification or transformation of member performances, interactions, and expectations in terms of group productivity, integration, and morale. When the group operates upon physical inputs and creates material values, these must be reckoned with in evaluating achievement.

This generalized statement of the structure of the system represents an extreme oversimplification of the nature of, and relationships between, the factors involved.

## Plan of the Book

Chapters 2, 3, and 4 define the input variables that are needed to develop a theory of group achievement. These variables (interactions, performances, and expectations) are regarded as behaviors of the group members, individually and in reaction to each other. The transformation of the input behaviors into group structure and operations is described in Chapter 5. Chapter 6 describes the effects of the individual input be- haviors, mediated through group structure and operations, in pro- ducing the complex and interrelated achievements of the group.

An attempt is made to develop fully the basic concepts needed for the theory, but no effort is made to elucidate every nuance of meaning and relationship that has ever been mentioned in the theoretical or experimental literature. Simplification of the theoretical discussion for the sake of clarity and understanding is accomplished at the expense of numerous by-products and sub- ordinate outcomes that are specific to particular kinds of groups. The discussions of research are permitted to carry some of the burden of illuminating the theory, showing the richness and complexity of the subject matter, and pointing out some of the limiting conditions that apply to the general findings. This procedure has the positive advantages of narrowing the field of speculation and of increasing the area of experimentally es- tablished information.

Theory and research are discussed separately in various chap- ters. It is not the author's intent to imply by this separation that theory and research have progressed independently of each other. However, there appear to be valid reasons for distinguish- ing between theory and research. Much of the research to be considered was conducted to support theories which differ markedly from the one presented in this book. The author be- lieves that the research which he reports has been conscientiously performed and, within the limitations of the design and sam- pling of each experiment, must be accepted as sound. Since some may doubt that the same experiment can lend equal sup- port to various theories and subtheories which differ in their basic premises, it seems desirable to separate the discussion of theory from the evaluation of research.

Whenever a number of related experiments is available, the studies are described seriatim and are examined to isolate any generalizations that are supported in common by the various experiments. This procedure, while somewhat tedious, increases confidence in the findings that receive consistent support and reveals various limiting conditions that need to be considered.

It will be noted in some chapters that previous research does not emphasize the same factors that receive emphasis in the theoretical discussion. However, except for a serious deficiency in the amount of research bearing on group morale, the experimental evidence is found to lend support to the theory.

# 2

## Interaction and Group Structure

Social interaction requires the presence of two or more individuals who are responding to each other. Although it is based upon the behaviors of individuals, it is not a characteristic of an individual. Social interaction is an interpersonal rather than a personal characteristic of behavior. It takes place in a group situation. In fact, interaction may be regarded as the essential concept for a definition of social groups.

The existence of a group is assumed when people are observed doing things together. However, since one could list thousands of activities that people do in groups, it would be very cumbersome to try to define a group in terms of each of the different kinds of things that people do together. It would be even more cumbersome to define a group in terms of the persons who are members of it. Each particular group would need to be described separately. An additional difficulty would be encountered when a group is observed in which old members drop out and new members enter under such circumstances that, in spite of the turnover in membership, we are able to identify it as the same group today that it was yesterday. The fact that the membership may change while the identity of the group remains the same suggests that we need a definition which is independent of the physical bodies that constitute the membership of a group. Further, the concept of "doing things together" is so general that it seems to imply a number of things that we do not wish to include in a precise definition of a group. It might be argued that people who are walking along the street in the same direction are doing things together and, thus, should be regarded as a group. But that is not what we mean to imply by "doing things together." It takes more than being in the same neighborhood at the same time to make a number of people into a group. We mean to imply that a special relationship exists between people who are doing things together so as to constitute a group, and that the relationship is more than accidental or instantaneous in duration. We look to see whether this duration is the result of the successive reactions of the members to each other. If we judge this to be the case, we are likely to assume that the members constitute a group.

## Definition of Group

Sociologists use the term *interaction* to describe the situation in which the reaction of any member is a response to the reactions of another member. In order for interaction to take place it is necessary for physical bodies to be present in order to carry on the interactions. However, the presence of physical bodies does not in itself guarantee the existence of a group. Interaction does appear to characterize a group. Since we need a general definition — one that will characterize a group wherever it may be found — we shall define a group in terms of interaction.

*A group may be regarded as an open interaction system in which actions determine the structure of the system and successive interactions exert coequal effects upon the identity of the system.*

This means that the structure of the system is determined solely by the actions of the members and that the identity (continuance) of the system is dependent upon the interactions taking place rather than upon the presence within the structure of any specified member.

By *interaction* is meant that, in a system composed of two members, A reacts to B and B reacts to A in such a manner that the response of each is a reaction to the behavior of the other.

By *open system* is meant that, within limits necessary to maintain interaction, members may leave or enter the system without destroying the identity of the system.

By *structure* is meant that the system is so differentiated or ordered that member A is not identical with member B, and the reaction of A to B is not identical with the reaction of B to A.

By *identity* is meant the continuity of interaction which permits the system to be recognized as the same group during successive periods of observation.

It is necessary to distinguish carefully between reaction and interaction. Reaction is a one way process which may be represented by the statement, "A responds to B." In this statement, we are interested in the behavior (reaction) of A, while our interest, if any, in B is incidental to the fact that he serves as a stimulus to the behavior (reaction) of A. Interaction, on the other hand, is a process which involves the reactions of two or more persons to each other.

It is not necessary to assume that the reaction of A to B is the same as the reaction of B to A in an interaction system. That is, the reaction of A to B may be one of threat or aggression, while the reaction of B to A may be one of submission or retreat. However, it is necessary to assume that, in an interaction system composed of members A and B, the effects of A and B in interaction are the same as the effects of B and A in interaction for the identical instant of interaction. That is, if A threatens and B retreats in response to the threat, the effect is the same as saying that B retreats in response to the threat of A. Thus, for every statement of interaction there may be stated an inverse which is its equivalent. For example, interaction AB is equivalent in its effects to interaction BA. This is true, for the two statements:

A retreats, B advances and
B advances, A retreats

are descriptions of the same (identical) interaction.

The content of an interaction is to be found in a description of the actions and reactions of the participants. A complete description may require a report from the participants of their own reactions and of their perceptions of the incident, including their perceptions of the actions of the other participants. Interaction, as a concept or unit of analysis, derives its specific content from a description of still smaller components — the actions and reactions which constitute the interaction. Each action and each reaction may be regarded as a response or performance. This fact does not detract in any way from the status or power of the interaction concept as a unit of analysis.

It is the distinction between reaction and interaction which gives us insight into the advantages to be gained from defining a group in terms of interaction. Since the reaction of A to B is not identical with the reaction of B to A, the reactions of these two members will exert different effects upon the structure of the interaction system. But since the interaction of A with B is merely an inverse description of the interaction of B with A, then interactions AB and BA must necessarily exert identical effects upon the identity of the system. Similarly, it is apparent that although interactions ABC, A.BC, and AB.C exert equivalent effects upon the identity of the system, they describe different structures of interaction.

In a group consisting of more than two members, it is possible for subgroups to be formed. A subgroup is an interaction system within a larger interaction system. In a group consisting of members A, B, and C, a subgroup composed of members B and C may interact with member A. In this event, the interaction of member A with subgroup BC and the interaction of subgroup BC with member A exert co-equal effects upon the identity of the system. This is necessarily true, since interaction A.BC is merely the inverse description of interaction BC.A.

These operations, which are directly suggested by the definition, are rather obvious. However, there are other, less obvious, operations which also aid in defining a group. If a group is just a group and not a particular kind of group, then it should be possible to demonstrate that various combinations and recombinations of subgroups within the system may be made without altering the identity of the group. Thus, insofar as the identity of the group is concerned, A.BC, AB.C, B.AC, BA.C, C.AB, and CA.B are equivalent in their effects, even though each represents a structure which differs from that of the others. In a larger group, still more complicated subgroups may be formed without altering the identity of the group. That is, interactions may take place between individual and individual, between individual and subgroup, and between subgroup and subgroup. In addition, individuals as well as subgroups may interact independently of other individuals or subgroups within the system. Thus, A and B may interact independently of C. Subgroup AB may interact with subgroup CDE independently of subgroup FG.

Since a group is by definition an open system, it can be demonstrated that in group ABC one of the members, A, may leave the system without destroying the identity of the group so long as any two members, BC, remain to carry on the continuity of interaction. Further, a member D may join the group so that the continuity of interaction is maintained by members BCD. In other words, the members of the group are potentially replaceable without destroying the identity of the group.

To recapitulate, the operations which define a group are the demonstration that (1) an interaction system exists; (2) it is an open system; (3) successive interactions maintain the identity (continued existence) of the system; and (4) the structure of the system is determined by the actions and reactions of its members.

## Group Identity: Performance and Interaction

The members tend to perceive a group as a collection of individual members rather than in terms of abstract structures. Furthermore, in a very large group, the perceptions of the members are more or less limited to the subgroups of which they are members. The personalization of perception is not surprising when it is realized that face-to-face interaction is an immediate, involving, and often demanding process. Members are perceived as pleasant, co-operative, hard to get along with, and so on. These reactions are personal, and often involve considerable feeling. The immediate, personalized experience tends to obscure the perception of the organization as an abstract process and structure.

The members of a group may vary as to age, sex, appearance, intelligence, training, strength, skill, and the like. However, groups that are quite homogeneous in these respects may be observed. Hemphill [314] uses the term "homogeneity" to identify the group dimension that describes the degree of uniformity among the personal characteristics of the members. Cattell [116] uses the term "population traits" to describe the same dimension.

A member's age, sex, physical appearance, and the like, identify him as an individual. These characteristics do not identify him as a participant in any particular group, but characterize and differentiate him as an individual in all the groups to which he belongs. It must be admitted that a description of the personal characteristics of the members may constitute an important set of facts about a group. It must be recognized, however, that these facts describe the members as aggregates of individuals. They do not describe the behaviors and interactions that differentiate a group from an aggregate.

A group is identified by factors which define the system. That is, the group is identified by the fact that successive interactions give the system continuity through time. The identity of the group is further grounded in the fact that each action and each reaction may be regarded as a performance that identifies the actor as a member of the group. The personal characteristics of the members do not contribute to the definition of a group as such, but they do serve to differentiate one group from another.

Interaction exists only so long as action and reaction exist. There is no interaction apart from the reactions of the members to each other. An act by one member may initiate interaction. The reaction of the same or of another member may terminate interaction. It is apparent that the actions and reactions of the members do not necessarily exert equivalent effects upon the identity of the system. Certain acts bring the group into being. Further actions and reactions keep the group going, while others' reactions terminate or destroy the group. Interaction describes a relationship. The components of this relationship are action and reaction.

The definition of a group is not dependent upon the manner of its coming into existence, nor upon whether the members associate voluntarily or involuntarily. Furthermore, it is not affected by the fact that members may be removed from or injected into the system by external force. The definition holds provided that interaction continues after such additions and subtractions are made. In other words, the physical composition of, and the reactions of the participating agents in, an interaction system may be altered by external forces without destroying the identity (continuity) of the interaction system.

The formulation of a useful definition of a group does not solve all the problems concerned with isolating social groups. It is not always easy to determine whether the members of an aggregation are in mutual interaction or which members are involved in interaction. The boundaries of groups often appear to be vague and indeterminate. Another difficulty encountered in the application of the definition of a group involves the continuation of interaction. How long must interaction continue before a system can be called a group? If an interaction system splits into two parts, each of which continues its separate and independent identity as an interaction system, which is to be identified with the original group?

These difficulties are not confined to the definition. They are characteristic also of the thing defined. Aggregations may form and disperse with such rapidity that it is difficult to determine whether or not they were groups. The congregation of a church may split into factions, one of which withdraws to form a separate congregation. In such instances, one faction is likely to claim to be the "parent body" and to retain the name of the original group, while the dissenters may add the word "reformed" to the title of their group in order to differentiate it from the parent group. If both factions lay claim to being the parent group, then a determination of the facts may require the application of empirical operations. Facts so obtained must be evaluated judgmentally. It remains an act of judgment to determine whether the operations being performed constitute a definition of the event upon which defining operations are being performed.

Physical objects such as chairs and beds exhibit such well-recognized characteristics that the operations for defining them might appear to be quite clear and unequivocal. Nevertheless, one may encounter objects in furniture stores which would put quite a strain on the operations designed to determine whether they are beds or chairs. It is the responsibility of the observer to decide whether or not a set of operations accurately defines the event under observation.

The definition of a group in terms of its continued existence may appear to be equivalent to saying that "a group is a group so long as it is a group." This equivalence is implied by the definition, but something additional is also implied. Since a group is an interaction system, there is likely to be constant change in the actions and reactions that are taking place. Nevertheless, we are able to observe a group today and identify it as the same group that we observed yesterday or the day before. We are able to make this identification by virtue of the fact that the interaction system exhibits stability through time. The identification of a group must account for the fact that interactional stability is based upon a substructure of constant change. This continuity in the presence of change is explained on the basis of the assumption that successive interactions (but not successive actions and reactions) exert co-equal effects upon the identity of the system.

## Groups of Minimum Structure

Most of the human and animal groups that come under observation appear to be differentially ordered. It seems probable that one will seldom encounter in nature a group that is totally unstructured. A school of minnows swimming freely at the edge of a stream appears upon casual observation to offer the nearest approach to an undifferentiated interaction system; they appear to exchange positions in the system freely. But the zoologist who observes such things systematically might tell us that some members occupy positions in the system that are not freely interchanged with other members.

A group of minimum structure is one in which each member may successively exchange positions with every other member without destroying the identity of the system. Among human aggregations, a group of children "taking turns" in their play would appear to meet our conception of a system in which the positions are freely interchangeable. This does not necessarily imply that the positions in the system are equivalent. In fact, the taking of turns suggests a differentiation in the nature of the positions, such that some posts are more highly valued than others. It is a matter of common observation that groups exist in which the positions of the members cannot be interchanged without disrupting the system.

Positions become differentiated in a group because the members exhibit characteristic differences in action and reaction; that is, they differ in the extent to which they initiate interaction and acquiesce to interaction initiated by others. The *position* of a member in an interaction system is defined by that predictability of action and reaction which operates as a stimulus to predictable reaction by other members of the system. Each position is defined in relation to the total system. When this definition is applied to the position of each member, it becomes apparent that the structure of an interaction system is determined by the reciprocal actions and reactions of its members.

Although the structure of an interaction system is determined by the actions and reactions of its members, action is not completely determined by the structure of the system. Individuals are free to initiate action, and they react differently to actions initiated by others. A structured system increases the area of freedom for its members because the predictable individual differences in performance which define the positions in the system permit areas of action (initiative) which are not responses to the actions of other members.

An interaction system defines an area of freedom of action for each member. Freedom is minimal in a group of minimum structure. Since a group can exist only so long as the members remain in the system and continue to interact with each other, it imposes constraints upon the behavior of the individual. The structure and identity of the group are dependent upon the continuance of action and reaction. Individual freedom of action in a group of minimum structure is limited to staying in the system or leaving the system. With maximum group structure, individual behavior becomes entirely determined or controlled by the system. The individual has no freedom except that of acquiescence to action initiated in the determining position in the system. We should expect to find, then, that freedom of action is at a maximum under moderate degrees of group structure.

Although a structured group provides a greater degree of freedom than does a group of minimum structure, both observation and research results suggest that after an optimum degree of structure is attained, additional increases in structure tend to decrease freedom of action. What constitutes an optimum degree of structure for a given group is a matter that must be determined empirically.

A group that is nothing but a group exists only so long as interaction is taking place. Observation suggests that groups of minimum structure exist, if at all, only for very short periods of time. In fact, the concept of a group of minimum structure is useful for theoretical purposes rather than for its close correspondence with objective events. The concept merely points to the fact that the identity of a group is dependent upon the continuation of interaction. Interaction is not necessarily self-perpetuating.

Groups are observed to exist over periods of time during which no interaction among the members is taking place. It can be shown that these are groups of more than minimum structure. They exhibit differentiated structures of positions and a common intent among their members to reassemble for the purpose of continuing their activities. The latter of these characteristics cannot be explained on the basis of the interaction concept. Group intent appears to be based upon intermember expectation.

## Individual Differences in Interaction

It has been stated that interaction is not a characteristic of individuals. Nevertheless, it can be observed that individuals differ in their capacity or inclination to enter into interaction with other persons. Certain individuals appear to be at ease with themselves only when they have the companionship of other persons. At the opposite extreme are to be found persons who exhibit acute embarrassment in any new social situation.

Some individuals interact effectively in pair relationships, others are effective in small groups, and still others are at their best when confronted by large groups of people. There are persons who interact comfortably only with their superiors, others with their peers, and others with their subordinates. Perhaps the most highly valued person is the one who is able to interact effectively with a wide range of people — the person who is "all things to all men."

Individuals may be observed to differ from time to time in their tendencies to interact. Some persons interact freely and comfortably in informal social situations but not in working situations. Others interact effectively in formally structured situations but not in informal social gatherings.

The origination of structure in social groups is made possible by the fact that the individual members of a group do not exhibit identical performances while interacting with their fellow members.

## RESEARCH ON INTERACTION

The research on social interaction does not closely parallel the theory being presented. The primary reason for this discrepancy is that many experimenters fail to differentiate between performance (action and reaction) and interaction. They describe interaction in terms of the performances of the group members. The results of their research will be described in other chapters.

In the theory being developed, interaction is regarded as a structure of relationships between persons. The content, or specific nature, of the actions and reactions involved is regarded as descriptive of performance rather than of interaction. This view is in accord with the practice of those experimenters who are working in the fields of sociometry and mathematical models. The content of interaction is not regarded as essential to the description of structure.

Despite the lack of correspondence between the definitions of interaction as required by theory and as utilized for experimental purposes, the research results throw much light on the nature of the interaction process. This fact will become apparent as the discussion progresses. It is very difficult when considering any one element of group behavior separately to show the richness of the factors involved in group life. It is only when interactions, performances, and expectations are considered in combination that the complexities of individual behavior patterns and group structures are revealed.

## Mathematical Group Theory and the Definition of Groups

The definition of interaction proposed for the present theory is based on a conception of interaction which has its origin in mathematical group theory developed by Galois [18, 98, 108]. This theory defines the criteria for determining whether or not a given mathematical system may be regarded as constituting a group.

Given a mathematical system of $n$ elements upon which a specified operation is to be performed, the system is a group if the following conditions are satisfied.

1. If any two elements are combined by the specified operation, then the result of the operation must be an element of the system. That is, if $a$ and $b$ are elements of G and the operation to be performed is multiplication, then $ab$ is an element of G.

2. The associative law must hold in the multiplication of the elements of the system. If *a*, *b*, and *c* are the elements of G to be operated upon, then $a(bc) = ab(c)$.

3. The system must contain an element known as the identity element, which when combined with any other element in the system leaves that element unchanged. That is, if *a* is an element of G, then there exists an element *i*, such that $ai = ia = a$. If multiplication is the operation to be performed then the identity element for all numbers, except 0, is 1.

4. There must exist for each element in the system its inverse, such that if the element is combined with its inverse by the specified operation, the result is the identity element. That is, if *a* is an element of G, then there is an element $a^{-1}$ such that $aa^{-1} = a^{-1}a = i$. When multiplication is the operation, the inverse of an element is its reciprocal.

Other operations besides multiplication, addition, and the like can be performed to define a group. The operations on an ordered series of objects or numbers that can be rotated through successive permutations until the original order of the series is restored, the final operation which restores the original order of the series being the identical operation, can be regarded as a group.

It is not suggested that men behave as do numbers or inanimate objects. Nevertheless, Galois theory suggests a useful approach to the formulation of a theory of social interaction. Harary and Norman [294] have demonstrated that graph theory is applicable to the development of interaction theory. Graph theory is a special case of the more general Galois theory. Kemeny, Snell, and Thompson [384] have demonstrated the relevance of the theory of "sets" and of "chains" to the study of social structure.

Moreno and Jennings [503] and Bronfenbrenner [86] developed statistical methods for assigning scores to persons that indicate the magnitude of their individual contributions to an interaction system. The methods of matrix algebra, as employed by Forsyth and Katz [219], Festinger [198], Luce [439], and others, seem best suited to the task of representing structure. These methods are particularly useful for isolating the structure of "cliques" in a group. A clique is a subgroup of persons who interact in terms of their mutual interactions with each other. A clique is to be differentiated from a subgroup of positions. Since a position is defined in terms of the predictable regularity of performances, a subgroup of positions is not described or measured in terms of interaction alone. Riley, Riley, and Toby [564] have shown that the method of scale analysis can be used for the measurement of social structure. Gardner and Thompson [235] have used psychophysical scaling methods for measuring sociometric status.

The literature on mathematical models of group structure is accumulating at a very rapid rate. Although Hertz and Livingston [320] and Petersen [537] find that these studies offer more in the way of hope for the future than of realized achievements, their importance can hardly be overestimated. Luce and Raiffa [440] have compiled an excellent evaluation and summary of game theories. The pioneering work of Dodd [181], Zipf [792], Rashevsky [551], Rapoport [550], Simon [646], Lienau [421], Wiener [767], Miller [492], and Von Neumann and Morgenstern [742] in the development of generalized mathematical models of social behavior have provided a valuable stimulus to the group theorist. It is the author's belief that the mathematical models of games and decision-making, despite their sophistication, are incapable of generating a full-bodied theory of group organization. The economic models described by Allen [6] appear to provide a more adequate starting point for the organization theorist who is interested in systems with complex inputs and complex outputs.

## The Origins of Structure

It is an interesting, if futile pastime, to speculate on the origin of human social institutions. We know that organization did not originate with man. All animal species exhibit some sort of group life. Allee's [4] summary of the biological literature indicates that even one-cell organisms tend to cluster in colonies and that the survival of the individual organism is facilitated not only by an optimum population density but by the fact that the presence of a preceding generation conditions the immediate environment for its progeny. Allee also observes some structuring of social interaction in terms of dominance or leadership among vertebrates in general. This structuring is most evident to the casual observer among species that maintain a continuous group or herd life.

Barker [32] has demonstrated that a group of strangers, after a few moments of being acquainted, exhibits a high degree of unanimity, not only in describing each other's behavior and appearance but also in choosing members for seatmates. Further, expressions of choice are highly related to descriptions of behavior and appearance. Suchman [692] found that the members of small experimental groups, after 30 minutes of interaction in the performance of a task, were most accurate in estimating the expressed feelings of those other members toward whom they reacted favorably. Tagiuri, Blake, and Bruner [696] also report that the members of experimental groups are able to estimate each other's expressed feelings with a higher degree of accuracy than expected by chance variation. These studies suggest that differential structure is perceived almost immediately by the members of a newly created group.

Newcomb [520] studied the structure of intermember choices among 17 men who lived in the same house. It was found that the distribution of an individual's liking of his associates is related to their liking of him. It was still more highly related to his estimates of their liking him. Since the relationship is as high for non-roommates as for roommates, it cannot be attributed to propinquity or communication. Individuals in close agreement about the 15 others clearly tended to like each other. Frequency of interaction, personality characteristics, and attitude agreement were also found to predict interpersonal attractiveness. The relation between an individual's liking of his associates and their liking of him was as high at the end of four weeks as at the end of four months.

Members of animal as well as human groups exhibit a remarkable sensitivity to the structure of groups. Gronlund [266] has shown that members of human groups not only have a fairly accurate perception of their own positions but also of the positions of other members in a group. If the structure is in doubt, it can usually be observed that certain members continue to test the structure until a stable ordering of positions is accomplished. Murchison [509] observed this effect among barnyard fowl. Allee [5] reports the same process to characterize mammalian groups in general. These results suggest that groups of minimum structure tend to gain structure.

The ideal, if it can be called such, of a totally unstructured group, community, or society is based on an erroneous conception of the nature of interaction. A number of human beings cannot interact for any period of time without one of them, because of his greater spontaneity or attractiveness in some other respect, becoming differentiated from others. Moreno [502] has accumulated a convincing mass of data which enables him to state as a general principle that the "income of emotional choices" is unevenly divided among the members of a group regardless of its size or type, such that comparatively few members receive the larger share of available choices. As groups increase in size, the highly chosen tend to receive an increased proportion of choices due to the greater availability of choices, thus widening the gap between the overchosen and the underchosen.

Jennings [364] studied the sociometric choices among 133 girls in a training school. When the girls expressed their choices for "living with" and "working with," it was found that the choices showed a very uneven distribution among the girls who were chosen. Approximately 20 per cent of the girls were designated as overchosen, and 20 per cent as underchosen. The overchosen received 43 per cent of the total choices made, while the underchosen received fewer than 3 per cent of the total choices. In the choice of leisure time partners, 28 per cent were also chosen to live with, but only 8 per cent chosen for leisure time were also chosen as work partners. The subjects actually contacted approximately six times as many subjects on the average as they chose as work or living partners. It is apparent that the structure of choices and the structure of interactions are not identical.

Price [547] reports that the distribution of choices in a group differs in relation to the criterion for which the members express their choices. In a group of 223 members, 15 per cent received no choices whatsoever for roommate, whereas 60 per cent of the members received no choices for leader. The roommate choices tended to be more evenly divided among the members, with a few members receiving a disproportionately large number of choices. The leadership choices tended to concentrate upon a small number of members. It is apparent that a stricter criterion was employed in choosing leaders than in choosing roommates.

Since groups become structured in such a manner that only one or a few members occupy the more highly valued positions, it is not surprising that conflict and tension are sometimes involved in the process of achieving structure. However, the fact that structure is readily perceived and stabilized when once acknowledged tends to reduce conflict among the members. Guetzkow and Gyr [280], observing adult conference groups in business and government, noted the development of "substantive" conflicts relative to the subject to be discussed, and "emotional" conflicts relative to the resolution of structure. It was observed that consensus is achieved in both types of conflict when (1) there is little expression of self-oriented need; (2) expressed needs are satisfied in the meeting; (3) the need for unified action is recognized; and (4) problem solving is understandable and orderly.

Heinicke and Bales [308] report that tension and conflict are involved in the development of structure in experimentally created groups given the task of discussing a social problem and preparing a written solution. Initially the members exhibit a high degree of task-oriented performance, but this preoccupation with the task decreases in later sessions. Comparatively small amounts of disagreement and tension are exhibited in the first session, but these show a sharp increase in the second session and thereafter decline. Agreement declines sharply from an initial high level, but this is compensated for by an equally sharp rise in solidarity and tension release. These changes in rate of performance are paralleled by changes in interaction. The groups differed in the extent to which they became structured in terms of sharply differentiated positions in the system. The second session was generally the critical one for the differentiation and establishment of structure. This was especially true for the more highly task-oriented groups and for those members of the groups who were in direct competition relative to the initiation of interaction and determination of group operations. After the crisis had passed, and structure was established, those members who had achieved high status tended to initiate fewer of the performances which enabled them to achieve their positions in the group. Their positions continued to be acknowledged by other members, and their influence on group operations persisted, but, once having established their positions, they were able to permit other members to play a more active role without any loss of status. The more highly structured groups were more efficient than the less highly structured groups and were better satisfied with their groups and with the solutions achieved.

The last two studies described above indicate that the process of arriving at structure develops not only tensions but also mechanisms for reducing tensions. It is also apparent that interaction always involves some substantive content, which is described in terms of the performances of the members.

## Structure Within Structure

The differentiation of interaction tends to define a structure of positions within the system. A stable structure of positions has the effect of eliminating the necessity of having the structure constantly under contest. The members are no longer required to contend for position, a process involving unpleasant tensions, but can devote their energies to other purposes.

Since the structure of positions in an interaction system grows out of the interaction process itself, it appears to be a contradiction in terms to speak of a structure of positions that is independent of the interaction structure. In fact, it can be observed in groups of all sorts that the two structures, insofar as they can be differentiated, are seldom, if ever, entirely independent.

However, the structure of positions and the structure of interactions can usually be clearly differentiated in a group. Organization theorists were able to solve the problem of isolating, defining, and charting the structure of positions in a group long before the behavior scientist was able to solve the problems involved in measuring interaction. An "organization chart" may be drawn to depict the structure of positions in any kind of organized group. Organization theorists use the term "formal organization" to refer to the structure of positions in a group.

One of the notable achievements of the behavior sciences has been the development of methods for measuring personal interaction. No systematic investigation of group process was possible until the methods were made available. Chapple [135] and Bales [28] have made particularly valuable contributions toward the development of methods for observing and recording interaction. Bales's method includes a description and categorization of the performances involved in interaction.

Moreno's [502] sociometry is a method for describing the structure of choice or preference relationships among the members of a group. The method may also be used to measure the frequency or duration of observed contacts among the members of a group. Chapin [129] and Weschler, Tannenbaum, and Talbot [758] have demonstrated the utility of multidimensional sociograms as a method for depicting the overlap among different structures of intermember choices.

Stogdill [675] and Stogdill and Shartle [680] have shown that a sociogram can be superimposed on an organization chart to show the relationship between the interaction structure and the structure of positions within a group. Although those members who occupy high level positions in a group tend to serve as focal points of interaction, they are seldom found to do so equally. Interaction often centers around the member (or his subgroup) who is engaged in some key phase of the group operations. A high status member who is unpleasant to deal with may be bypassed whenever possible by the members of his own subgroup and avoided by members of other subgroups. Interaction between the members of different subgroups may usually be observed. Interaction structure seldom parallels exactly the structure of positions in the group or the channels of interaction that the formal organization defines and specifies.

Stogdill and Haase [676] report that interaction structure tends to parallel, but is not identical with, choice structure. Low, but statistically significant, correlations were found between the number of persons who mention a member as a work partner and the number who choose him as a leader. The choice structure is highly related to the formal structure of positions, with those occupying high status positions receiving a greater number of choices. Interaction structure is also significantly related to the structure of positions, but not as highly as the choice structure.

Roethlisberger and Dickson [571], Moreno [502], and others, have shown that groups tend to develop informal subgroups or "cliques" of persons who are attracted to each other and who may be drawn from the same subgroups of positions or from different subgroups of positions in the larger group.

Stogdill and Haase [676], using sociometric methods to measure interaction structure, report the same statistically significant structures appearing in different large naval organizations, as well as in the same organization under different operating conditions, ashore and at sea. Jaynes [362] and Fleishman [216] find that organizations, not only of the same type (submarines) but also of different types (military and industrial), develop stable patterns of operations that are similar from one organization to another. Superimposed upon these stable substructures are other factors which are subject to change under the influence of different operating conditions, and which characteristically differentiate one organization from another. Despite the many surface characteristics by means of which organized groups may be identified, the study of a variety of organizations using the same methods suggests the presence of basic substructures which appear in all. It is also apparent that groups tend to develop a variety of structures which are conceptually independent but which overlap and are mutually interdetermined in varying degrees.

## Individual Differences in Interaction

A member of a group interacts not only with individuals but with other members in various combinations. Graicunas [263] has shown that a member is confronted by 4 possible interactional combinations in a group of 3, by 26 combinations in a group of 5, and by 57 combinations in a group of 6 persons, not including himself and not considering the factor of initiation by different members. In view of the time factor involved in interacting with individuals as well as with different subgroups, Graicunas concluded that an executive is likely to be overburdened if he attempts to supervise more than four or five immediate subordinates. Healey [307], however, reports that many executives in industrial organizations are able to find time to interact with 12 to 15 assistants, and the larger the organization the greater the number of subordinates an executive is able to supervise without feeling overburdened or pressed for time. Healey's study suggests that individuals differ in capacity to interact.

Jennings [364] shows that individuals differ not only in the number of persons they characteristically choose as interaction partners (emotional expansiveness) but also in the number they contact as interaction partners (social expansiveness). There is a low but statistically significant relationship between emotional expansiveness and social expansiveness. Those who express a greater number of choices also tend to interact with a greater number of persons. There is a slight but significant relationship between the emotional expansiveness shown by an individual and the expansiveness shown by others toward him. However, the degree to which an individual's choice of others is reciprocated by them is highly related to the degree of his own expansiveness and to the degree of expansiveness shown by others toward him. Emotional expansiveness does not insure the receipt of choices from other persons, but the ability to choose others who reciprocate the choice greatly improves the individual's chances of being frequently chosen by others. Age, intelligence, and length of residence are not related to emotional expansiveness. However, length of residence is significantly related to social expansiveness. Those who have lived longer in the group initiate more interactions. However, emotional expansiveness does not increase with increased residence or acquaintanceship. Thus, it appears that the capacity of the individual to maintain choice relationships with other persons is a highly stable characteristic. Although a group may present equal opportunities for interaction to each member, the opportunity is not utilized equally by the members. They differ not only in the number of members with whom they interact but also in the number of members with whom they can initiate and accommodate reciprocal choice relationships.

Borgatta and Bales [76] organized and reorganized experimental groups so that each subject in a group of four men had three new co-workers in each of four sessions. It was hypothesized that if the group was composed all of high (or low) interacters, the members would inhibit each other's activities. The hypothesis was confirmed for all high participators but rejected for low participators. Regardless of a member's characteristic performance, his rate of initiation was found to be an inverse function of the average characteristic rate of interaction of his fellow group members. Each individual appeared to exhibit an upper boundary which represented the limits of his capacity to initiate interaction no matter how much opportunity he had to participate. Stogdill, Shartle, Scott, Coons, and Jaynes [682] studied naval officers in positions that they had occupied for some time, then restudied them six months later in different positions. It was found that patterns of interaction with other persons tend to be carried from one position to another, while patterns of individual performance tend to change in conformity to the demands of the new position. Stogdill and Haase [676] present data which suggest that individuals differ not only in the number of persons with whom they maintain interaction but also in the ease with which they interact with superiors, subordinates, and peers.

There is strong evidence to support the view that individuals differ in their capacity to initiate and maintain interaction with other persons. It will be shown in the discussion of social roles (Chapter 5) that these differences account to a very large degree for the differentiation of structure in groups.

# 3

# Performance and Group Operations

ONE of the most obvious characteristics of a group in action is that of task performance. A brief period of observation is usually sufficient to enable one to decide whether the members of a group are working, playing, conducting a business meeting, or carrying out some other kind of activity. The work that a member does in behalf of a group may contribute to the accomplishment of its purpose even though his work does not involve continuous interaction with other members. The "dramatic performance" of an actor and the "task performance" of a machinist may differ in the amount of social interaction involved, but both may represent observable aspects of group operations.

Each member of a group exhibits behaviors which identify him as an individual. These behaviors may or may not identify him as a member of a group. But a group derives its identity from the actions and reactions of its members. This fact suggests a clue to the nature of performance. The system being developed requires that performance be defined in terms of its social context. Instead of inventing a new word, the term *performance* will be given a definition that is specific to the system.

## Definition of Performance

*Performance is defined as a response which may be identified as one of the actions or reactions that constitute the operations of an interaction system.* A performance, then, is any response which is perceived by other members to identify the actor as a participant in the operations of a group. An act exhibited by an individual is a performance if it identifies him as a member of a group.

A *member* is defined as a participant in interaction whose performances exert effects upon the operations of a group. A performance may or may not exert effects upon the structure of an interaction system. Therefore neither *performance* nor *membership* can be defined in relation to group structure.

By *operations* is meant all the actions and interactions which maintain the structure and accomplish the purpose of a group. A performance may or may not be one of the actions or reactions involved in an interaction sequence. Performance therefore may, but need not, exert effects upon the structure of an interaction system. Both individual and interpersonal performances are involved in group operations.

A valuable contribution toward the definition of the term *response* has been made by Logan, Olmsted, Rosner, Schwartz and Stevens [433]. They note that the problem of defining responses has been approached from four different directions. Responses have been defined in terms of (1) movements of the organism, (2) changes exerted upon an apparatus, (3) effects upon another organism, and (4) presumed internal states of the organism being observed. In some cases, two or more of these definitions are combined. The authors conclude that the choice of a system of definitions will depend upon the nature of the problem being considered.

All of these meanings will be utilized in the system being developed. Performance, here defined as any act which identifies the actor as a member of a group, will almost always imply movement of the organism. Performance will also be used to imply (1) a combination of movements and effects on other persons (as in co-operative work); (2) a combination of movements and changes exerted upon some object or apparatus (as in working at a lathe); and (3) a combination of movements and presumed internal states (as in planning, evaluating, and making decisions). Performances are exhibited by the individual members of a group. Performance implies action or the observable effects of action and always occurs in response to stimuli which may or may not be observable.

In experiments involving the observation and measurement of group behavior, performance is usually described as a complex referent. The various combinations of meanings are seldom untangled. The same condition pertains in the description of interaction and expectation. In some experiments to be discussed, interaction is described in terms of the performance components of interaction, while in other research the specific nature of interaction is ignored. Expectation is variously described (1) as a presumed determiner of action or decision, (2) as an inference drawn on the basis of observed action, and (3) as a presumed internal state of affairs with a future orientation. In many cases it is difficult to determine which part of the definition above is being used. This state of affairs reflects the complex nature of the behaviors being observed, as well as the need for definitions that have some stability of meaning.

Difficulties may be encountered at times in attempting to apply the definition of performance. A customer who is not wearing a hat in a store may be mistaken for a clerk, and similarly a clever person may manage to get himself misidentified as a member of a group to which he does not actually belong. This fact does not invalidate the definition of performance but rather the judgment of the person who incorrectly identifies a nonmember as a member. Another problem arises in connection with the application of the definition of performance, which is not so easily solved. Performances such as talking, listening, reading, writing, using tools, and operating machines are observable. Performances involving thinking and "mental planning" are not so readily identified as performances. If a member spends a great deal of time "staring into space" while attempting to formulate a plan or solve a problem, his actions may not appear to identify him as a member of the group. His fellow members may accuse him of loafing, of failing to do his part as a member. It is only when he communicates his plan to other members that the true nature of his apparent nonperformance is revealed. However, it is not safe to conclude that the group members are generally incapable of detecting and identifying the more subjective aspects of performance.

Communication has come to be recognized as an important aspect of member performance. However, the emphasis on verbal communication tends, at times, to obscure the fact that a member's gestures, facial expressions, postures, and bodily tensions may communicate more to his fellow members than the words he utters. Ruesch and Kees [596] have shown that a great variety of nonverbal behaviors may be communicative in nature. All performance, in so far as it is perceived by other members, tends to be communicative. Verbal communication (spoken and written) represents but one aspect of performance, all of which is communicative in nature when it is perceived by other members.

Communication between any two members may be regarded as a kind of interaction and as a kind of performance. The act of giving information and the act of receiving information, in addition to involving interaction, each represents a different kind of performance. This distinction becomes even clearer when acts such as the passing of boxes and the receiving and stacking of boxes are considered. These acts involve interactions between two members, but the behavior of each member may also be regarded as a form of task performance.

The members of a group may exhibit behaviors that do not involve interaction. Two members may work in separate rooms, one sorting objects while the other writes reports. Behaviors such as these, and the use of tools and the operation of machines, represent performances that do not necessarily involve direct interaction with other persons. These performances, however, accomplish the work of the group.

It is apparent that the same action may be regarded as exhibiting a dual aspect, representing a kind of task performance and component of interaction. For reasons which seem necessary for the logical development of the point of view being presented, an action that is a component of interaction will always be regarded as a performance. However, as noted above, not all performances involve interaction.

The use of job analysis and time and motion study to determine and describe the acts involved in performing the duties attached to a given position usually reveal that even the simplest of individual performances are complex in nature. This complexity is further apparent when it is realized that performance includes a great variety of actions involved in interaction and in the carrying out of tasks, as well as any other action that identifies an individual as a member of a group.

## Individual Differences in Performance

Individual differences in performance provide the basis for the differentiation of structure in groups, both animal and human. Individual performance when analyzed in detail appears to be infinitely varied. However, the members of a group tend to perceive each individual member as exhibiting a homogeneous pattern of behaviors which makes him particularly fitted to perform a specific task in the group. The members may overestimate or underestimate the capacity of the individual to perform the task. Nevertheless, both the individual and his fellow members may accept the evaluation for the benefit of the group.

Individual differences in skills make collaborative effort advantageous to the individual and the group. The subdivision of the group task makes it possible to apply individual member skills in places where they can be used most effectively for the accomplishment of the group purpose. Both the possibility of structural differentiation in groups and the advantage of collaborative effort are based on the fact that the performances of different individuals and the successive performances of the same individual are not identical.

Members who occupy similar positions in a group tend to exhibit similar performances. Considerable overlap is often observed in the performances of persons who occupy different positions. The task requirements of a group tend to limit the range of performances exhibited by its members.

## Dimensions of Performance and Interaction

The performances of all the members in interaction describe the operations of a group. Performance and interaction also generate group structure. The operations of a group represent the task or activity being carried out by the members; structure represents the differences between the members in the positions they occupy and in the tasks they perform. Both predictable differences between individuals and predictable regularities in the performance and interaction patterns of individuals provide the basis for structure.

Group structure and operations represent summation effects of the performances of all the members in interaction. Both observation and theory suggest that group structure and operations are very complex in structure. However, factorial studies suggest that they can be analyzed in terms of a limited number of dimensions. These dimensions differ markedly from the factors that describe individual performance. Of five factors found in common by several investigators studying a variety of groups, two represent group structure (the structure of positions, and interaction structures), while three represent the end effects of group operations. These factors have been identified as goal direction, group integration, and within-group interaction facilitation. It will be shown in a later chapter that these three factors represent different aspects of group achievement. They represent end effects of individual performance and group operations rather than direct descriptions of performance and operations.

## Group Operations and Activities

Ordinarily one thinks of group operations in terms of the work that the members do and the material objects upon which they operate. However, a group, such as a discussion group, may not operate upon material objects of any sort. The essential variable for describing the operations of groups in general is the performance of the members. If material objects are involved, they may influence the nature of the group's operations but are not the essential factors for defining group operations. It is not the warehouse full of materials that describe a group's operations, but the individual and interpersonal performances of its members.

It becomes important, both for theoretical and experimental purposes, to distinguish performance from the effects of performance. It is also necessary to differentiate between the characteristics of individuals and the characteristics of groups. The task performances of all the group members combined describe the operations of the group. The effects of the task performances of all the members describe the achievement of the group. Performance is a characteristic of individuals; operations and achievement are characteristics of groups.

A distinction is sometimes made between group operations and group activities. The latter is a more inclusive term. The former is usually employed to designate all those performances of individuals and subgroups of individuals that contribute directly toward the achievement of the primary goals of the group. The term *activities* is used to designate all the performances of members and subgroups that contribute to the achievement of primary goals and secondary objectives. For example, the group may participate in community welfare projects and conduct recreational and training programs for its members, which do not contribute directly to the attainment of its stated goals. These activities are designed to accomplish secondary objectives. As a matter of convenience, we shall confine our discussion to a consideration of group operations and primary goals.

Since the operations of a group are described in terms of the performance of its members, it is apparent that operations may become unbalanced as a result of under-performance or over-performance on the part of individual members or subgroups of members. The performances of individual members become matters of concern when the group has any important task to accomplish. No matter what the nature or purpose of a group, all its accomplishments and all values created by it are products of the performances of its members. In fact, the very existence and identity of the group is dependent upon a degree of performance sufficient to maintain interaction.

## RESEARCH ON PERFORMANCE

Performances are exhibited by the individual members of a group. Group research has been strongly oriented toward the task of discovering regularities of response in a variety of situations. The effect of different group situations upon various response syndromes has not been explored in an equally systematic fashion.

Experimenters differ in their views relative to which aspects of behavior are significant for a study of groups. These views appear to reflect differences in theoretical orientation and in the nature of the problems being investigated. It is of some interest to note that although most students of groups regard productivity to be an important measure of group achievement, some do not appear to regard instrumental work performance as a significant aspect of group behavior.

### *Dimensions of Individual Performance*

Performance must be regarded as a multidimensional element of individual behavior. It can be described in broad, general terms or it can be described in minute detail. To say that an individual spends his day in "working, sleeping, eating, and playing" is to describe his behavior in very general terms. To say that he "picks up pencil, looks at point, places pencil on sheet of paper, writes name, lays pencil down" is to describe his behavior in considerable detail. Descriptions of interpersonal performance in groups, in order to be meaningful and useful, are usually made at some level between these two extremes. Arrington [16] describes various methods of obtaining quantitative descriptions of group behavior by means of repeated observations over short periods of time. Most of the recent studies of group behavior are based on records of continuous observations made by two or more observers. Heyns and Lippitt [322] survey these methods.

Descriptions of individual performance are often reduced to minute details of the component motions involved in complex sequences of performance. This is particularly true in industrial organizations and also in military installations. However, instead of concentrating attention upon the individual, numbers of individuals who occupy similar positions are likely to be considered. In other words, member behavior is described primarily in terms of performances that characterize different jobs. Shartle [622] discusses the development and use of methods for describing job performance. He defines a *position* as "a group of tasks performed by one person," while a *job* is defined as "a group of similar positions in a single plant" or organization. It is apparent from these definitions that there are as many positions as there are members in a group, but there are likely to be fewer jobs than positions.

Descriptions of performance are usually quantified in terms of (1) frequency of occurrence, (2) duration in time, or (3) successes or errors in relation to some criterion of accuracy. Time and motion analysis, as discussed by Barnes [37] and others, involves a highly detailed description of job performance. Stogdill and Shartle [680] and Carlson [107] describe methods for obtaining estimates of time spent in several general, rather than detailed, aspects of performance. Flanagan's [214] critical incidents technique is a method for obtaining descriptions of behavior which differentiate effective performance from ineffective performance.

It might be assumed that the more highly subjective aspects of individual performance would be more difficult to observe and evaluate than performances that are objectively observable. However, Siegel [641] reports that different workers in a maintenance task are able to agree as closely in checking the intangible as the tangible aspects of task performance. Trattner, Fine, and Kubis [727] also find that one group of job analysts using written job descriptions, and another group making direct observations of job performance, agreed better in rating mental and perceptual aptitude than physical aptitude. These results suggest that individuals in a work situation tend to become highly sensitized to the subjective aspects of performance.

Shartle [622] estimates that there are approximately 30,000 occupations in the United States. These are groups of jobs which exhibit similar performances in different organizations. A large percentage of these involve manual performances. In view of the number and diversity of such occupations, it might be assumed that manual performance would be almost infinitely varied. Factorial studies, however, suggest that this is not the case. Fleishman and Hempel [217] report that the performances measured by different dexterity tests can be reduced to five elements. These are fine dexterity, manual dexterity, wrist-finger speed, aiming, and positioning. The reviews by French [229] and Fleishman [215], and the experimental work of Harrell [299], Melton [482], and others suggest that manual performance can be described by a limited number of factors, but the components of performance so described are very general in nature.

The structure of factors that describe on-the-job performance is likely to be more complex than that of factors that describe manual test performance. McQuitty, Wrigley, and Gaier [460] found 23 factors to describe the performance of highly skilled and poorly skilled aircraft maintenance mechanics. The six most clearly defined factors were interest in aircraft maintenance, sense of responsibility, willingness to work, weakness of character, lack of initiative, and failure to use knowledge effectively. McCormick and North [451] isolated six factors that describe performance in 119 enlisted naval jobs. These factors are work knowledge required, guidance and supervision required, inherent job hazards, physical effort required, potential combat hazards, and responsibility for the safety of others.

Wilson, High, and Comrey [773], using 108 items to describe the behavior of civilian supervisors, isolated the following eight factors: communication, lack of arbitrariness, social nearness, congenial work group, informal control, group unity, pride in work group, and safety enforcement. Shartle, Stogdill, and Campbell [625] found four factors that described naval officer performance in each of three different shore based organizations. These were high level policy-making, co-ordination control, methods planning, and personnel administration. Two additional factors, each specific to a single organization, were identified as (1) technical consultation and (2) investigation-report writing. The results of these studies are sufficient to indicate that performance differs not only with the type of work being performed, the type of organization, and the level in the organization hierarchy but also with the methods of observation and measurement employed.

Sorokin and Berger [657] asked 103 adult men and women to fill out daily schedules of the amount of time spent in different activities over a period of one month. Most time (673 minutes per day) was spent on physical needs, such as sleeping, eating, and personal care. Next most time (505 minutes) was spent in economic activities such as work, household duties, and transportation. The remainder of the day was divided equally (about 90 minutes each) among social (visiting, entertaining), intellectual (reading, radio), and pleasurable (riding, playing) activities. It is apparent that both interpersonal and solitary activities are included in this list.

Shartle and Stogdill [624] in a study of the work activities of 470 navy officers found that 59.6 per cent of the working day was spent in personal contacts (attending conferences, consulting other members, conferring with outsiders, interviewing, making speeches, attending meetings, and instruction). The remaining 40.4 per cent of the working day was spent in individual effort (observation, reading and answering mail, examining reports, writing reports, reflection, mathematical computation, using machines and equipment). Insofar as the achievement of an organization is concerned, individual effort appears to be as important as interpersonal performance.

Wallace and Gallagher [745] obtained 260 observations of more than two hours each on 171 foremen in industry. The observations were reduced to 3,765 incidents descriptive of specific job behaviors. It was found that about one-third of all supervisory behavior is devoted to the maintenance of machines and equipment and provision of supplies, about one-third to the implementation of production schedules, about one-fourth to the maintenance of quality standards, and about one-tenth to the administration of special personnel policies. Talking constitutes about one-half of the mode of action, while looking at something and doing manual work are the next most frequent actions.

Florence [218] made a factor analysis of 300 items describing successful student behavior. Six factors were identified as general achievement, organizational leadership, academic achievement, normative conformity, social acceptability, and self-direction.

McCormick, Finn, and Scheips [450] studied 4,000 jobs that had been analyzed by the United States Employment Service. The jobs were described in terms of 44 items descriptive of training, aptitudes, physical capacities, temperaments, interests, and working conditions. The job descriptions were intercorrelated and factor analyzed. Seven factors were identified as mental and educational development versus adaptability to routine, adaptability to precision operations, body agility, artistic ability, manual art ability, personal contact ability versus adaptability to routine, and heavy manual work versus clerical ability. These factors are descriptive of job requirements rather than of individual performance. Because of the wide variety of jobs sampled, these factors do not correspond exactly with the factors found in various studies of performance.

Performance must be regarded as complex in nature. The use of job analysis or time and motion study to determine and describe the acts involved in performing the duties attached to a given position usually reveals that even the simplest of individual performances are quite complex. This complexity is further apparent when it is realized that performance includes a great variety of actions involved in interaction and in the carrying out of tasks, as well as any other action that identifies an individual as a member of a group.

## Individual Differences in Performance

In his study of the division of labor, Durkheim [186] observed that in primitive groups, as well as in highly civilized societies, there usually emerge certain craftsmen and specialists who are regarded as the masters and dictators of their own trades. The traditions of the European guild system persist today, even in our highly mechanized society. The self-determination of the acknowledged specialist is specially apparent in the arts, professions, and custom trades. Each practitioner finds reason for satisfaction and pride in the fact that his personal style and skill lend a value to his performances and products not found in those of his colleagues. Caplow [105] observes that the members of a group are able to observe individual differences and to make evaluations of them.

Studies of individual differences summarized by Tyler [733] and Roe [568] indicate that individuals vary widely not only in ability to learn new skills but in the upper level of skill attained after training. Evidence that successful job performance is related to intelligence and special aptitudes is summarized by Burtt [99], Harrell [300], Tiffin [714], and others. These authors also review the evidence which indicates that factors such as the length of the working day, the pace of work, the spacing of rest periods, lighting conditions, and the like may exert marked effects upon performance in the industrial situation. Strong [691] has shown that individual interests are not only highly related to the choice of an occupation but also to successful performance in it. Those who exhibit an interest in the kind of work they are doing tend to exhibit a higher degree of successful performance.

Caplow [105] points out the fact that the position occupied by an individual or his family in the status structure of the community may tend to determine his occupational placement. Miller and Form [490] summarize the research on occupational mobility. This research indicates a strong tendency for sons to follow the occupations of their fathers. If the sons move into occupational levels that differ from those occupied by their fathers, they tend to move upward rather than downward. However, once started at a given occupational level, the individual tends to remain there. Caplow [105] observes that each occupation is so structured as to control and regulate the opportunities for upward mobility. Those that provide the greatest opportunities for mobility (salesman, politician, artist, entertainer) also provide the least security and the greatest possibilities of rapid downward mobility.

Two well-documented bodies of literature have been cited. One indicates a rather high relationship between individual ability and performance. The other indicates a rather close relationship between an individual's status in the community and the level of the status positions available to him in various groups which he may enter. Harrell and Harrell [301] and others have shown that intelligence and occupational status are also related. A fact often ignored in studies of group performance is that individual ability and social status may operate singly or in combination to determine not only the type of position that a member will seek in a group but also his performance in the position that he acquires. In addition, the group members are usually able to perceive quite readily an individual's standing in these respects relative to other members, and this perception, consciously or unconsciously, influences their reactions to him and the status position they assign to him in the group. Allee [4] reports that infrahuman groups may drive away the member that is perceived to be different. It can be observed that human groups often are reluctant to accept a member who is perceived to deviate too far from the average of the group in ability or social status. These various observations suggest that individual ability, social status, and within-group factors may interact to determine an individual's position in a group and his performance in the position.

Studies conducted by Shartle, Stogdill, and associates [681] indicate that persons who occupy similar positions tend to exhibit similar performances whether the positions are located in the same organization or in different organizations. Greater variance was found between different positions within the same organization than between similar positions in different organizations. Carter and Nixon [111] have reported a high correlation between performances in intellectual and clerical tasks. However, performance in mechanical tasks was not highly related to performance in intellectual and clerical tasks. The results of these studies suggest that performance is related to the kind of position occupied in the group and to the type of task being performed by the group.

Abruzzi [1] concludes from an analysis of the literature on work measurement that each worker tends to organize his work according to his characteristic style of performance even when required to follow a carefully detailed set of job specifications. There is no "one best way" of performing a task that is best for all workers. In addition, some variation of performance alleviates the effects of monotony and fatigue.

## Dimensions of Group Performance and Interaction

As groups develop in size and complexity and as they engage in a variety of technical operations, they appear to exhibit dimensions of behavior not fully encompassed in the basic dimensions of personal performance and interaction. The dimensions that emerge from the study of large, highly structured organizations depend upon the nature and generality of the units of behavior that are observed. Comrey [151] and Comrey and Staats [153] report that, depending upon the nature of the task, the amount of variance in group performance of two-man groups that can be predicted on the basis of individual performance varies from 50 to 80 per cent. The remainder can be attributed to group performance effects. However, it would be expected that as the size of the group increases the total group effect will also increase. Thus, Bales and Borgatta [29] report that the relative talking time per individual member in a discussion task decreases as the size of the group increases. Rosenberg, Erlick, and Berkowitz [585] found that when three-man groups perform a task requiring co-operation, both the individuals and the three men combined contribute significantly to achievement. However, subgroups of two do not contribute significantly more to the achievement of the group than does the single member.

Various categorizing schemes have been developed for observing and describing interpersonal performance in groups. The methods of Benne and Sheats [56], Bales [28], Steinzor [669], and Fouriezos, Hutt, and Guetzkow [220] were devised for the description of verbal interaction in discussion groups. The categorizing scheme devised by Carter, Haythorn, Meirowitz, and Lanzetta [110] includes motor as well as verbal performances. These systems differ markedly in the number of observational categories employed. Fouriezos, Hutt, and Guetzkow [220] used five items of need (dependency, status, dominance, aggression, and catharsis). Steinzor [669] employed 18 items describing the intent of the actor. Benne and Sheats [56] used 27 items to measure three kinds of role enactment (group task roles, group building and maintenance roles, and individual roles). Bales [28] employed six bipolar items for measuring performances related to problems of communication, evaluation, control, decision, tension reduction, and reintegration.

One might expect to find that the more detailed and precisely defined the units of behavior under observation, the more useful and revealing would be the results. Experimental findings do not always bear out this expectation. Various units of response, which might be regarded as different in nature, appear to combine to exert a unitary effect upon the group members. To list all the kinds of performance that an individual can exhibit in a group would result in a veritable dictionary of verbs. However, the group members do not appear to respond differentially to each discernible aspect of behavior. Campbell [101] reports that leaders tend to be more discriminating in describing different aspects of their own behavior than are followers in describing the behavior of the leaders. Followers tend to describe all aspects of the behavior of their superiors as a single behavior. Perhaps this tendency to respond non-differentially to diverse behaviors represents a form of perceptual defense, protecting the group member from a continuous state of alertness, reactivity, and selective discrimination in coping with the behavior of other group members. This interpretation is admittedly hypothetical.

Carter [109] has made a comparative analysis of five different studies that employed factor analysis as a method of determining the minimum number of dimensions needed to describe the behavior of individuals as group members. Although different descriptive items and different kinds of groups were employed in the five studies, three factors were found in each which exhibit considerable parallelism. Carter [109] found three factors which were identified as individual prominence, group goal facilitation, and group sociability; while those found by Wherry [760] were called forceful initiative and leadership, proper attitude toward job, successful interpersonal relations, and job competence and performance. Sakoda [599] found three factors which were identified as physical energy, intelligence, and social adjustment. Hemphill and Coons [315] found that ten hypothesized dimensions were reduced to three: the structuring of objective attainment, group interaction facilitation, and maintenance of membership. Clark's [142] dimensions were identified as individual prominence or leadership, group orientation, and social relations. Carter summarizes the findings of the studies above by proposing that three factors are needed to describe the behavior of individuals as members of groups. He identifies these factors as individual prominence and achievement, aiding group attainment, and sociability. These three factors represent interpersonal forms of performance that one may expect to find in any kind of social group. They do not take into account the various kinds of individual, non-interpersonal performances that are exhibited in many kinds of groups. Wherry, for example, found four factors, one of which he identified as job competence and performance. Nevertheless, these factors describe individual rather than group performance.

Hemphill [314] has developed a set of scales for measuring 14 dimensions of social groups. The dimensions are size, viscidity, homogeneity, flexibility, permeability, polarization, stability, intimacy, autonomy, control, potency, hedonic tone, participation, and dependence. The scales have proved their utility in the study of a wide variety of groups. A different set of dimensions was arrived at by Cattell [116] as a result of his factor analytic studies of experimental groups. He isolated syntality dimensions (characteristics of the group as an acting entity), structural dimensions (status, communication channels, etc.), and population dimensions (sex, average age, intelligence, etc., of the members). In contrasting the solutions achieved by Hemphill and Cattell, it is apparent that groups can be studied from a variety of viewpoints, and can be described at different levels of generality.

Except for population characteristics and group size, the dimensions proposed by Hemphill and Cattell may be regarded as representing complex behaviors that develop as a result of the performances, interactions, and expectations of the members of a group. Since these dimensions isolate patterns of interpersonal behavior that emerge as end products of a great variety of group processes, they must be regarded as dimensions of group rather than of individual behavior.

Cattell and Stice [118] obtained a variety of individual and group measures on 80 groups that performed verbal, intellectual, and motor tasks. From the intercorrelations among more than 90 different measures, 12 factors were isolated as dimensions of group behavior that showed stability in two or more sessions. These factors were identified as (1) high synergy through leadership, (2) high individual synergy through personalities, (3) adventurous forcefulness of population, (4) plodding fortitudinous morale, (5) intellectually effective role interaction, (6) sophisticated democratic determination, (7) frustration through temperamental heterogeneity, (8) frustration of group through high individual dominance, (9) garrulous nervous emotionality, (10) indifference or low group synergy, (11) slow, rigid, unintegrated deliberation with frustration, and (12) low integration of goal orientation.

Borgatta and Cottrell [79] intercorrelated 34 measures of interpersonal behavior and status in the study of 166 groups engaged in a role-playing task. Seven factors were found to account for the variance in interpersonal behavior. These were identified as emotionally neutral activity, involvement activity, group identification, leadership structure, discussional involvement, task interest, and maturity. These dimensions, as well as those isolated by Cattell and Stice, appear to describe group behaviors in which performance, interaction, and expectation combine to produce complex effects on group structure and achievement.

Borgatta, Cottrell, and Meyer [80] compared and matched the factored dimensions found by Borgatta and Cottrell [79] and Cattell, Saunders, and Stice [117] with the a priori dimensions prepared by Hemphill and Westie [319]. Five parallel dimensions were found in the three studies. The author has taken the liberty of naming these factors. The names assigned are (1) differentiated role structure, (2) informal interaction, (3) goal direction, (4) group integration, and (5) within-group interaction facilitation. The last three of these dimensions are practically identical with those identified by Hemphill and Coons [315]. The first three are similar to those which Carter found in five different studies that isolated only three or four factors each. In addition to the fact that the studies analyzed by Borgatta, Cottrell, and Meyer are based on a wider array of variables, the author believes that there are strong theoretical reasons for accepting their solution of five factors in preference to Carter's proposal of three factors. The former analysis identifies not only two independent structures (structures of positions and structures of interaction) but also three independent factors that describe aspects of group achievement (productivity, integration, and morale).

The factorial studies tend to support the hypothesis that group structure and operations are founded on a substructure of individual performances and interactions. Individual expectation does not appear as one of the basic elements of the substructure because it was not isolated as an input variable in the factorial studies. That there is strong reason to infer its presence and operation, particularly in the emergence of the factor identified as "differentiated role structure," will be shown in the following chapter.

# 4

## *Expectation and Group Purpose*

THE variables *interaction* and *performance* provide a basis for describing group structure and operations. However, they can not account for group purpose. Nor can they account for the differentiation of member roles or answer a number of questions related to group stability. Why is it, for example, that the members of a group may be observed to exhibit attitudes of expectancy and to depend upon each other as if their expectations would be fulfilled? Why do some members, more than others, serve as sources of anticipatory attitudes? Why may some members exchange positions quite freely in various kinds of groups, while those who originate expectations do not exchange positions as readily with other members? When members exchange places, why is each expected to behave according to the new position he occupies? The concepts of performance and interaction are not well designed to answer these and other questions related to group purpose, member affiliation, and role definition.

The value of positing expectation as a basic dimension of group organization was suggested to the author by the works of Mead [478], Barnard [35], Mayo [477], and Roethlisberger and Dickson [571]. Although none of these authors developed a full-fledged expectation theory, their comments and interpretations of previously obscure group processes suggested the utility of the concept for descriptive and analytical purposes. Mead and Barnard suggested that group organization is founded on a system of stable expectations which gives predictability to the behavior of the members. Mayo commented that a socialized person is one who acts in accordance with the expectations of others. Roethlisberger and Dickson and Mayo found that a great variety of experimental manipulations of the work group situation produced changes in the performance of workers in a manufacturing plant. The changes in performance were not always in the direction predicted. However, the seemingly discrepant results began to make sense when interpreted in terms of the hypothesis that the experimental situation tended to alter the level of expectation of the subjects. When factors were introduced into the work group situation which met or failed to meet these expectations, performance was correspondingly elevated or depressed. The students of group processes have used the concept of expectation to explain a variety of effects, but they have failed to define the term in any precise manner.

Historically, expectation has been a concern of the statistician and the gambler — persons interested in the probability of uncertain events. More recently, contributions to expectation theory have been made by workers in the fields of economics, decision theory, learning, and perception. Since the acquisition of social expectation may be regarded as a learning process, the work of the learning theorist would appear to provide a relevant starting point for the development of a theory of interpersonal expectation. Therefore, any conception of expectation employed in the present system should be able to stand as a theory, or rather as a subtheory, of learning.

## Formal Expectation Theory

Kelly [383] bases his theory of personality on the fundamental postulate that *"a person's processes are psychologically channelized by the ways in which he anticipates events."* The concept of expectation has come to play an increasingly important part in personality theory and in learning theory during the past decade.

Tolman [717], Mowrer [508], MacCorquodale and Meehl [452], and Rotter [589] view learning in terms of the reinforcement of expectation. According to these theorists, expectation is raised by reinforcement and depressed by the experience of failure to effect reinforcement. That is, the confirmation of an expectation increases the probability estimate by the individual that a course of action which has been successful will, under similar circumstances in the future, result in similarly satisfying outcomes. However, in a series of action-satisfaction sequences, successive reinforcements of expectation appear to produce a diminishing effect upon expectation. That is, the initial satisfactions of an expectation are more effective in increasing expectation than later ones. It may also be observed at times that the satisfaction of one expectation may generalize to the strengthening of related expectations.

It is generally assumed that reinforcement is a necessary condition to learning. Hilgard [325] and McGeoch and Irion [456] review a mass of literature which supports the view that reinforcement rather than frequency of response is the essential factor in learning. However, repeated reinforcements increase the probability of response at a decelerated rate. Tolman [720], although he does not deny the possibility of reinforcement, maintains that what is learned is the belief or expectation that some responses rather than others will increase the likelihood of satisfying the needs of the organism. A response sequence that leads to the satisfaction of need confirms the hypothesized means-end relationship between response and the satisfaction derivable from goal utilization. Thus, drive activates response and attaches valence to perceived stimuli. Readiness for response is considered to be a function of strength of expectation and stimulus valence. The valence of a stimulus is a measure of the organism's need and cathexis (the perceived gratification value of the goal object). Cathexis is regarded as rather highly resistant to extinction.

In Tolman's system, experience confirms not only expectation relative to the comparative values of different stimulus objects for satisfying needs but also belief relative to the comparative utility of various means (responses) for obtaining goal objects. When two goal objects are encountered together, the cathexis attached to one may become attached to the other. The concept of "equivalence beliefs," rather than secondary reinforcement, is used to explain the fact that a previously ineffective stimulus may acquire effectiveness for eliciting a given response.

The concept of need plays an important role in Tolman's theory. Hull [342] and Skinner [647] also regard need or drive as a necessary condition for learning. Skinner, however, refuses to speculate regarding the nature of drive. He measures drive for experimental purposes in terms of the length of time during which an animal has been deprived of food. Hull included *drive* and *drive stimulus* as concepts in his theory. His point of view and that of Tolman's were similar in regarding drive (or need) as a strong determiner of reaction potential. For Tolman, however, the effects of drive are exhibited upon responsiveness, while Hull regards drive as a facilitator of learning.

Although expectation theory accepts as valid the experimental findings produced by other schools of theorists and assumes that all these findings can be somehow explained, it must be admitted that expectation theory has not provided all the needed explanations. Neither does any other available theory of learning. Expectation theory is rapidly gaining in sophistication and in experimental support. It is the only variant of learning theory which appears to provide a promising access to problems of social learning.

## Definition and Nature of Expectation

The author's definition of expectation differs in three respects from that proposed by the learning theorists. First, expectation is regarded as a readiness for reinforcement. Second, estimates of desirability and estimates of probability are assumed to be affected differentially by reinforcement. Third, drive is assumed to operate in expectation.

*Expectation, defined as readiness for reinforcement, is a function of drive, the estimated probability of occurrence of a possible outcome, and the estimated desirability of the outcome.*

By *reinforcement* is meant the experiencing of an outcome which tends to meet, fulfill, satisfy, or confirm an expectation.

By *readiness for reinforcement* is meant the extent to which an individual is prepared or unprepared to experience, or reconciled or unreconciled to the prospect of experiencing, a possible outcome.

By *drive* is meant the level of tension and reactivity exhibited by an organism.

The *estimated probability of occurrence of an outcome* refers to an individual's prediction, judgment, or guess relative to the likelihood that a given event will occur.

By the *estimated desirability of an outcome* is meant an individual's judgment relative to the satisfyingness of, need for, demand for, appropriateness of, or pleasantness or unpleasantness of, a possible outcome.

According to the definitions given above, estimates of probability and estimates of desirability are not opposite ends of the same continuum, and desirability is not to be regarded as a mere modifier of probability estimates. Rather, estimates of probability and estimates of desirability interact to determine the level of expectation. The operation of probability estimates is inferred if the individual is observed to exhibit a persistent postural or behavioral orientation toward, and a preparatory readiness for experiencing, an outcome. The operation of desirability estimates is inferred if the individual is observed to exhibit satisfaction or disappointment with an outcome for which he was prepared. An individual tends either to accept or reject an outcome for which no prior preparation was possible.

The validity of a concept such as expectation is dependent upon its utility for explaining the effects which are observed rather than upon its direct visibility. Thus, we may observe that we have disappointed an individual's expectations, but we cannot state the exact nature of his expectations. It is not always safe to rely upon a person's verbal report of his expectations because custom and convention make it difficult or embarrassing to express certain kinds of hopes and ambitions, particularly those which might conflict with the interests of other persons. Nor is it safe to assume that all persons entertain identical expectations. Despite the difficulty of interpreting the exact nature of an individual's hopes and aspirations, we assume the operation of expectations because of his perceived readiness to experience certain kinds of outcomes and because of his perceived disappointment when the outcomes are not forthcoming.

In postulating a two-dimensional conception of expectation in which probability estimates and desirability estimates respond differentially to the same reinforcement, considerable departure has been made from formal theories of learning and expectation. It is usually postulated that value is highly contingent upon probability. Although this assumption has the merit of theoretical simplicity, it does not necessarily account for all that may take place in the response of an organism to a stimulus situation. It is generally recognized that the human organism becomes differentially sensitized to different stimuli and is capable of responding differentially to the visual, auditory, and other stimuli presented by the same situation. Differentiation does not reside in the stimulus; it is a response of the organism. There is reason to believe that the organism is capable of responding differentially to its own responses. The author suggests that probability estimates and desirability estimates represent such differentiated reactions to any situation which elicits expectation. With habituation, the process of weighing desirability against probability, and vice versa, may be carried out at a very low level of awareness. The deliberate weighing of probability estimates against desirability estimates is most likely to occur in new situations and when a difficult decision is to be made. Expectation is formulated in terms of what is uncertain in the future as well as in relation to what has been learned in the past.

An individual may estimate it to be very probable that he will inherit a large sum of money and that he will have to undergo a serious operation. Although one is estimated as desirable and the other as undesirable, he may be equally willing to experience both outcomes because of the high probability of their occurrence. However, if both outcomes are estimated to be desirable, but the estimated probability of the first is low and the second is high, his expectation of receiving the inheritance may be depressed and that of undergoing surgery may be raised. Again, an individual may estimate that he is likely to die unless he undergoes surgery, but his dread of surgery may be so great as to suppress the estimated probability of dying. Estimates of probability and of desirability may act either to enhance each other, or one to lower the other.

There is reason to believe that positively valued and negatively valued desirability estimates exert somewhat different effects upon expectation. Probability estimates tend to be overestimated when expectation is positively valued, and underestimated when it is negatively valued. It may be observed, however, that this is not always true. Continued failure, emotional depression, and inconsistent reinforcement often have the effect of inducing overestimation of the probability of undesirable outcomes. Probability estimates may also exert effects on desirability estimates. The perceived possibility of attainment as well as actual attainment (reinforcement) enhances desirability under some circumstances. On the other hand, the "sour grapes" reaction is often observed when a highly valued outcome is perceived to be unattainable. There is need for careful experimentation to determine the extent to which desirability estimates and probability estimates affect each other.

It is important not only in a theory of learning but also in a theory of group achievement to account for individual drive and group motive power. Drive is difficult to define in any precise manner. The operation of drive is inferred when the organism exhibits tension, heightened reactivity, and persistent or vigorous action. It is generally agreed that drive may arise from a great variety of internal conditions, including glandular activity, the lack of food or water, and the like. Drive may also be induced in response to painful stimulation, the perception of danger, or the perception of a highly valued stimulus object. Thus, drive may be inferred from the observation of stimulus avoidance as well as stimulus approach. Drive provides the basis for the differential outputs of energy exhibited by an organism in response to various internal and external stimulus situations.

Tension and reactivity appear to be exhibited in all drive states. However, the instrumental and consummatory activities which lead to drive reduction often have to be inhibited in animal as well as in human groups. The weaker members of a group may have to stand aside until a stronger has had his fill. Most human societies require that their members meet certain standards and observe certain rituals as conditions for exhibiting permissible action toward drive reduction involving the use of food or sexual objects. Therefore, although drive may not be exhibited in overt instrumental behaviors, it is likely to be exhibited in tension and heightened reactivity to specific classes of stimuli.

Motivation may be regarded as a function of drive and confirmed desirability estimates. When consummatory actions reduce drive and confirm desirability estimates, probability estimates also receive some degree of confirmation. Similar conditions of expectation and stimulus situation serve to reactivate those patterns of behavior that previously ended in reinforcement. Through the confirmation of desirability estimates, behaviors activated by drive acquire goal direction. The strength of motivation for a specific kind of reinforcing outcome is a function of drive and of the level of estimated desirability of the outcome confirmed by prior reinforcement. The confirmation of a given level of estimated desirability need not necessarily have been accomplished by reinforcement with the specific class of goal objects which is the referent of expectation. For example, an individual may be strongly motivated to buy an automobile even though he has never owned one. Experiences other than the actual possession of a car may confirm the estimated desirability of ownership.

Expectation and motivation are overlapping concepts. Drive and desirability estimates contribute both to motivation and expectation. Ordinarily, consummatory outcomes reduce drive and confirm some level of estimated desirability and probability. Eating a full meal reduces tension and reactivity, but this does not eliminate the expectation that a particular kind of food being eaten will prove desirable (or undesirable) when encountered in the future. With satiation, food as a stimulus provides decreasing confirmation of the desirability of continued eating for the time being. In addition, previous experience may operate to confirm the undesirability of gorging to the point of nausea. Although the "act" of eating is described as singular, it involves a complex sequence of responses. A reinforcement, although described as singular, involves the interaction of drive with a variety of desirability estimates and probability estimates which overlap in time.

Not all consummatory experiences reduce drive. Strongly aroused drive does not subside immediately. A living organism continuously exhibits some level of drive. With drive held constant, variation in expectation becomes a function of desirability estimates and probability estimates.

A great variety of responses during the history of an expectation make some contribution toward the confirmation or disconfirmation of probability estimates and desirability estimates. Let us consider a sequence of complex behaviors such as the following: restless activity, looking at clock, walking to dining room, sitting at table, watching food being served, eating food. We ordinarily think only of the last set of performances (eating) as constituting a reinforcing event. However, all the acts in a sequence such as that described above may confirm expectation to some degree, even though they do not all reduce drive. All the enumerated actions, plus a great many not specified, serve to place the organism in a stimulus situation in which the reduction of drive and the confirmation of estimates may occur. Although the utilization of stimulus objects may be necessary under many circumstances for the reduction of drive and the confirmation of probability estimates, it is not the environmental object which confirms expectation. It is the response of the organism to the stimulus object which does or does not confirm the desirability of further readiness for reinforcement. The differential effects of an outcome upon drive, desirability estimates, and probability estimates provide a basis for the continuity and variability of patterned behavior and for the different levels of readiness for reinforcement exhibited by the organism in different stimulus situations as they are encountered simultaneously and in succession.

Expectational theories have been challenged at times on the ground that they fail to provide any connecting link between expectancy and overt response. This criticism loses much of its force when expectation is defined as readiness for reinforcement. Expectation, as the initial stage in the preparatory — instrumental — consummatory response sequence, and continuing throughout the sequence, is defined within the same system of concepts in which response is defined. Desirability estimates and probability estimates, as inferred concepts, are necessarily measured in terms of the responses of the organism to stimulus objects. Such measurement constitutes the operational definition of the concepts. Although it may be doubted that probability and desirability estimates can be measured adequately with any instruments or methods now available, some progress appears to have been made toward the definition of expectation within the system of natural science concepts.

## Reinforcement and Generalization of Expectation

Expectation is neither an overt response nor a "state of mind." It is a readiness for specific reinforcements or classes of reinforcements. To say that an organism may exhibit several expectations simultaneously is not to imply that these expectations exist as separate entities. However, it does seem necessary to explain the fact that some expectations, such as vocational aspirations, are made manifest in consistent patterns of behaviors that may be exhibited over a period of years; while others, such as the expectation that a gentleman will hold the door open for a lady, may be manifested in behaviors which require only a moment for execution. Still others, such as expectations relating to time of eating, sleeping, and working, may involve behaviors which exhibit a high degree of periodicity that corresponds closely with socially or environmentally determined schedules.

The activation of drive may increase the reactivity of the organism to any stimulus to which it responds. However, it is the confirmation of expectation which accounts primarily for the differential reactivity to specific aspects of the stimulus environment. Although drive appears to affect response thresholds selectively, the goal direction of drive is enhanced by confirming experiences. The actions which are instrumental to reinforcement tend to maintain the dominance of the expectation being served. Consummatory actions, such as the acquisition and utilization of goal objects, represent the end stages in the temporary history of an expectation. The reduction of drive and the lowering of the estimated desirability of excessive consummatory action permits other expectations to be elicited in response to the stimulus environment.

The expectation of having lunch with a friend may increase the anticipated pleasure of eating. One expectation generalizes to strengthen another. The arrival of the friend may not only confirm the anticipated pleasure of companionship but may also strengthen the expectation of pleasure in eating. The reinforcement of one expectation may strengthen a second which is present at the same time. However, should the friend fail to arrive, the resulting disappointment may generalize to reduce any anticipation of pleasure in eating alone. The generalization of expectation may take place in the absence of any positively valued reinforcing outcome.

An expectation, once aroused and reinforced, tends to persist, particularly if a high level of estimated desirability or undesirability has been confirmed. Successive reinforcements of the same expectation tend after a time to produce a smaller increase in the desirability estimate because of the operation of satiation and monotony. However, repeated reinforcements tend to raise the level of probability estimate, thus maintaining a residual level of expectation that is highly recoverable after a period of nonreinforcement.

The administration of reinforcement at irregular and unpredictable intervals during a sequence or series of responses induces a level of expectation that is quite resistant to extinction. Any inability of the organism to predict reinforcing outcomes or to control its behavior in effecting outcomes constitutes a threat to its well being and serves as a stimulus to drive. If drive is mobilized in response to a reinforcement, it is not reduced by that reinforcement or by successive reinforcements with the same reward or punishment. That is, if drive is mobilized and maintained by a series of negatively valued reinforcements which cannot be predicted and from which there is no escape, the organism exhibits a state of continued tension, uncertainty, alertness, and stereotypy of behavior. Its freedom of action is bound and limited by the dominating expectation of being unable to effect drive-reducing reinforcement and by the continued motivation for such reinforcement.

The organism may exhibit a readiness for negatively valued outcomes, particularly if they cannot be avoided. Thus, an individual may prepare himself for punishment and other kinds of undesirable outcomes, even though he would prefer to avoid them.

Both reward and punishment reinforce expectation. They confirm the estimated desirability or undesirability of an outcome. Any difference in effect is exerted on the polarity (positive or negative) of the desirability estimate. The probability estimate of a negatively valued outcome may be as high as that of a positively valued outcome reinforced an equal number of times. Therefore, reward and punishment do not differ in that one is reinforcing and the other not. Although punishment may suppress response for an interval of time, its end effect is to increase the probability of response. Furthermore, since strong punishment stimulates drive, responses that are learned under punishment become highly resistant to extinction.

It is suggested that a single reinforcement is sufficient to confirm a desirability estimate at or near its maximum value for a given set of relevant outcomes. However, more than one reinforcement is required to confirm a probability estimate at its maximum level for the same set of outcomes. Estimated desirability rises rapidly to its maximum value in response to reinforcement, and further reinforcements exert diminishing effects in increasing the desirability estimates. Estimates of probability tend to rise more slowly and continue to rise until the scale of estimated probability reaches a value that corresponds with the objective probability of reinforcement. Level or strength of expectation is a function of drive and of the levels of estimated desirability and estimated probability confirmed at a particular stage in the reinforcement history of the expectation.

In the ordinary course of events, unreinforced expectations tend to diminish and undergo extinction. However, the possibility should be considered that, since desirability estimates are highly generalizable, expectations may persist although not reinforced by relevant environmental outcomes. A desirability estimate, confirmed at a high level of value, may persist. Probability estimates, since they tend to assume a level that corresponds with the objective probability of reinforcement, are likely to decline when reinforcing outcomes are no longer available. Desirability estimates and probability estimates exhibit differential rates of extinction in response to continued nonreinforcement.

An event that fails to reinforce expectation differs in its effects on the organism from an event that has no relevance to expectation. The latter leaves expectation unchanged, while the former tends to lower the probability estimate. The consistent reinforcement of expectation provides the individual with freedom of action to do other things after drive is reduced. Under an erratic and unpredictable series of reinforcements, drive is mobilized and serves to maintain the expectation of uncertainty and crisis so that freedom of action is limited to the continued preparation for emergency. Freedom of action is related to the ability of the individual to predict outcomes. The failure to reinforce expectation reduces, while consistent reinforcement increases, predictability and freedom of action.

## Scales and Norms of Value

A confirmed expectation provides a set of reference experiences for evaluating related expectations. The reinforcement of one expectation may also act to strengthen other expectations. The

child who cries after being denied a toy and is then given it may
come to expect that not only toys but other objects may be obtained by crying. It is difficult to estimate the degree of conscious
estimation of probabilities in the behavior of the young child.
However, conscious estimation and generalization is often apparent in the reports of adults. For example, the workers who describe their supervisor as "easy" because he permits them  to do
a great deal of loafing may also conclude that he will be equally
lenient in his treatment of absenteeism, wastage, and violations
of minor rules.

Individuals tend to formulate judgments in terms of scales of
estimate that appear to be related not only to the objective situation but also to their past experiences. Thus, an individual's perception of a situation is determined both by the information that
he derives from the situation and by the set or expectation in
terms of which he views the situation. The desirability of a situation is estimated in reference to internalized scales and norms of
value which are determined by past experience. That which conforms to these norms tends to be most readily perceived, and that
which departs from the norms tends to be rejected.

Since the strong reinforcement of expectation tends not only
to confirm desirability estimates but also to strengthen other related expectations that are highly valued, the individual develops
systems of more or less highly interrelated value expectations relative to his family, school, community, church, political party, nation, work group, and so on. These different systems may be mutually reinforcing or they may be in conflict with each other.
Young people frequently experience conflict between the values
acquired from their parents and those acquired from their age
peers. They may also perceive conflict between the values acquired at church and those acquired from their science teachers.

A personal *value system* may be defined as a highly generalized
set of expectations in which desirability estimates are mutually
confirmed with little reference to probability estimates, and
which serves as a referent or criterion for evaluating the desirability of alternative outcomes. The degree of generalization

among these value systems may be conceived as so great that they are reinforced by almost all relevant outcomes. Since they are reinforced by satisfying as well as unsatisfying outcomes, and are little diminished by the failure of outcomes to confirm their validity, they are very resistant to modification and are essentially non-extinguishable. Because of their high degree of independence of validating outcomes, they come to serve as stable reference points in terms of which experienced outcomes are evaluated as satisfying or unsatisfying. They also serve as comparing criteria and, as such, enable the individual to evaluate the values of other persons, groups, and subgroups. The prejudiced person is one who makes evaluations in terms of his value systems without reference to the objective validity of his judgments.

According to Tolman [717], experience tends either to confirm or disconfirm expectations. It is here proposed that the *validity* of an expectation is determined by the confirmation of probability estimates. A rational expectation is one that is formulated in terms of the estimated probability of outcomes. The estimate need not be accurate in order to be rational, but the criterion of its validity is the occurrence or non-occurrence of the predicted outcomes. Validation is the confirming reinforcement of a rational expectation.

Experienced outcomes which reinforce, or correspond with, a desirability estimate confirm the *value* of an expectation. It is proposed that desirability estimates are highly reinforcable by related expectations and may exhibit very little decrement despite the lack of reinforcement of probability estimates. However, the value of an expectation may be diminished by an outcome which confirms probability estimates but fails to confirm desirability estimates.

Outcomes may confirm estimates of probability but not of desirability; or they may confirm estimates of desirability but not of probability. Either set of outcomes may prove unsatisfying. More important is the fact that it is only when desirability estimates and probability estimates are reinforced simultaneously that value systems are subjected to reality testing. A highly valued outcome may not prove to be a validating outcome if the individual entertains little or no expectation of its occurrence, is uncertain, misestimates the probability of its occurrence, or experiences the outcome under such inconsistent and discrepant circumstances that no rational prediction is possible. Thus, although an outcome may prove to be highly valued, it may provide no valid basis for estimating the probability of its occurrence in the future.

That values are reinforced by satisfying as well as unsatisfying outcomes is evidenced in political beliefs. If the political party of one's choice is in power, good times are attributed to the wise action of the politicians, while bad times are explained by the force of circumstances. When the opposing party is in power, good times are attributed to the rising trend of events, and bad times to stupid politics. Strongly reinforced value systems appear to be affected very little by reality testing.

The integrity of the individual is founded on the consistency of his value systems. A member may withdraw his vote from the party of his choice or may withdraw his membership from a group if he perceives it as being no longer capable of acting in accord with his personal values. These values need not be personally oriented. They may be concerned with the welfare of family, friends, nation, or humanity at large. They may refer to the welfare of various groups to which the individual belongs. But, no matter what their objective reference, they can be traced back to the individual. Whatever happens to family, friends, and membership groups has an impact on the individual. It is due to the fact that he exhibits a preference for certain outcomes (for self and others) that his generalized expectation systems may be called value systems.

Individuals differ in what they value. The same objectively observable outcomes are not responded to alike by all persons. When alternative outcomes are available, a more highly valued reward tends to exert a stronger reinforcing effect than does a reward of lesser perceived value. However, the effect of a reward in a series of reinforcements is determined not by its absolute magnitude, but by the range of magnitudes perceived to be available. In order to estimate the satisfyingness of an outcome to an individual, it is necessary to know the frame of reference in terms of which his expectations have been formulated.

## Individual Values and Group Affiliation

The individual is thrust at birth into a social situation. Both the quality of nurturance and the schedule of care which he receives in infancy may establish expectations relative to the good will and dependability of other persons that last through adult life. Since initial reinforcements exert stronger effects than later reinforcements, and since strongly reinforced desirability estimates appear to be resistant to extinction, it seems reasonable to accept as valid the conclusions of numerous clinical observers who report that enduring patterns of behavior and belief are fixed early in childhood. Many of the child's expectations are set by the training and treatment he receives in the home. Other expectations are acquired in the classroom, on the playground, and in other social situations. The expectations acquired in one group may be exhibited by the individual in other groups.

It seems unnecessary to postulate any biologically determined drive or need for group affiliation or social co-operation. Any patterns of social behavior which suggest the possible operation of such factors can be more simply explained in terms of learning and reinforcement of expectation. As soon as habitable frontiers become accessible to human exploitation they are sought by individuals who exhibit little evidence of drive for affiliation or co-operation. Many individuals who are compelled by necessity to participate in group life exhibit only a marginal degree of membership. The clinician encounters numerous clients who have experienced such inconsistent and painful reinforcement of expectation that they not only mistrust all affiliative interaction but feel no secure sense of personal identity.

An individual's sense of personal identity and his identification of himself with other persons and groups seems best understood in the light of his history of social reinforcements. He tends to identify himself in some degree, either positively or negatively, with those individuals and groups that have been influential in shaping his expectations. According to Newcomb [518], any group with which an individual identifies or compares himself, either positively or negatively, may be regarded as a reference group. The individual evaluates possible outcomes not only in terms of his value systems but also in terms of the perceived values and experiences of his reference groups. An individual may or may not be a member of one or more of his reference groups.

When individuals are free to choose, they appear to seek the companionship of persons whose values are similar to their own and to join groups whose goals and activities tend to reinforce their own value systems. It seems probable that the individual will continue to identify himself with a membership group that initiates a strongly reinforced expectation and continues to reinforce it. However, if reinforcement of a highly valued expectation is discontinued, the individual may either reject the group or experience a conflict of loyalties in relation to it. A group that arouses a strong negative or unpleasant expectation may be rejected.

The willingness of a member to permit a group to structure his expectations is likely to be determined by the extent to which he perceives the goals of the group and the value systems of its members to be in accord with his own value systems and those of the reference groups with which he most strongly identifies himself. Thus, some individuals appear to identify themselves quickly with a new group, while others never seem to accept the group or identify themselves with it. Individuals not only differ in their value systems and reference group identifications, but they also appear to differ in the extent to which they are willing to accept structure that is initiated and controlled by other persons. The individual is likely to accept, or even to demand, structure in a new group if he perceives a stable system of goals, norms, and related expectations to reinforce his own value systems and to increase the probability of experiencing satisfying outcomes. However, the individual who expects to experience negatively valued outcomes and who perceives the goals of the group to be in conflict with his own value systems may oppose the group structure even though he accepts membership in it and conforms sufficiently to retain his membership. Thus, an individual's performance in a group may be determined not only by those expectations that are structured by the group but also by the expectations that he brings into the group. However, some persons may enter the group because they perceive no more satisfying alternatives to be available or because they seek to avoid certain unpleasant consequences attendant upon avoiding membership in the group. They may participate voluntarily even though they find the experience unpleasant or disapprove of the activities of the group. It is apparent that membership in a group is not necessarily dependent upon a correspondence between individual values and group purpose. It seems probable that value systems and reference group identifications interact to determine to a large extent an individual's acceptance or rejection of the goals and structures of the groups to which he belongs.

## The Structuring of Expectation by the Group

Among the most highly valued expectations exhibited by an individual are those which, when reinforced, confirm his perception of his own worth and identity. Because he acquires these expectations in social situations, he becomes highly sensitized to the positive and negative reactions of others toward him. His ability to gain membership in a variety of groups (occupational, educational, social, fraternal, recreational) may depend upon the extent to which he can convince others of his worth as a member. Because of the operation of a variety of motivated expectations, most individuals are highly susceptible to reinforcement by the groups of which they are members.

A new member enters a group with a great variety of expectations already formed. Some of these expectations may be unrelated to the group. Those that are related to the group may be realistic or unrealistic in terms of the ability of the group to reinforce them. However, Sherif [631] has shown that groups tend to develop norms of belief, expectation, and performance. A new member who enters the group with a response that deviates from the norm of the group tends, after observing other members, to exhibit a response that is closer to the group norm. This normative response tends to persist even after the member leaves the group. The norms of a group tend to induce conformity in belief and conduct as well as in performance when these are perceived to be related to the purpose and operations of the group.

Groups exhibit strong capabilities for structuring the expectations of members. The goals, norms, rules, traditions, and rituals of the group represent such mutually reinforced sets of expectations. These are characteristics of groups, not of individuals. The goals and norms are likely to persist after any single member has left the group. Goals and norms are to the group as value systems are to the individual. They represent sets of values in terms of which alternative outcomes are evaluated and the norms or purposes of other groups are compared.

The members usually assume that a new member will accept the group purpose, norms, and related structures of expectations. Once the members of a newly formed group accept a common goal and develop a mutually reinforced structure of expectations, they exhibit a concern for the conformity of all members to the norm. The deviating member becomes the recipient of a high rate of interaction and of pressure exerted by other members to induce his conformity to the norm. If he refuses to conform, he is likely to be isolated or rejected by other members.

Conformity to expectation not only increases the predictability of the performance of individuals but also facilitates the coordination of action, unity of goal striving, freedom of action, and integration of the group. Whether or not the members are conscious of these specific effects, they do act to induce and to reward conformity. Since individual values and reference group identifications are essentially private in nature, it is often difficult for the group to assess the effect of these individual factors upon the group. It is for this reason that the overt and visible acceptance of the group structure and purpose becomes important as a means toward maintaining the integration of the group.

The purpose of a group represents merely a statement, or understanding among the members, of the outcomes the group expects to experience. The operations of the group, or the performances of its members, are designed to bring about these outcomes. The more closely knit the group, and the more important its goal, the more essential it becomes that the performances of each member contribute toward the accomplishment of the group purpose. The structuring of interaction and expectation, and the differentiation of performance, whether accomplished directly or incidentally, are found to facilitate the accomplishment of the group purpose. This structuring reduces interactional conflict and the continued necessity of redefining individual performance and group structure, and it defines a common goal for the group, thus permitting unity of action.

Whereas the larger group is concerned with the accomplishment of over-all goals, a subgroup may have specific subgoals to achieve. A subgroup may develop its own norms, which tend to structure the expectations and regulate the performances of its members. Such norms not only serve to protect the subgroup from pressures exerted by the larger group but may also serve to legitimize and reinforce the norms and values of the larger group. Once an individual accepts the norms of a group or subgroup, he surrenders some degree of personal freedom for the benefit of the group.

The structural integrity of a group is dependent to a large degree upon the commonality of expectations and values among its members, particularly as these relate to the group purpose and operations. A lack of integration is exhibited when peripheral members or independent subgroups operate upon tasks which have little or no relation to the purpose of the larger group. Conformity to the norms of a group is facilitated when the members are strongly motivated to remain in the group, when they exhibit a desire for group reinforcement of their value systems, when the group norms are clearly defined, when the members have access to accurate information relative to the norms, when the group is more highly valued than other reference groups with conflicting values, and when the group is able to reinforce expectations.

Although groups tend to formulate their norms as universally applicable they do not always expect all members to conform to the norms in equal degrees. Certain members, or certain classes of members, may be expected to deviate from the norms in varying degrees. Most of the members may be allowed to deviate from the norms under highly specified circumstances. However, marginal members and members who are perceived to constitute a potential threat to the group may be required to conform to the norms under all circumstances in order to retain their membership.

Group structures of expectation, once differentiated and reinforced by the performances and interactions of the members over a period of time, tend to exhibit a high degree of stability. The stability of these structures increases the predictability of the behavior of the members of the group. Just as the power of the group to produce outcomes exceeds that of the individual, stable structures also increase the probability of experiencing anticipated outcomes. The individual who has not experienced a high degree of personal success in confirming his probability estimates may find that membership in a group with stable structure provides him with higher degrees of certainty and reward than he could obtain by acting alone. Thus, there is a real sense in which a structured group is able to provide a higher degree of predictability than does the larger environment in which it operates. In addition, the goals and norms developed by a group may provide a high degree of satisfaction and comfort to a member through the reinforcement of his value systems. The individual derives his sense of personal integrity from the internal consistency of his value systems and from the support given his value systems by the groups with which he identifies himself. The strength of this support is enhanced if the group in which he is a member is also a valued reference group.

It is apparent that individual, group, subgroup, and reference group factors exert effects upon the individual member which structure his expectations. The members in interaction exert determining effects upon each other. All of these effects in combination acting upon the members determine the motivation of the group. A group derives its motive power from the fact that the experiencing of an anticipated outcome reinforces the expectation of further outcomes. The satisfaction of one expectation creates a new expectation which requires action and movement in order to be satisfied. There is no end to expectation, nor any permanent satisfying of it, so long as the group exists. It is this fact which gives the group continuity, purpose, future oriented action, and motivation. A group may be regarded as highly motivated when the level of group goal expectancy among its members is high, when the probability of experiencing satisfying outcomes is perceived to be high, and when experienced outcomes reinforce expectation. The factors that contribute toward this condition are numerous and complex.

Not only is it observed that the same reward is not valued alike by all members of a group, but value estimates and probability estimates interact to determine the motivating potential of a reward. An outcome that is easily brought about is not likely to raise expectation, while a goal that is perceived as impossible to attain is likely to depress expectation. An outcome that is attainable, but requires some effort, is likely to provide the greatest motivating potential for most of the group members and for the group as a whole.

Since initial reinforcements exert the strongest effects, it would appear that mutual satisfaction between a new member and the group would be facilitated by a realistic initial structuring of the new member's expectations relative to the contribution he is to make to the group and the return he is to receive from the group. This mutual satisfaction would then appear to be most easily perpetuated by insuring the fulfillment of both sets of expectations.

## Discussion

Learning theory is concerned with the acquisition of responses by the individual organism. So is expectation theory, even when it is used to explain group behavior. Thus, it is not necessary to introduce concepts such as "group mind," "herd instinct," and the like in order to explain group phenomena. If the group possesses any memory, it exists in its repository of written records, in the memories of its individual members, and in the rituals, customs, traditions, and routines passed on from old members to new. Constitutions, by-laws, rules, and the like serve the purpose of maintaining stability of structure in expectations.

A group derives its motive power from the drive of its individual members and from the reinforcement they give to each other's expectations relative to the goal to be reached. The ability of group members to stimulate strong drive in each other is readily apparent in games, contests, and emergency situations. The presence of numbers appears to give a group the capability of generating effects that are multiplicative rather than additive functions of the characteristics and behaviors of its individual members. This capability would appear to be derived from the ready generalizability and reinforceability of expectation and from the high degree of sensitivity and readiness for reinforcement which the members exhibit toward each other. Previous theories have been hard pressed to account for the motive power that groups are able to generate.

The conception of expectation as a function of desirability estimates and probability estimates which respond differentially to reinforcement results in a formulation that is able to account for individual value systems. The interaction of drive and desirability estimates accounts for goal direction. Each member of a group carries his personal values and motivations into the group. However, the ability of the members to originate expectations for each other and to reinforce each other's value systems accounts for the fact that groups are able to exhibit singleness of purpose. The members in interaction reinforce in each other the expectation of experiencing valued outcomes as a result of working toward a common goal.

The concept *expectation* has been developed in considerable detail because it has remained the least well defined of the input variables needed to construct a theory of group achievement. It is not suggested that the concept as here developed constitutes a complete theory of learning. Rather, it is to be regarded as an input variable which is required to account for individual value systems, reference group identifications, group norms, and group purpose without summoning the aid of variables which are extraneous to the theoretical system.

The basic variables (performances, interactions, and expectations) for a theory of group achievement have now been built into the system. An attempt will be made in the following chapter to show that these three variables, in combination, are able to account for the differentiation of member roles and for the differentiation of various structures that may be observed in groups.

## RESEARCH ON EXPECTATION

Recent research on expectation has been concerned primarily with problems of learning and perception. However, experimentation has been extended to include the investigation of level of aspiration, decision making, choice behavior, and predictive behavior. Little of the latter research has been designed to test a well-developed theory of expectation. In fact, expectation theories, as formal systems, have been developed primarily for the purpose of explaining the large body of data already accumulated in the field of learning.

Mowrer [507] and McGeogh and Irion [456] have reviewed the earlier experimental work which indicates that preparatory set and expectancy facilitate learning. Vernon's [738] review of research on perception suggests that set and expectation may determine to a large degree what is perceived in a stimulus field. Early experimenters tended to use the concepts of set and expectation only as a last resort to account for findings that could not be explained by other solutions. Hilgard [325] observes that there is little difference of opinion about the experimentally established facts of learning, but that there is considerable controversy regarding their explanation. Since expectation theories, as alternative solutions, have been developed after the fact and are comparatively recent in origin, they are not as well documented as are the stimulus-response theories of learning. Nevertheless, experimental data accumulated in the study of a wide variety of problems have direct relevance to expectation theory.


## Research on the Formal Theory of Expectation

An examination of Hull's [342] systematic theory of learning impresses one with the extreme complexity of the learning process. Any attempt to sort out a set of findings for a particular purpose is certain to ignore many exceptions and qualifying conditions that must be reckoned with in a theory of learning. The attempt to translate well-validated experimental findings into a theory of expectation does not necessarily substantiate the theory. However, if expectation is reinforcible, then it is hypothesized that the facts of reinforcement discovered in learning experiments apply to the reinforcement of expectation. This transferability from learning experiments to expectation theory is presented as an assumption, not as a demonstrated fact.

Thorndike's [710] experiments led him to propose the view that reward (or punishment) acts in an all or none manner to produce a confirming reaction. Tolman [719] holds that reward or punishment associated with a response serves primarily to confirm hypotheses or expectations regarding means-ends events. Guthrie's [283] research suggested that some degree of learning takes place completely during a single trial and that reward merely prevents the response from being unlearned. Skinner [647] found that extinction is more rapid following a single reinforcement than following 250 reinforcements, but that a single reinforcement is sufficient to produce a number of responses without further reward.

Hilgard [325] and McGeogh and Irion [456] regard the facts of primary and secondary reinforcement to have been convincingly demonstrated. Frequency of reinforcement increases the probability of response to the primary reinforcing stimulus, but with decreasing increments after an initial rapid rate of gain. Secondary stimuli which accompany, or are associated with, a reinforcement may also acquire reinforcing value. A secondary reinforcer may serve to elicit the relevant response when the primary stimulus is absent. In addition, closely related or generalized stimuli, even though not reinforced, may elicit responses associated with the primary reinforcer. Responses learned under reinforcement tend to be extinguished under the continued absence of reinforcement.

Stone [684] has reviewed the literature which indicates that responses are reinforced by punishment as well as by reward. Evidence presented by Estes [192] supports the conclusions of Thorndike [711] and Skinner [647] that, although punishment may suppress the rate of responding in the early stages of extinction, it does not decrease the time required for extinction. Skinner [647], Humphreys [345], and others have shown that responses learned under irregularly administered reinforcements are more highly resistant to extinction than those learned under consistent reinforcement. Miller and Dollard [493] suggest that less stimulus generalization takes place under consistent than under partial reinforcement. Wickens [764] has demonstrated the operation of response generalization as well as of stimulus generalization in learning experiments.

Pavlov [528], Hamilton and Krechevsky [293], Maier [462], Liddell [420], Spence [661], Mowrer [508], Skinner [647], and others have demonstrated that the flexibility and variability of behavior is reduced by several variations of reinforcement sequences. Among those are the intermixing of reward and punishment in a reinforcement situation, the administration of punishment in connection with a reinforcement, and the differential reinforcement of two stimuli that are made more and more similar until the individual is no longer able to discriminate between them. Under such demanding conditions the individual exhibits a marked restriction in variability of behavior, a tendency to repeat the same pattern of behavior over and over again, and a persistent state of vigilance.

A comparison of the results cited above with the theoretical discussion presented earlier in this chapter suggests that the hypotheses relative to the reinforcement of expectation, if not directly substantiated by experimentation on learning, are at least in conformity with the research findings.

The perception of positively and negatively valued discrepancies between expected and experienced outcomes is not dependent upon the absolute value of the expected reward when alternative outcomes are available. Tinklepaugh [715], in a study of delayed responses in monkeys, found that when a less well-liked reward was secretly substituted for a better-liked reward, the subjects exhibited searching behavior, bewilderment, disappointment, and often anger. Children also expressed disappointment when a substitute reward was found in place of the expected reward. Cowles and Nissen [159] used chimpanzees as subjects in an experiment to determine whether a large, as contrasted with a small, reward would be more effective as an incentive in making delayed discriminative choices. Although accuracy of choice tended to be somewhat higher with constantly large than with constantly small rewards, the results were not so clear cut when large and small rewards were alternated. The authors conclude that accuracy of response is not a function of size of reward alone but also of anticipation aroused by the perception of large and small incentives. The latter factor may be regarded as the "expectancy value of the incentive," its effect on the subject as "reward expectancy." Reward expectancy, rather than the absolute size of the reward, appeared to be the determining factor in explaining the results obtained.

Meyer [488] carried out a carefully designed experiment to determine the effects of large and small rewards on discrimination reversal learning by monkeys. The subjects were rewarded with a small reward for the correct choice of one of a pair of objects until a criterion of performance was attained. Choices between 64 pairs of objects were then studied under four different reward conditions: (1) large reward for one object, small reward after reversal to the second object; (2) large reward before reversal, large reward after; (3) small reward before reversal, large reward after; and (4) small reward before reversal, small reward after. At the beginning of the experimental trials, the four different reward conditions exhibited equal effects. However, after

64 problems had been solved the following results were clearly apparent. Performance was most accurate when a small reward was followed by a large reward. Next in effectiveness was a large reward followed by a large reward; and next was a small reward followed by a small reward. Least effective was a large reward followed by a small reward. Crespi [163] reports parallel results. He found that white rats ran more rapidly toward a goal for large reward following a small reward then for a constant reward. They ran more slowly for a small reward following a large reward. Meyer [488] concluded that "the range of rewards presented for the performance of a given task is a major determinant of the effectiveness of individual rewards."

Results obtained by Rotter [589] and his students indicate that human subjects respond differentially to increments and decrements of reward. In various experiments involving choice and preference behavior, it was found that the choice or preference behavior of the subjects could not be explained on the basis of frequency of reinforcements alone, but that both the strength of reinforcements and their place in the sequence of reinforcements were significant. Castaneda [115], studying betting behavior, calculated increments of expectancy following each reinforcement. He found that level of expectancy is elevated in response to positive reinforcement and depressed in response to negative reinforcement. His results are interpreted as supporting both the frequency hypothesis and the increment hypothesis.

Tolman has conducted numerous experiments the results of which are difficult to explain in terms of the hypothesis that reward reinforces the learning of responses. Illustrative of these is the experiment by Tolman and Honzik [723] in which three groups of rats were permitted to run in a maze. One group, which was rewarded with food, rapidly improved in efficiency (made fewer errors) from day to day. The two unrewarded groups improved very slowly in performance. However, when on the eleventh day, one of the unrewarded groups was given food, its performance on the following day and on succeeding days equaled that of the group which had been consistently rewarded. Tolman interprets these results as indicating that learning took place during exploration of the maze before food was encountered. Reward established the expectation of finding food. When again placed in the maze, the operation of expectation and the utilization of knowledge acquired about the maze enabled the previously unrewarded rats to find food as efficiently as those that had been consistently rewarded.

Experimental evidence presented by Wickens [765] indicates that perception in a learning situation cannot be explained solely in terms of direct stimulus effects upon the organism. Responses of the organism to its selective reactions to different aspects of the stimulus situation are involved in perceptual learning. In dealing with a stimulus complex, "the actual conditioned stimulus is the combination of the results of the unconditioned responses which are independently produced by the separate physical stimuli of the complex." Wickens' research provides a significant linkage between stimulus-response and expectational theories of learning.

In summary, Tinklepaugh's early experiments directed attention to the importance of differential expectations of outcome in learning experiments. The more carefully controlled experiments conducted by Cowles and Nissen, Crespi, and particularly by Meyer, indicate that it is not the absolute size of a reward, but its magnitude in comparison with a range or scale of possible rewards, that determines its value as a reinforcer. Rotter and Castaneda have demonstrated that a curve drawn to portray the acquisition of successive increments of expectation is similar to the curves used to represent the acquisition of increments of response in learning experiments. Tolman's experiments are ingeniously designed to support a theory of expectation. Research on expectation is well anchored in formal learning theory.

## Reinforcement and Generalization of Expectation

According to Tolman [718], an expectation acquires cathexis (positive or negative value) as a result of confirming experiences, and cathected expectations are highly resistant to extinction. The valence or motivating value of a stimulus is regarded as a function of need and acquired cathexis. Lewin [413] observed that the valence, or goal attractiveness, of a stimulus may change as a result of association with pleasant or unpleasant outcomes, satiation or monotony, and reactions to success or failure in attaining the stimulus object. It is apparent that value estimates play an important role in these theories. Although Tolman and Brunswick [722] recognized the operation of probability estimates in learning, probability is not utilized as one of the formally defined variables in Tolman's theory.

The research on choice, prediction, and betting suggests that Tolman and Lewin did not overemphasize the importance of value in expectation. Marks [467] observed that desirability rather than probability determined children's predictions of outcomes for which they had expressed a prior preference. Stated expectations were higher when drawing a desirable than an undesirable object. Irwin [351] also found that the stated expectations of adults are higher for desirable than undesirable outcomes in drawing (selecting) objects. An excess of stated expectations for desired outcomes increased confidence in the expectations. Cantril [104] found that the prediction of social events is influenced by preference for alternative outcomes. The lack of objective information and the lack of strong preference operate to reduce the certainty of predictions. McGregor [457] also found that attitude toward coming social events influences predictions. Students and experts who exhibit the same attitudes toward an issue do not differ significantly in their predictions relative to the issue. The more ambiguous the stimulus situation and the more important the outcome to the individual, the greater is the effect of attitude (value) upon prediction. The results of these studies indicate that the extent to which desirability estimates dominate expectation is related to existing attitude (value systems) and the degree of predictability provided by the relevant environment.

It might be expected that the occurrence of relevant environmental outcomes would provide a basis for confirming probability estimates and would enable the individual to predict more accurately. However, some kinds of events do not provide a valid basis for predicting future similar events. This is particularly true of events such as horse racing. In a study of betting behavior, Edwards [189] found that the choice of bets of equal value was determined primarily by the avoidance of long shots and by individual preference for specific probabilities. The studies of Cohen and Hansel [149] suggest that individuals differ in levels of risk taking in ways that are constant from one situation to another for the same individual. McClothlin [448] analyzed parimutuel statistics in 9,605 horse races. The bets made for win, place, and show indicated significantly positive expectations for low odds horses and a significant avoidance of horses for which the odds suggested a low probability of success. Bettors tended to increase the size of their bets as the racing day proceeded, and to bet more frequently on high odds horses. Losing bettors wagered larger amounts on succeeding races than did winning bettors. These results suggest that when expectation is highly motivated, and probability estimates are not validated by experienced outcomes, behavior tends to be more highly controlled by desirability estimates than by probability estimates.

Evidence is available from several studies which indicates that desirability estimates and probability estimates are differentially reinforcible. Hunt [346] reinforced children's expectations by varying the expression of approval for their rankings of toys. Preference changes after one day were related either to the expectation of reinforcement or to the frequency of reinforcement. Changes in preference, after eight days, were not related to reinforcement, suggesting that value is not related to the prediction of reinforcement. Phares [540] tested the hypothesis: since reinforcement scores in a skill situation are direct outcomes of performance, expectation as measured by a betting technique should be more realistic than when reinforcement is controlled by chance experimental variation. Support for the hypothesis was provided by the finding that shifts in expectation were not only significantly more frequent but also significantly greater in magnitude in the skill than in the chance situation. Worell [782] studied the level of aspiration of 102 boys with and without penalty for error in estimating performance on the next trial in a variety of tasks. It was found that expectation was lower for highly valued goals than for goals of low or medium value. When a penalty was imposed as a reinforcement, expectations continued to be lower for highly valued goals but were more realistic. Although desirability estimates may be high, Worell's results suggest that the individual may exhibit only a moderate level of expectation and may protect himself against disappointment by lowering his estimate of the probability of outcomes.

Jessor and Readio [366] rewarded the maze performance of college students with nickels and dimes. They found weak support for the hypothesis that the value of an event influences the expectation for its occurrence, especially when the probability is at the chance (.50) level. Peterson's [539] subjects predicted the appearance or non-appearance of two lights with different reward or loss values, under conditions of .75 and .50 probability, and with a money reward for success or a money loss for failure. The proportion of predictions with a higher expected value gradually increased over 250 trials. Crandall, Solomon, and Kellaway [161] announced before each of 100 random trials whether their subjects would gain or lose ten cents for success in estimating the appearance of a red light which appeared in 70 per cent of the trials. No loss or gain attended a green light which appeared in 30 per cent of the trials. During learning, expectancy for the red light increased significantly whether positively or negatively valued, but acquisition was more rapid with positive than with negative values. By the end of 100 trials, the red light was expected no more frequently with positive than with negative values. At the beginning of extinction (30 trials, all green, following 100 random trials), red light expectancies with positive value were more frequent than with negative value, but this difference diminished as the 30 trials progressed. These results suggest that value estimates operate to determine expectation to a greater degree in the early stages than in the later stages of reinforcement and extinction. Probability estimates tend to determine expectation in greater degrees as they are based on outcomes that exceed chance occurrence by increasing degrees.

The experiments discussed above provide consistent evidence

in support of the view that desirability estimates and probability estimates respond differentially to reinforcement.

Evidence is available from a number of studies which indicates that estimates of probability tend eventually to reach a level that corresponds with the objective probability of reinforcement. Humphreys [344] asked subjects to predict whether or not a second light would be flashed following the presentation of a signal light. For half the subjects, the second light appeared uniformly following the signal. The predictions of those subjects approached the 1.0 level. For the other half of the subjects, the second light was presented only 50 per cent of the time in random order. The predictions of this group approached the .5 level. During twelve extinction trials in which the second light was not presented following the signal, the predictions of the group that had received uniform reinforcement rapidly dropped to the zero level. However, the predictions of the group that had received random reinforcement showed a sharp rise in the first several extinction trials, then slowly declined. Inconsistent reinforcement is here shown to increase the resistance of expectation to extinction.

Grant, Hake, and Hornseth [264] repeated Humphreys' experiment, but varied it so that the second light appeared in 0, 25, 50, 75, and 100 per cent of the trials. Under each of the five experimental conditions, the predictions by the end of 60 trials had reached a level which approximated the percentage of reinforcements (appearance of the second light). Estes [193] has conducted a variety of experiments which indicate that if the probabilities of reinforcement are held constant, estimates of probability tend to rise or fall until they reach a value that corresponds with the probability of reinforcement.

Bruner, Goodnow, and Austin [93], in a series of studies on concept formation, found that categorizations over a series of trials tend to correspond closely to event probabilities even when the subjects are unable to identify the cues which they used in formulating categories. They observed three forms of behavior which accounted for variation of response in prediction or event matching. These were hope of a unique solution, need for direct test, and interest in the less frequent alternative. With validation, the subjects exhibited greater variability of response. Without validation, they tended to follow the lead of one or two cues and to disregard the evidence of other available cues. However, the abhorrence of monotony and the willingness to take a chance in hopes of gain also operated to produce variability of response. Cue preference or the valuing of cue impressiveness was found to disrupt estimates of probability. The preferred cue tends to be chosen in the face of conflict. If probability is obscure and if desirability is operative, the latter may operate on expectation as if the validity of external cues were 100:0 rather than 67:33, for example. The varied experiments described by Bruner, Goodnow, and Austin provide considerable detailed insight into the factors that operate in the formation of concepts and expectations.

The results of a number of experiments indicate that experienced success and expected success exert different effects upon the attractiveness of a task. Cartwright [112] reports that the expectation of failure tends to reduce the attractiveness of an activity more than the actual experience of failure. Gebhard [237] finds that both experienced and expected success increase the attractiveness of a task, while both expected and experienced failure reduce task attractiveness. Gebhard [238] reports also that the attractiveness of an activity rises when experienced success follows expected failure and falls when experienced failure follows expected success. Attractiveness rises when expected success follows expected success and also rises to some extent when expected failure follows expected failure. According to Filer [209], the attainment of a goal object tends to increase its attractiveness, while non-attainment tends to decrease its attractiveness. However, the expectation of attainment or non-attainment has little effect on its attractiveness after attainment or non-attainment.

The findings reported above can be interpreted to support the view that positively valued and negatively valued outcomes exert different effects on expectation, although both are reinforcing. A valued expectation, once aroused, does not necessarily undergo immediate extinction as a result of failure to effect reinforcement. A desirability estimate (attractiveness of a goal object) once established by reinforcement (goal attainment) is little affected by further reinforcement or non-reinforcement.

In order to study the generalization of expectation, Jessor [365] asked subjects to estimate their expected scores on four different tasks. They were then required to work on one of the tasks, and level of success was determined by experimental manipulation. A second set of estimates was then made for expected success on the four tasks. Generalization of expectation, as measured by changes in estimates, was greatest for the closely related task but occurred in relation to the other three tasks as well.

Irwin [350] analyzed the results of five studies bearing on the realism of expectations. He concluded that the correlation between levels of expectation and the immediately preceding performance scores reported to the subject are higher for realistic than for unrealistic expectations. The correlation between levels of expectation for the same task are higher for unrealistic than for realistic expectations. Also, the levels of expectation in different tasks are higher for unrealistic than for realistic expectations. The latter conclusion suggests that unrealistic expectations exhibit a higher degree of generalization than do realistic expectations.

Results from a variety of experiments conducted by Postman [543] and Bruner and Postman [94] suggest that both positively and negatively valued objects accentuate perceptual and judgmental responses more strongly than do objects which are neutral in value. Postman and Crutchfield [544] studied the relationships between need, set, and stimulus structure in perception. These authors prepared lists of incomplete words which could be completed to form a word representing either a food or a non-food. Selective set was established by forcing the subjects to give different numbers of food responses before beginning the experimental series. Need was measured by number of hours of food deprivation and by subjective ratings of hunger made at the close of the experiment. Lists which presented a greater probability of forming food responses elicited more food responses than did low or medium probability lists. The stronger the set, the greater the number of food responses elicited, especially by the medium probability lists. Hunger also increased the number of food responses, and hungry subjects gave more food responses with increasing degrees of set. Non-hungry subjects gave more food responses under median degrees of set, and fewer under high degrees of set. These results, while not directly applicable, suggest that drive may bear a complicated relationship to desirability estimates and probability estimates in determining level of expectation.

Experiments in the reinforcement and generalization of expectation, employing a variety of approaches, have produced findings which suggest that probability and value are differentially reinforced by the same outcome, that value dominates probability in the early stages of expectation, that value continues to maintain expectation when probability estimates are not confirmed, that probability estimates tend to assume a level which corresponds with the objective probability of reinforcement, that expectations become more realistic as the probability of outcomes increasingly exceeds the level of chance occurrence, and that unrealistic expectations undergo a higher degree of generalization than do realistic expectations. These findings are in accord with the theory presented in this chapter.


## Scales and Norms of Value

There is a great deal of experimental work which indicates that judgments and evaluations are made in relation to scales of estimation rather than on an all or none basis. Gibson [248] and Sherif and Sherif [633], have reviewed various aspects of this research.

Luchins and Luchins [442] and Coffin [145] have demonstrated that the greater the ambiguity of a perceived stimulus situation the more readily does the subject respond to distorting suggestions by the experimenter. Chapman and Volkman [132] found that they could influence the level of aspiration of their subjects by introducing standards which could not be tested for accuracy. However, after establishing their own standards of judgment and scales of evaluation, the subjects were not influenced by experimentally introduced standards. These studies suggest that an individual's reality orientation is related not only to the stability of his own scales of judgment but also to his ability to perceive structure in the stimulus situation.

Rogers [572] found that changing the anchorage stimulus as a standard of comparison for judging future stimuli (lifted weights, for example) tends to narrow or expand the scale of judgment as the anchorage point moves closer to, or farther from, the scale of stimuli being judged. Sherif and Sherif [633] also review research which indicates that the further a stimulus is moved away from the end points of a scale of judgment the more the scale tends to shrink rather than expand. Tresselt [728] reports that the more firmly a reference point is learned, the greater its effect upon, or utility as a reference point for, other scales of judgment. These results suggest not only that scales of judgment and value tend toward conservancy and the avoidance of disruption but also that they are generalizable to other scales of value.

Festinger [201] has advanced the hypothesis that individuals act to reduce cognitive dissonance, or to bring cognition into correspondence with reality. He cites numerous studies which indicate that individuals tend to interpret environmental events in terms of the opinions they hold, thus enhancing cognitive consonance. However, he found that under some experimental circumstances an individual may make a stronger effort to reduce dissonance under moderate degrees of uncertainty than under high degrees of probable success or failure.

Smock [655] found that subjects under psychologically stressful conditions who are confronted with ambiguous task situations tend to structure the stimulus elements into a complete figure relatively earlier in a task series and to achieve correct recognition of the stimulus later in the series. In other words, it appears that prerecognition or prior expectancy tends to reduce perceptual accuracy under stress and that stress in a discrepant situation induces a tendency to adhere to prevailing expectancies.

The evidence from these experiments indicates that stress, uncertainty, and stimulus ambiguity tend to fixate, or induce
closure in, expectation.

Wyatt and Campbell [785] investigated the effects of prior experience with objects perceived with varying degrees of blurring
or clarity upon later recognition. The authors report that hypothesis or expectancy formed in a highly undifferentiated situation inhibits accuracy of perception in a more clearly differentiated situation. They conclude that their experiment constitutes
a "demonstration of stereotypy, in its psychological sense, and illustrates one of the conditions under which prior experience may
be a liability." Luchins and Luchins [442] asked subjects to identify figures after observing a bystander identify the figures correctly or incorrectly. Conformity with false communication was
higher for ambiguous than for clear figures. Agreement with
either a true or false communication inhibited the perception of
an emerging percept. These experiments suggest that what an individual perceives may be more highly determined by prior
perceptual experiences than by the objective nature of the object
observed.

Postman [542] has presented experimental evidence which indicates that the strength of "hypothesis" or expectation is determined by the following factors: (1) the frequency with
which it has been confirmed in the past, (2) the absence of alternative hypotheses requiring large amounts of stimulus information for confirmation, (3) strong motivational support,
which reduces the amount of stimulus information required for
confirmation, and, (4) firm embedment in a larger cognitive
organization, which reduces the amount of confirming information required. Bruner [92], Bruner, Postman, and Rodrigues
[95], and Postman [542] also present experimental results which
suggest that when the amount of appropriate stimulus information is reduced, the individual's perceptual organization is more
highly determined by the dominant hypothesis. In other words,
the stronger an expectation, the more readily will it be reinforced by discrepant information. It may also be inferred from
Postman's conditions (2) and (4), that the more closely struc-

tured and all-inclusive an individual's value system, the more readily will it be reinforced by all relevant outcomes.

The experiments on level of aspiration provide further evidence on interpersonal norms and scales. According to Lewin, Dembo, Festinger, and Sears [416], the subjective experience of success or failure is a function of the relationship between an individual's level of aspiration and his level of performance, rather than a direct function of his level of performance. Level of aspiration is related to seeking of success, avoidance of failure, and judgments of probability. Frank [221], summarizing the literature to 1941, found that the personality of the individual, the properties of the task, and the meaning of the experimental situation to the individual may all operate to affect level of aspiration. In general, level of aspiration tends to follow level of performance, but is more strongly influenced by success than failure. Escalona [191] and Gould [260] found that subjects tend more often to raise their goals after success than to lower them after failure. Anderson and Brandt [11] and Sears [612] found that the group tends to exert influences on the individual which shift his level of aspiration toward the mean (norm) of the group, particularly if his performance is considerably below the group average. Those members whose performance is below the mean exhibit an exalted level of aspiration, while those whose performance is above the group average tend to be little affected by comparisons with the group. Chapman and Volkman [132] found, however, that when the task is one in which the subject has had past experience and has fairly accurate knowledge of his ability to perform, his level of aspiration is not affected by comparisons with the group norm.

Festinger [197] found that level of aspiration may be determined by reference group comparisons. The level of aspiration of college students was observed to vary when the average high school student, the average college student, and the average graduate student was used successively as a reference group. According to Festinger, reference group identification serves to establish scales of value in terms of which a given level of performance is judged to be desirable or undesirable. The individual tends to compare himself in terms of these scales with other persons whom he perceives to be comparable with himself. He tends to withdraw from competition with others whom he perceives to be much superior or inferior to himself. Dreyer [183], in a test of the latter hypothesis, found that under conditions of experimentally induced success and failure, only the average performers competed against the group average. When permitted to stop at various stages in the experimental procedure, the high performers stopped significantly sooner than the low performers. Once the high performers had established their superior status to their own satisfaction, they allocated inferior status to the group and withdrew from competition. Under conditions of high expectancy, the average performers continued longer than the high and low performers. Under conditions of low expectancy, the low performers continued longer than the high or average performers.

The findings from the various studies discussed above indicate that judgments and evaluations are made in terms of scales of estimate and value. These scales are related to the perceived environment. Both the lack of a well-anchored scale of judgment and the lack of structure in the relevant environment reduce the certainty of judgment and render it vulnerable to unrealistic suggestions. However, scales tend toward conservancy and the maintenance of their own integrity through the process of constriction and closure under stress. One means by which individuals maintain the integrity of their scales of estimate in interpersonal situations is to compare themselves with their perceived equals rather than with persons estimated to be superior or inferior to themselves. An additional source of reality testing is the group norm, which serves as a more or less stable reference point for comparing self with others. Individuals are found to shift their scales of expectation to conform with the group norm.

The conception of value as reinforced by all outcomes receives some support in the experimental literature. Haigh and Fiske [285] report that speed of recognition is significantly higher for words which represent a subject's most highly ranked value preferences than for words which represent less highly preferred values. Gilchrist, Ludeman, and Lysak [252] found that the recognition threshold for words with negative and positive value connotations is lowered in comparison with words which are neutral in value. However, when words are shown in contexts with other words which imply a disagreeable or socially tabooed association, the effect is to raise the threshold of both positively and negatively valued words while lowering that of neutral words. The results of these experiments suggest that value systems exert a selective effect upon perception and that selection is displaced in the direction of confirming or reinforcing the value system.

Adorno, Frenkel-Brunswick, Levinson, and Sanford [3] have posited the existence of an authoritarian personality structure, characterized by conservatism, emotional coldness, power seeking, hostility toward minority groups, and other undesirable reactions. An anti-authoritarian personality is said to exhibit liberal attitudes toward political and social issues and other traits more or less the opposites of those presented by the authoritarian. Luchins [441], Rokeach [576], Christie [138], Shils [638], Titus and Hollander [716], and others have criticized these hypotheses on methodological grounds as well as on the basis of contradictory evidence.

Sullivan and Adelson [693] prepared a scale which parallels that used by Adorno and associates for measuring ethnocentrism. However, the words "people" or "most people" were substituted for the words "Negroes," "Jews," and the like. Responses to the two scales were significantly correlated. The authors conclude that attitudes of suspicion and prejudice tend to be highly generalized and that for many persons "there may be no in-group other than the self." Bass [43] constructed a scale which consisted of items from the ethnocentrism scale and of additional statements which paralleled those in the ethnocentrism scale but were stated in the opposite direction. Different degrees of contradiction were represented in the pairs of statements. He found that set to acquiesce to contradictory statements increases as the pairs become more ambivalent. Bass concludes that these results may be interpreted on the basis of a response set to acquiesce to *any* generalization about social issues. Jackson and Messick [353] found ethnocentrism scores to be positively related to reversed items on the authoritarianism scale, and Rokeach [576] reports a negative correlation between narrow-mindedness and ethnocentrism. Chapman and Campbell [133] and Cohn [150] observe a tendency for response set to operate in answering the authoritarianism scale.

Rokeach [575] asked college students to describe ways in which they thought different religious and political ideologies were interrelated. They were also given a scale of ethnocentric attitudes. The least ethnocentric subjects showed the highest degree of comprehensive organization (ability to interrelate). Rokeach [574] suggests that value systems vary in degree of organization and inclusiveness, ranging on a continuum from comprehensive, though isolated, to narrow. Vidulich and Rokeach [740] report that high dogmatic subjects experience greater difficulty than low dogmatic subjects in integrating new sets into a problem solution, and that such difficulty is a function of greater rejection of, and poorer memory for, the new sets to be integrated. Brown [89] summarized the results of his research by concluding that the person with a rigid value system "has a formula to fit every case," thus providing reassurance and reducing anxiety. The anxious person, when ego-involved regarding his achievement, and once having found a solution to a type of problem, tends to reformulate relevant new problems to fit the same solution.

The results of the research described above lend strong support to the hypothesis that value systems are reinforced by all relevant outcomes and tend to become highly generalized. Perception is found to be highly selective. The direction of selectivity tends toward the confirmation and protection of value systems, particularly when the objective environment fails to provide clearly unambiguous information for the rejection of preconception. Individuals differ in the degree of rigidity of perception and in the flexibility of value systems. However, the liberal person differs from the conservative individual, not in being unprejudiced and free from value estimates but in being able to integrate a greater variety of elements in his value systems.

Edwards [188] reports the results of a wide variety of studies which indicate that "social desirability," rather than response set, determines reactions to the items of personality tests. The individual tends to accept those items which describe him in socially desirable terms and to reject those which describe him in socially undesirable terms. The tendency of individuals to describe their personality reactions in terms of estimates of social desirability might well be regarded as an expression of conformity to a general social norm of self-perception. Whereas estimates of social desirability serve to protect the integrity of the individual's perception of himself as a personality in public interaction with other members of society, response set operates to protect the integrity of his value systems, which are perceived as private to himself.

Numerous studies have revealed a relationship between value systems and personality patterns. Value systems have been measured by means of scales of attitude, opinion, and strength of belief. Both projective tests and tests composed of items that are descriptive or non-descriptive of various patterns of behavior have been used to measure personality. Kogan [393] found that high scorers on authoritarian attitude scales differed from low scores in exhibiting a higher degree of defense against the perception of visually presented statements which disparaged the subject. High and low scorers on ethnocentric attitude scales do not differ in this respect. Scodel and Freedman [608] observed that high scorers on authoritarian attitude scales exceed low scorers in response stereotypy in that they tend to estimate co-workers as making high scores on the same scales whether their scores are high or low. Low scorers were more discriminating in estimating the attitudes of their co-workers. Brim and Hoff [84] asked subjects to estimate the probability of events and the degree of certainty of the estimates. Extremity of response to attitude scales was found to be significantly related to desire for certainty scores, but response to individual attitude items was not. It was found that both high and low scores on a scale of authoritarian attitudes were significantly related to desire for certainty scores. Davids [170] also reports that the intolerance of ambiguity (desire for certainty) is exhibited by persons who make extremely liberal, as well as by those who make extremely conservative, scores on scales of authoritarian attitudes.

Cohen [146] found that self-esteem and situational structure interact to determine the perception of threat in the power exercised by other persons. Those individuals who are high in self-esteem exhibit less threat-oriented behavior in structured situations than do individuals who are low in self-esteem and in unstructured situations. The effects of self-esteem alone on threat are not significant, but the effects of structure alone are highly significant in that a reduction of structure increases the perception of threat at all levels of self-esteem. Cohen concludes that his subjects differed, not on the presence or absence of threat reactions but in their handling of threat. Those high in self-esteem act to protect their perceptual integrity by excuses, blame avoidance, and rigidity in their reactions to the threat inherent in perceived power. Those low in self-esteem bring more threat into the situation, are more sensitive to discrepancy, are more vulnerable and dependent upon the power-laden situation, and show a greater need for structure. In another experiment, Cohen [147] paired subjects in discussion tasks according to similarity or dissimilarity of personality defense syndromes. When paired on the basis of projective reactions, subjects were found to be more hostile in interacting with other projectors than with non-projectors. Lindzey [426] compared the reactions to frustration of subjects who exhibited a high degree of minority group prejudice with persons scoring low in minority group prejudice. Individuals high in prejudice were found to be more susceptible to frustration than those low in prejudice, but did not show more evidence of overt aggression. A restricted value system does not necessarily lead to violence or aggression.

Evidence from a great variety of experiments indicates that individuals differ in the response patterns they exhibit to maintain self-integrity and the integration of value systems. Uncertainty, discrepancy, and the lack of structure tend to induce the closure of value systems and the structuring of perception in accord with existing expectation. Persons high in emotional security and self-esteem tend to respond to threat and stress by perceptual closure and the rejection of discrepant values, while those low in emotional security exhibit a heightened sensitivity to discrepancy and a greater need for situational structure which is in conformity with their value systems. The greater the extent to which an individual's value systems deviate from the norm of the group, the greater his desire for certainty, whether his attitudes be liberal or conservative. Individuals prefer the association of other persons whose values are similar to their own; hence are mutually reinforcing. Narrowness of value systems is closely related to response stereotypy and to the projection of own values and motives upon other persons. Predictive ability (accuracy) is related to cognitive complexity and openness of value systems, but with demand for situational structure which reinforces value systems. The liberal differs from the conservative person not in exhibiting a greater degree of freedom from value systems but in the types of defensive reactions he employs to protect his value systems and in the greater range of discrepant elements he is able to reconcile in his value systems.

## Individual Values and Group Affiliation

The importance of individual value systems in the motivation of voluntary associations has been demonstrated in a variety of research approaches. French [222] instructed subjects in a group session to rate their own achievement motivation and affiliation motivation, and to rate each other according to degree of friendship. The subjects were then divided into groups of four in which three were mutual friends and one was not considered a friend by the other three. In an assembly task only the non-friend was permitted to succeed. The subjects then nominated one or two members with whom they would like to work again. Friendship was found to be more important than success in making the second choice for all subjects combined. However, those subjects who valued achievement very highly made significantly more choices of success partners, while those who valued group affiliation chose few success partners. There is apparent in these results a tendency for persons to choose in the direction of increasing the probability of reinforcing their own value systems. Other investigators report similar results. Atkinson and Walker [21] found that the greater the extent to which an individual values group affiliation the greater his ability to differentiate faces from geometric figures presented subliminally on a screen. According to Precker [545] students prefer as associates those peers (other students) and superiors (faculty advisors) whose values (measured attitudes) most closely resemble their own. Fiedler, Warrington, and Blaisdell [208] found that group members perceived their best-liked fellow members as more like self and ideal self than least-liked members. Fensterheim and Tresselt [196] report that college students express a greater liking for other persons the more closely their values are perceived to resemble their own. Smith's [651] subjects, after completing a scale of values, were given two incomplete scales to complete as they might have been filled out by the persons who supposedly started them. One was made similar, and the other dissimilar, to the subject's own responses. Subjects tended to prefer as work partners or companions the persons on whom they projected their own values. Persons perceived as more similar to self were more highly accepted. The results of the six studies described above lend support to the point of view that values operate to lower perceptual thresholds and that individuals seek affiliation with other persons who are perceived to raise the probability of reinforcing value systems.

Various aspects of group functioning are found to exert differential effects upon the choice of associates, the desire to continue affiliation with the group, and the perception of the nature of the group. The success or failure of the group in which one is a participating member may reinforce expectations relative to self and the group. Steiner and Dodge [668] manipulated the success and failure of small groups working on a construction task and then had the group members describe themselves on interest and personality items. The subjects used the same items to indicate how their partners ought to describe themselves and again to indicate how they thought their partners would describe themselves. Discrepancies between descriptions of "ought" and "predicted" behavior were significantly greater for the unchosen than for the chosen partner in the failure condition, but not in the success condition. A significant tendency was observed for subjects in the failure situation to think that the unchosen subject would rate himself as more like the rater than was warranted by the facts. Also in the failure situation, the chosen partner was described as more similar to the rater than was warranted by the self-description of the chosen partner. In Fiedler's [207] research, members of successful basketball teams and surveying teams were found to choose as a preferred co-worker a differentiating member who is concerned with effective task performance. Members of unsuccessful teams tended to choose a warm, emotionally involved member as preferred co-worker. Torrance [726] reports the results of research in which highly effective and less effective air crews wrote stories about pictures of formal and informal groups. Once a crew story had been agreed upon, the individual members of more effective crews accepted the story as their own. The members of more effective crews, in response to pictures of formal group interaction, more frequently perceived successful outcomes, remaining in the group, orderliness, and productivity; but, in response to pictures of informal interaction, perceived less harmony and more friendship than the less effective crews. Similar results are reported by Horwitz and Lee [338], who found that members who were interrupted at different stages of a group performance task tended to recall disagreement in decision states and to recall agreement in indecision states. Cervin and Ketchum [125] studied the individual and group performance of persons who differed in emotional stability. As predicted, both individuals and groups showed an initial increase in performance and then a decline in response to continued frustration. Contrary to hypothesis, stable and unstable persons did not differ in the amount of time spent on frustrating tasks.

Not only do individuals value the kinds of persons and groups that will reinforce their value systems, but experiences of group success and failure exert effects upon perceptions of the nature of the group. In addition, such experiences appear to change the demands that the individual makes upon his associates. He requires one kind of personality structure to bolster his expectations of continued group success, and a different kind of personality to support his disappointment under group failure.

Group success and failure also exert effects upon the individual's perception of the value of the group as a medium for the accomplishment of valued tasks. Lichtenberg [419] asked subjects to estimate the probability of successful task performance under different conditions of available time and perceived time needed to complete a co-operative construction task. It was found that group members tend to work as individuals when the perceived time required to initiate co-operation lowers the probability of success by group effort. Gerard [242] observed the reactions of group members to experimentally induced success and failure when the outcome was attributed to the differing abilities of the group members. After he had experienced group success or failure, each subject was asked to estimate his chances of future success when working with other members whose skills were known with different degrees of certainty. It was found that the more successful an individual had been in the past the more favorable was his estimate of future success by means of group action. However, the more equivocal the information possessed by the individual relative to the abilities of his co-workers, the less certain he was in estimating the future success of the group.

The success or failure of a group may affect not only a member's perception of the group, but also his evaluation of himself. Evidence to support this point of view is provided by Stotland, Thorley, Thomas, Cohen, and Zander [686]. These authors studied the aspirations and self-esteem of subjects working alone or in groups under conditions of induced success or failure and with varying relevance of individual task to the group task. The subjects were told that the group had either high or low expectations for them in completing a performance task. It was found that a member is more likely to accept as a personal goal the level of aspiration set by the group when the activity is relevant to the group than when it is not. Failure on a relevant, but not irrelevant, task induces a member to evaluate his performance as poorer when the group's expectations are high than if low for the member and for the group as a whole. Group expectations do not affect self-evaluation when performance is successful. Under failure, the individual is more dependent upon the group for reality testing. Group expectation appears to be more potent than self-esteem as a reference point in evaluating self-performance.

The results of these varied studies indicate that a membership group, even though an experimental group of very short duration, provides a valued reference scale for self-evaluation. Group members are found to act to further the success of the group and to preserve their self-esteem. Group success contributes toward the latter effect, while the failure of the group tends to jeopardize the individual's self-esteem as well as his esteem for other members who are perceived to be responsible for the group failure. Those members whose aspirations are closer to the norm of the group exhibit greater emotional freedom for becoming task involved. Group expectations do not affect self-evaluation as much when the group is successful as when it fails. Group failure disrupts the individual's group anchored scale of estimation and throws him back upon his own defenses to maintain the integrity of his scale of values.

Experimental evidence has been found which supports the point of view that individuals seek affiliation with other persons and groups who are perceived to be potential reinforcers of value systems. Continued affiliation with such persons and groups is valued so long as they are perceived to provide a means for maintaining the integration of value systems, the accomplishment of personal goals, and the maintenance of self-esteem.

## The Structuring of Expectation by the Group

A new member enters a group with certain expectations already structured by his experiences in other places and by the groups with which he identifies himself. But his expectations also come to be structured by the new group and by his experiences in it. Sherif [631] reports the results of an extensive body of experimentation which indicate that participation in a group tends to bring the responses of deviant members into conformity with the normative response for the group. Individuals judging the perceived movement of a light shown on a screen in a darkened room exhibit differences in estimate that are specific to the individual when tested alone. When retested in a group situation, the estimates of individuals converge toward the average judgment of the group and tend to persist after leaving the group. When newly assembled groups are brought into an unstructured experimental situation, each tends to develop a characteristic norm relative to the situation. Kidd and Campbell [391], using an adaptation of Sherif's experiment, found that group members when asked to judge a light flicker after having experienced success showed more movement toward a purported group norm than did those who had previously experienced task failure.

Asch [19] reports a series of experiments in which groups were given the task of comparing the lengths of successive sets of lines. All the members except one were instructed by the experimenter to respond erroneously. The single uninstructed member was then confronted by a situation in which all other members of the group were perceived to be in error. Two-thirds of the uninstructed subjects gave the correct response even though in a minority, and one-third of the subjects gave responses which corresponded with the erroneous reports of the unanimous majority. A majority of three was as effective as a majority of 8 or 16 members in producing conforming errors. The introduction of a "partner" instructed to agree with the uninstructed subject markedly reduced the number of errors made in conformity with the majority.

The experiments of Sherif and Asch demonstrate very clearly the power of the group to infleunce the expectations and actions of its members in conformity with the norms of the group. However, they also demonstrate the fact that the group is not all-powerful in structuring the behavior of its individual members. Many individuals maintain their independence in spite of all pressures for conformity exerted by the group. Asch [19] reports that independence of group pressure was exhibited in three different forms based (1) on confidence in own perceptions in opposition to group pressure, (2) on the necessity of maintaining individual integrity, and (3) on the felt necessity of dealing adequately with the task. Subjects who yielded to group pressure appeared either (1) to suffer actual distortion of perception, (2) to judge their perceptions to be in error, or (3) to conform deliberately and knowingly because of the discomfort attendant upon appearing different or inferior in the eyes of the group.

Conformity to group norms is exhibited not only in judgments but also in value systems and goals and aspirations. McKeachie [459] used attitude scales for measuring personal values and estimated group attitudes or norms. He found that changes in individual attitudes are significantly correlated with changes in the subjects' estimates of the group norms. Gerard [241] required his subjects to make judgments in larger experimental groups and then divided them into subgroups which differed in the degree of mutual liking among the members. Greater convergence of opinions was found in the high attraction than in the low attraction subgroups. Those members who were in agreement with the norm of the larger group made more attempts in the subgroups to influence members who expressed divergent opinions. Rasmussen and Zander [553] report that the level of aspiration of teachers resembles the perceived norm of their own subgroup in the school system more closely than the perceived norms of subgroups in which they are not members. Perceived personal performance falls below "ideal" performance the more the individual deviates from the standard attributed to own group and the more attractive the group is to him. Results of the latter two experiments suggest that norms may be structured by subgroups as well as by the larger group.

According to Sherif [631], "social norms of any description represent standardized generalizations concerning expected behavior of consequence to the group." Norms may develop relative to judgments, values, conduct, and other aspects of member and group behavior. Mutual interaction is more effective than observation alone as a means of enabling the members of a group to arrive at a common norm. Scott [611] suggests that if values are reinforced, the more people who profess a value in a group, the more important it should become for those who hold it. Results in 14 experimental groups confirmed the hypothesis. The relationship between the number of members stating a value and the importance of the value to them was found to be greatest when group cohesiveness was high, interaction intense, and communication about the value was high. Argyle [14] found that the public expression of opinion is more effective than the private expression of opinion in changing the communicator's own opinion. Brodbeck [85] presented members of experimental groups with the opportunity to change their attitudes in response to different conditions of reinforcement, counterpropaganda, and group discussion. She found that when an individual's confidence in a belief is shaken by propaganda, he prefers to hear arguments in support of the belief. Members of discussion groups tended to listen to persons who agreed with them and to ignore the arguments of their opponents. Although there is much evidence which supports the view that interaction facilitates the formation of group norms, a number of investigators have produced results which indicate that reinforcement prior to interaction limits the reinforcing effects of interaction. Mausner [474] required subjects working alone to compare the lengths of lines. Half were told they were right 82 per cent of the time; the other half that they were wrong 82 per cent of the time. Later, when working in pairs both of whom had been positively reinforced, subjects tended to maintain their former judgments in the group situation. When both had been negatively reinforced, or when one had been positively and the other negatively reinforced, their judgments in the group tended to converge. Mausner [473] and Gilchrist [251] conducted experiments on the reinforcing effects of group success and failure upon judgment and material choice. Mausner found that subjects who had worked with previously successful partners converged significantly more toward those partners on a group judgment task than did those who had worked with previously unsuccessful partners. Gilchrist successively paired and re-paired the members of groups consisting of four members each under different conditions of success and failure. Initially successful pairs of subjects tended to choose other successful subjects so long as their successes continued. They also tended to choose other previously successful subjects after experiencing failure. Initially failing subjects tended to distribute their choices between successes and other failures. However, when permitted to succeed after repeated failure, previously failing subjects were then able to choose each other. Those who failed to the end continued to distribute their choices between previous successes and failures. The author concludes that initial reinforcements are more effective than later ones in determining mutual choices. However, the eventual experience of success appears to reinforce the expectation of success for those who initially failed.

Mausner and Bloch [475] tested the hypothesis that a pair of subjects in a task situation should converge (change own estimate to conform with partner's estimate) less when they are positively reinforced, when they are successful, and when they have not worked together co-operatively in the past. Convergence was found to be lowest when all three conditions were fulfilled, with the forces of all the variables operating in the same direction. Partner success and prior reinforcement were found to be additive in their effects on convergence, except when the partner had failed in a previous task. Kidd and Campbell [391] studied experimental groups under different conditions of success and failure. Members of groups with three successes and no failures showed significantly more movement toward the group norm than did those in groups with three failures or in a control situation with no relevant group experience.

When an individual's judgment has been confirmed by prior experience, he is less strongly influenced by a group norm than when he has failed to receive positive prior reinforcement. Evidence on the effects of the prior success or failure of a partner is contradictory, but suggests that partner success facilitates convergence of judgments toward a norm. Experiencing success after continued failure enables the individual to choose as partners other persons who have also failed. It is clear that prior reinforcement exerts influence upon expectation that conditions the effects of different reinforcements which may follow. The exact nature of these limiting effects is not always easy to predict when reinforcement occurs in the course of interaction with other group members. Further evidence along this line is provided by Horwitz [337], who studied the effects of task interruption upon groups that were competing for points. Midway toward task solution the members voted either to accept the points already earned or to complete the task for additional points. Significantly more of the tasks were recalled when interrupted after a group vote to continue than when completed after a vote to discontinue. When the individual's vote is contrary to the group vote, task recall for both completed and interrupted tasks is higher than when the individual vote corresponds with the vote of the group. The author concludes that disagreement with the group, as well as task interruption, tends to induce tension. If a member agrees with the positive goal of the group, his tension is reduced when the task is completed, but increased when the task is interrupted. If the member accepts an avoidance goal of the group, his tension is reduced when the task is interrupted; but if his avoidance goal for the group is contrary to the group goal, his tension is increased by continuing with the task. Whether or not an individual exhibits tension in a group may be more closely related to his conformity or non-conformity to the group norm than with the success or failure of the group.

When a member joins a new group, the group provides a

stimulus for further expectation which may or may not be clearly defined and structured. If the group fails over a period of time to provide structure, the new member may be observed to test the situation in a variety of ways in an effort to arrive at a stable structuring of his expectations. Examples of such testing behavior may be observed in persons who report for work on a new job but can find no one to tell them what their duties are or who is to supervise their work. There is a considerable body of experimental work which indicates that many persons are comfortable only in a structured situation. Lippitt [428] reports that children in experimentally created groups, when given a great deal of freedom from leadership direction and programming, exhibit a strong tendency to "get things organized" and to "know where I stand." Hemphill [312] finds that the members of large groups exhibit a significantly greater tendency than those of small groups to approve a highly structuring type of leadership.

The expectations of most members are structured in conformity with the norms of the group. They tend also to be structured by membership in subgroups within the larger group. Roethlisberger and Dickson [571] observed that membership in "informal" subgroups serves a variety of functions. It provides a basis for a satisfying type of fact-to-face interaction that "formal" organization tends to inhibit. It often serves the function of sanctioning the norms of the larger group. However, it may also create a subgroup norm which differs from that of the larger group. Roethlisberger and Dickson, in attempting to explain why rest pauses, increased financial incentives, and the like were at times ineffective, observed that the members of a subgroup developed their own normative standards relative to what constituted a reasonable or fair rate of performance. The members tended to conform to this subgroup norm even though it might deviate considerably from the norm of performance set by the larger group, or rather by the management of the group. Members who attempted to deviate from the subgroup norm in the direction of the norm of the larger group were made to feel the active disapproval of the subgroup.

Mathewson [472] found that the "restriction of output" was a widespread practice in a great variety of business and industrial organizations. He was able to confirm Roethlisberger's observation of the power of subgroup norms to regulate the performance of individuals. Stouffer and his associates [688], in their study of soldiers' attitudes toward combat, found that many otherwise baffling results relative to combat morale could be explained satisfactorily in terms of the reference group hypothesis. It was discovered that married men with low morale were not comparing themselves with the other married men undergoing similar hardships in combat, but were comparing themselves with unmarried men who were perceived to be making a lesser personal sacrifice and with married men at home who were perceived as suffering relatively less deprivation. Shils [639] presents a systematic development of the reference group hypothesis and the concept of "relative deprivation." He maintains that the primary group develops standards and norms of conduct which support the individual member and enable him to bear up under stress. Individuals estimate their own experiences as satisfying or dissatisfying in comparison with the experiences of reference group members with whom they compare themselves. Newcomb [518], Sherif [631], Katz and Lazarsfeld [378], Merton and Kitt [486], and Shils [639] present evidence which indicates that the extent to which an individual will conform to the norms of a group is related to the extent of his identification with other reference groups whose normative values are similar to, rather than contrary to, the norms of the membership group.

Not only do the members of a group tend to shift their judgments and values in the direction of conforming to the norms of the group, but the members tend also to exert pressures designed to induce such conformity. Festinger [199] has advanced the hypothesis that the pressure exerted by the group members upon a given member relative to an issue will increase with increase in the perceived discrepancy between the group norm and the opinion held by the member, with increase in the relevance of the issue to the functioning of the group, and with increase in the cohesiveness of the group. Festinger [200] expands this system of hypotheses in his theory of social comparison processes.

The greater a member's attraction to a group, the greater his tendency to conform to the norms of the group and the greater the pressure that the group can exert upon him without driving him out of the group. When there is a range of opinion in the group, the members tend to reject those whose opinions are very divergent from the norms of the group.

Festinger's theories of communication and social comparison processes have stimulated a number of experiments on social norms. Festinger and Thibaut [205], Thibaut [705], and Back [22] found that as groups increase in cohesiveness and relevance of the issues being considered, they exert increased pressures upon deviant members, and deviating members exhibit greater change in the direction of the group norm. Deviates who will not conform tend to be rejected. Gerard [240], and Festinger, Gerard, Hymovitch, Kelley, and Raven [202] observed that conformers tend to communicate most with those members who express deviant opinions, and deviates tend more often than conformers to change their opinions. Greater change was observed in homogeneous than in heterogeneous groups, and on matters of opinion than on matters of fact. Gerard found that minority groups are less able than majority groups to accept the member who deviates from the norms of both groups. Festinger's theory is shown to receive support from a variety of experimental approaches.

According to Bovard [81], Israel [352], Festinger, Torrey, and Willerman [206], and others, the greater the extent to which a member values group affiliation the greater the likelihood that he will permit the group to structure his expectations. Hochbaum [326] observed that a member's perception of his deviation from the group norm tends to lower his self-confidence and increase the probability that he will change in the direction of the norm. Those who deviate and then change in response to pressure exhibit less confidence than those who change voluntarily or do not change at all. Whether or not a member will change under pressure depends upon his perception of his ability to handle the various problems involved in the situation. Dittes and Kelley [180] gave members of experimental groups fictitious ratings which indicated that they were rated by other members as high, average, or low in acceptability as group members. Those rated average in acceptability tended to conform to the group norms, while those rated high tended not to conform. Those rated low showed less uniformity, being about midway between the high and average in conformity. Those rated low in acceptability showed a higher degree of conformity when required to express their opinions publicly in the group than when not required to do so. The experimenters interpret the greater conformity under public conditions as an attempt to avoid rejection by the group. In a similar experiment, Jackson and Saltzstein [355] found that non-accepted members of experimental groups exhibit a greater need for reassurance than do members who are accepted, and that the need for reassurance is proportionate to the member's attraction to the group. The need for social reality and the perceived necessity of group locomotion and norm conformity are positively related to the degree of ambiguity of the stimulus situation, particularly for members who are highly attracted to the group.

Although groups are shown to exert potent forces in the direction of inducing conformity among their members, the individual is not entirely at the mercy of a group. Prior experience which confirms the value of desirability estimates and the validity of probability estimates strengthens his ability to withstand pressures exerted by the group. An objective group task which permits the individual to test and validate his probability estimates also increases the ability of the individual member to resist group pressure. Sherif and Harvey [632] report that the group tends to be resented and to produce increased feelings of insecurity under conditions of heightened uncertainty. Their subjects preferred to make their judgments of the group under high certainty conditions publicly, but alone under conditions of low certainty. The more uncertain the situation, the greater the difference between the group norm and individual judgment and the greater the scale along which individual judgments are scattered. Additional evidence is presented by Thibaut and Strickland [708], who studied groups which differed in experimentally determined task set and group set. They found that as the pressure to conform increases, the percentage of members whose judgments change to conformity increases under group set but decreases under task set. In group set, a member is concerned in maintaining membership with other persons whose attitudes are being communicated to him. In task set, he is interested in other persons as communicators of facts. Goldberg [255] found that knowledge of a group norm results in conformity toward the norm, but conformity is no greater in groups of four than in groups of two members. Blake, Helson, and Mouton [68] observed that conforming responses are more frequent with difficult items than with easy ones, and with small rather than large deviations of group opinion from the true response. Significant individual consistency in conforming to different norm situations was observed, indicating that personality as well as situational factors operate to induce conformity. Bass [41] found that individual conformity to group opinion regarding a matter of fact is related to the accuracy of the group opinion and the degree of certainty of the individual's initial judgment.

An analysis, by no means complete, of research concerned with the structuring of interpersonal expectation reveals an impressive number of variables at work in social groups. Few of the variables are found to exhibit any simple, one-to-one relationship with other variables. Nevertheless, a number of well-substantiated findings has emerged from the analysis. The studies discussed above indicate that groups exert strong pressures upon their members in an effort to induce conformity to their norms. The greater the cohesiveness of the group, the stronger the pressure it is able to exert. Members are more readily influenced to conform when they are strongly attracted to the group, when they do not wish to be rejected by the group members, when they are lacking in self-confidence, and when the norm concerns a matter of judgment or value rather than a matter of fact. Another factor that facilitates conformity is a correspondence between the norms of the membership group and the norms of reference groups with which the members identify themselves. Members tend not to conform to the norms of the group under conditions of uncertainty and group failure.

## Discussion

Although the main outlines of the expectation hypothesis receive experimental support, there are several detailed areas for which very little experimental evidence is available. There is particular need for research on the different rates of growth and extinction of expectation when high, medium, and low values respectively, are confirmed for desirability estimates. This research should be extended to include an investigation of the relationships of different levels of positively and negatively valued desirability estimates to different levels of estimated probability.

There is strong reason to believe that drive and desirability estimates interact. The theoretical system, as developed, imposes no necessity for advancing the hypothesis that drive and probability estimates interact. However, the lack of a strong hypothesis in this direction should not bar a thorough investigation of the problem. There is need for experimental definition of the relationship between drive and estimates of desirability and probability.

# 5

## Group Structure and Operations

THE concepts *performance, interaction,* and *expectation* refer to aspects of behavior that are recognized in our daily speech. Each concept is well established in the scientific literature. It is suggested that the use of these three concepts in combination is capable of explaining group structure and operations.

There is no denying the wholeness and continuity of behavior. Nevertheless, performances, interactions, and expectations are exhibited with varying degrees of independence of each other. Performance and expectation may be exhibited independently of interaction, as when a group member is working alone. It seems probable, even though an arbitrary assertion would be difficult to support, that some degree of expectation is always involved in performance and interaction. Performance, since it describes the nature of the actions and reactions involved in interaction, is always an element of interaction.

The three concepts have been described as if each could be exhibited separately. Each can be combined with another to generate specific conceptualized effects. If we recall some of the generalizations arrived at in Chapters 2 and 3, we can combine them to formulate further generalizations about the effects of interaction and performance. The two variables combine to account for structure in interaction. Structure is a characteristic of interaction, but is dependent upon differences in action and reaction (performance). The performances of the members, singly and in interaction, describe the work or operations of the group. The identity of a group is founded on the performances of its members and on the continuity of interaction. Predictability in action and reaction (performance) provides the basis for differentiating different positions in an interaction system. The factor of predictability suggests that expectation also operates in defining the structure of a system.

A comparison of findings in Chapters 3 and 4 suggests that performance and expectation are interdependent. Confirmed expectation establishes specific motivations. Performance provides the instrumentality for confirming expectation. The combined performances of all the members operate to achieve those mutually reinforced expectations which define the goals of the group.

Interaction and expectation, discussed in Chapters 2 and 4, combine to account for the mutual reinforcement of group norms and purpose and for the forces exerted to induce conformity to norms of value and conduct. The freedom of action exhibited by a group and by its individual members is related to its degree of structure and to the consistency with which expectations are reinforced.

The generalizations listed above represent some of the major concepts which may be used in combination and recombination to describe group structure and operations.

## Organization: The Differentiation of Structure

In a newly formed group, structure in interaction is based on the differential actions and reactions of the members. This is a reciprocating process. In addition, the structure thus formed appears to exert feedback effects upon the members which tend to reinforce expectations differentially in relation to various positions, and also normatively in relation to various values. It is apparent that each member exerts effects upon the structure of the system. In other words, the structure of the system may be described in terms of the differential performances, interactions, and expectations of the members. But the group also exerts effects upon each member which structure his expectations and interactions, and pattern his performances to some extent in conformity with the normative expectations of the group. This structuring is made possible by virtue of the fact that different members do not exert identical effects upon the group, and the group does not exert identical effects upon its various members.

We defined structure in interaction in terms of the differential regularities of action and reaction exhibited in the positions in a system. The *position* of a group member becomes differentiated from other positions by virtue of the fact that the member exhibits predictable patterns of performance which elicit predictable responses from other members. The greater the extent to which a member initiates actions which elicit acquiescent reactions from other members, the greater the extent to which he structures the interaction system and the greater the difference between his position and the positions of other members. Thus, Homans [331] explains social differentiation in terms of the "origination of structure in interaction," and Hemphill [313] defines leadership as the "initiation of structure in interaction."

Each individual enters a group with various personal motivations and goal orientations. Why then do some members yield to the initiative of others? Most individuals appear to learn through experience that in order to accomplish a task through group action, it is necessary for all members to work toward the same outcome or goal. More important is the fact that the members come to perceive in a newly formed group that they can make no progress in operating upon a task until they yield to the initiative of a member whose perception of the group goal represents the normative perception of the group or of a subgroup which determines the structure of the system.

Predictable regularities of performance by the members confirm probability estimates for each other. The perceived ability of a member to determine the structure of a system confirms the expectation of his continued ability to do so. The ability of the group to begin task operations once a goal and a structure of positions have been mutually accepted operates to confirm the estimated probability of being able to experience satisfying outcomes through group action. Experiences of group success reinforce this expectation. Thus, the structure of an organized group represents not only a predictable system of actions and reactions but also a system of mutually reinforced expectations. Both initiation and reaction to initiation may be regarded as responses which are instrumental to the confirmation of expectation relative to the value of each position for the maintenance of group structure and the accomplishment of group goals. Thus, the actions and reactions underlying the structure of positions established by interaction provide the behavioral instrumentalities for the confirmation of a system of mutually reinforced expectations which define for each position a set of predictive prescriptions relative to performances and interactions that accomplish group goals and maintain group structure.

Various members of a newly formed group may attempt to determine the structure and goal direction of the group. The consistency of the success or failure that a member exhibits in testing the effects of his initiative upon the structure of the interaction system exerts confirming effects upon the expectations of other members relative to the contribution he is capable of making to the group. The system of expectations thus reinforced defines the status and function of his position in the system.

The *status* of a position defines the degree of freedom granted its occupant in initiating and maintaining the goal direction and structure of the system in which the position is located. The status of a position is defined in relation to the status and functions of all other positions in the system. The *function* of a position defines the general nature of the contribution that its occupant is expected to make toward the accomplishment of the group purpose. Function varies in relation to differences in the status levels of the positions in a system. Both function and status are defined for a position rather than for any given occupant of the position.

It might be argued that there is inconsistency in the attempt to differentiate between function and status and in the further attempt to define status in relation to a specific set of functions. If we can agree, as we should be able to do, that status implies a hierarchical relationship between two or more referents, we are required to specify the nature of the relationship. Substituting a term such as *power, right,* or *privilege,* for *degree of freedom* to specify the relationship would not solve our problem. We should be required to ask, "Power for what purpose?" Power must then be defined in terms of some function. No matter what term is substituted for *degree of freedom* in defining status, the latter concept appears to have little meaning except in specifying a differential right of function in a hierarchy of positions. The adequacy of the present theory in specifying the nature of this function is subject to test by logical and experimental procedures.

The mutual acknowledgment among the members of the stability and legitimacy of the system of positions they have structured (or accepted) is sometimes referred to as *formal organization.* Formal organization implies (1) acknowledgment and confirmation of the suitability, legitimacy, and stability of the structure of positions, and (2) acknowledgment of the mutual obligations among the positions relative to the form and manner of initiative and response to initiative in interaction. This acknowledgment operates as a barrier to the initiation of interactions which might threaten the stability of the structure of positions. It may not succeed entirely in preventing various members from challenging the system, but it may serve to nullify the effects of their efforts.

A number of factors operates to stabilize the system of expectations which define the status and function of the different positions in a group. First is the fact that initial reinforcements exert strong effects upon expectation. The initial experiences of success or failure among the members confirm expectations which are highly resistant to extinction. Second, the group purpose represents a set of mutually confirmed desirability estimates relative to valued outcomes that may be experienced as a result of group structure and operations. Desirability estimates have been found to be highly generalizable and to be confirmed close to their maximum values by initial reinforcements. Such goal oriented expectations define the motivation of the group. That status and function apply to positions rather than to the members as individuals is evidenced in the fact that if two members exchange positions in a group, each is expected to act in accord with the status and function of his new position. If an old member leaves the group and a new member is recruited to fill his position, the new member acquires the status and functions of the position. Groups appear better able to sacrifice or lose the occupant of a position than to sacrifice the position, particularly if it is a high status position. As groups become more highly structured, the interchangeability of the members among the positions in different status levels of the system becomes increasingly restricted. The factor of reduced interchangeability may be regarded as the ultimate criterion of the difference between an organized and an unorganized group, in that it fulfills the requirement of a group of more than minimum structure. In terms of the present system, an organization is a group in which the positions in the system are differentiated relative to function and status.

Wilson [771] and Znaniecki [793], in tracing the historical development of group concepts, note that earlier scholars tended to differentiate between groups and organizations in respect to size, duration, intimacy, and the like. More recent investigators tend to emphasize structural and functional differences. For purposes of the point of view being developed, it is found convenient to differentiate organizations from groups only in terms of degree of structure, since both must be regarded as groups.

In organization theory, the terms *vertical differentiation* and *horizontal differentiation* are used to describe the structuring of groups in terms of status and function. Vertical organization refers to the ordering of positions in relation to status hierarchies. Horizontal organization describes the subdivision of the group task into segments of related operations, and the assignment of specific segments of operational requirements to specific subgroups of positions.

An additional factor which operates to define an organization is the possibility of prestructuring the positions in the system. If the structure of the positions is charted before any members are recruited, this charting predetermines the structure of the interaction system by the process of specifying the status and function of the various positions in the group. These formal definitions of status and function serve as models for both interaction and expectation when members are acquired to fill the positions in the system.

Function and status in combination describe the leadership potential of the different positions in the system. The leadership potential of a position may be defined as the degree of freedom it provides for the initiation and maintenance of structure in expectation and interaction. Thus, the occupants of different positions vary not only in freedom for initiative (status) but also in the extent to which they are expected to exert determining effects upon group structure and goal direction (function).

A clearly defined and stable system of positions provides a frame of reference which may be utilized for predictive purposes by each member of the group. Most individuals regard such a stable system to be an advantage. It establishes a model in terms of which performance and interaction may be initiated with a heightened expectation of experiencing satisfying outcomes for self, for other members, and for the group as a whole. However, the structure of a group is not necessarily viewed alike by all its members. Situations are encountered in which certain members of a group are dissatisfied with their positions. Some members dislike the functions (duties) of their positions. Other members may be discontented with the status aspects of their positions. Despite these facts, groups can be observed in which deliberate efforts are made to structure function and status of the members in relation to the purpose of the group. Business, military, and governmental organizations are frequently cited as examples of types of groups in which such efforts are made. But the structuring of positions relative to function and status is not confined to the types of groups cited. The process may be observed in groups of all types, even though the members may not be aware of the processes taking place. Ordinarily, if a group has any important task to accomplish, the members make a deliberate attempt to develop a structure which will best enable the group to accomplish its purpose.

## The Role System: Responsibility and Authority

The structuring and restructuring that takes place in a group does not end with the differentiation of a system of positions and the definition of function and status. A member who transfers from one position to another of equal status in a group may be expected to play a similar role in both even though the two positions differ in function. A new member who accepts a position in a group may be expected to exhibit a pattern of behavior which differs from that of his predecessor even though the status and functions of the position remain unchanged. Observations such as these suggest that groups become structured in terms of differential role expectations.

Role theory, stimulated by the work of Mead [478], and elaborated by Linton [427], has come to play an important part in sociological and psychological theories. Linton has defined roles as normative or ideal patterns of behavior that are culturally defined and which regulate the relationships between person and person as well as between individual and society. Each position occupied by an individual specifies a role for him, but he cannot play all the roles associated with those positions at the same time. Nadel [512] observes two kinds of roles in a social system. Recruitment roles impose not only changing but also inescapable patterns of behavior, as evidenced in the changing demands made upon the individual as he advances in age. Achievement roles are those which the individual is free to choose, but they also impose behavioral demands which are determined by the pre-history of the role.

Coutu [158] distinguishes between *role,* the behavior prescribed for a position, and *role playing,* the performance of the person in the position. Rommetveit [579] differentiates *prescribed roles* which incorporate imposed social norms from *subjective roles* which incorporate perceived social norms. Bennett and Tumin [58] call attention to the fact that role performance is not always in conformity with role definition, while Merton [484] and

Scott [610] observe that roles are not always clearly defined. Tolman [719] defines role in terms of the confirmation of expectations. He maintains that the concept of role implies not only that other members in an interaction situation expect an individual to behave in certain ways but also that the individual expects that, if he behaves as expected, his behavior will meet with approval or some form of response which confirms his expectation. Bates [47], Neiman and Hughes [517], and Gross, Mason, and McEachern [271] have reviewed the different definitions of the role concept. Sarbin [600] has summarized the literature on role theory and experimentation.

If role is defined in terms of a set of expectations bearing on a position, then it seems necessary to determine whether this is the same set of expectations that defines function and status. For the sake of clarity, let us remind ourselves that the term *set of expectations* is used to imply, not a psychic entity of any sort but a mutually confirmed readiness for reinforcement exhibited by the members in relation to the occupant of a position.

We have noted that function and status are attached to a position rather than to the occupant of the position. The function and status of a position may remain essentially unchanged in the expectations of the members over long periods of time during which several different persons may occupy the position. If the role concept is to have any meaning which differs from the concepts of status and function in combination, then it seems necessary to assume that role expectations are attached to the person rather than to the position he occupies.

The occupant of a position is expected to act in accord with the defined status and functions of his position. However, the members of a group may perceive no great deviation from this expectation in the fact that different occupants of a position do not exhibit identical patterns of behavior. In fact, the members may recruit a new member to fill a well-defined position in the expectation that he will exhibit a pattern of behavior which differs from that of his predecessor. They may expect him to play a role which will induce a heightened (or lessened) degree of group structure and induce renewed motivation toward task achievement. Whatever the pattern of role behavior expected of a new member, the status and function of his position are likely to be regarded as unchanged.

A versatile member, while occupying the same position, may play a changing role in response to changing demands or opportunities arising in a group. Two different occupants of a position, while exhibiting different patterns of performance and interaction, may prove equally effective in fulfilling the demands made upon the position. It seems clear that roles are not defined by the same expectations that define function and status.

At least three factors appear to operate in structuring those expectations that define a member's role in a group. First, is the nature (status and function) of the position he occupies. Second, is the demand made upon him by the members as a result of changes in the structural and operational requirements of the group. Third, is the members' perceptions of the kind of person he is. The second of these appears to provide the essential clue relative to the nature of roles as distinguished from positions. Status and function define a very general and durable set of expectations relative to the utility of a position for the accomplishment of the enduring group purpose. Role defines a set of less stable expectations relative to the performance of a member in fulfilling the changing operational demands made upon his position.

If role differs from position, then the pattern of performance and degree of freedom defined by role expectations must differ from those defined by function and status. The concepts *responsibility* and *authority*, derived from organization theory, appear useful in accounting for two distinct aspects of role differentiation. Organizational *authority* may be defined as the degree of freedom that the occupant of a position is expected to exercise in initiating performance and interaction within a formally acknowledged structure. *Responsibility* may be defined as the specific set or range of performances that a member is expected to exhibit by virtue of the operational demands made upon his position in a formally acknowledged structure.

The responsibility and authority that a member is expected to exercise in the performance of his role are closely, but by no means perfectly, related to the function and status of his position. In general, the higher a member's status the greater the area of freedom granted him in the initiation of operations for the group. No matter what a member's position, his responsibilities for performance are expected to bear a direct or indirect relationship to the functions of his position.

Responsibility and authority define two aspects of role expectation. They define, first of all, the nature of the role that an individual is expected to play. Second, they define the relationship between his role and specified other roles in the group. Thus, the occupant of the top status position in a group may be given authority to initiate group operations and may be held accountable for the responsible performance of all members or subgroups in carrying out the group operations. In carrying out the responsibilities of his role, he is held accountable for the initiation, co-ordination, and control of the entire group operations. Members who occupy lower status positions may be held accountable for the operations of subgroups, while the members who occupy the lowest status positions in the group are held accountable only for their own performances.

There is no gain from group formation or differentiation of structure if all right to action and initiative is assigned to a single member. That function of high status positions which defines the right to initiate structure for others implies acceptance of the correlative and inseparable obligation to provide freedom for others. Those expectations which specify the boundaries of roles define the authority of any one role in relation to the authority of other roles. The group tends, when possible, to elevate to high status a member whose performances, values, and responses to interaction confirm the expectation that, in maintaining group structure and in exercising the authority defined for his role, he will respect the rights of other members to initiate action in accordance with the degrees of freedom defined for their roles.

The concept *delegation,* derived from organization theory, defines the reciprocal relationship between the responsibility and authority dimensions of associated roles in different status levels of a group. Delegation may be regarded as the use of authority to define the responsibility and authority of subordinate roles in terms of their accountability to the delegant. According to the principle of delegation, a superior does not surrender his accountability to the group when he assigns a specific responsibility to a subordinate. At the same time, it is useless to assign a responsibility unless sufficient authority is delegated to carry the assignment to completion. Since group operations impose demands for changing, as well as for stable and repetitive, sets of performances, delegation is usually expected to define both a core of stable performance requirements and a range of freedom for initiative and response to change.

A member's responsibility, as well as his authority, may be restricted or expanded as a result of the actions of other members. A member may complain that he is being overloaded or that other members are infringing upon his responsibilities. In addition, if a member has assistants or subordinates, he is usually made responsible for their performance as well as his own. The success of his own performance is then dependent upon the efficiency of his subordinates. The scope for action available to a member represents his interpretation of the rights, obligations, limitations, and boundaries imposed upon him in making decisions and taking action as a member of an organization. He may make this interpretation in terms of the organization as an abstract concept or in terms of the expectations of seniors, peers, or juniors. Thus, his authority is conditioned and defined by a complex of variables. If he fails to take necessary action, or if he makes decisions which other members expect to have referred to them, he may find himself in an embarrassing position, particularly when he makes mistakes. In unusual situations, a member may question his right to act in behalf of the organization. He is likely to learn through more or less painful experience what the limits of his authority are in unusual circumstances.

The most troublesome aspects of authority are likely to be those which are determined by the member's relationships with his superiors and subordinates. Some members characteristically seek to exercise a high degree of control over the activities for which they are responsible. Others appear able to delegate freely to their assistants. Some subordinates are able to exercise initiative. Others wait to have decisions made for them. Still others have to be held in check. Each member entertains expectations relative to his own rights and obligations as well as to those of his fellow members.

Granted the subordination of the individual's personal aspiration in the interest of the group, he tends to seek two conditions in order to act for the benefit of the group. First, he attempts to determine what he is expected to do and with whom he is expected to co-operate. Second, he seeks a sufficient but not excessive degree of freedom for initiating action and interaction in order to carry out his own duties and co-operate with other members when necessary to do so. Members appear to be able to tolerate an almost unbelievable amount of personal frustration in a group if these two conditions are fulfilled. A group is ordinarily able to offer few other rewards which will compensate a member for the frustration of these two expectations relative to his contribution to the group.

Each role in a group is defined in relation to the total role system and the purpose of the group. A number of members may have similar roles. Some members may have overlapping roles. Others may have roles that are lacking in definition. The boundaries of roles are often as difficult to determine as the boundaries of groups. Insofar as the boundaries of a member's role are vague and indeterminate his freedom of action is restricted because he does not know how to act. This restriction may or may not be imposed by other members. However, any testing behavior that the member exhibits in an effort to determine boundaries may involve him in error, difficulty, reprimand, or rebuff. Yet, if he remains inactive he may be regarded as failing to do his share. Thus, the member whose role is lacking in definition is under compulsion either to seek structure which will permit him to act according to expectation or to resign himself to inaction as a means of avoiding the unpleasant consequences of possible error.

Freedom of action is restricted if roles are too closely defined. Merton [483], Hughes [340], and other students of bureaucratic structures point out the fact that the stabilization and habituation of a role structure may result in the performance patterns of various positions becoming so bound by ritual that the occupant becomes a symbol rather than a responsible agent. Role performance becomes so firmly habituated and closely prescribed by expectations relating to function and status that the members are unable to act freely in coping with the changing situational demands made upon the group. A differentiated role structure has utility in enabling the members to operate upon a complicated and continuing task, each in accord with his specialized skills and abilities. However, the survival of the group may be jeopardized when the maintenance of the role structure is given precedence over effective task performance and reaction to stresses bearing upon the group.

Function and status cannot possibly define in advance all the possible variations in performance and freedom for initiative that may be required of the occupant of a position. Those members who perceive group organization only as a structure of positions defined by function and status tend to become disturbed when the performances and interactions of the members deviate from formally acknowledged definitions of function and status. On the other hand, those members who perceive organization only as a structure of roles defined by responsibility and authority tend to become disturbed when the group attempts to induce compliance with those expectations which define group purpose and the structure of positions in the group. These observations suggest that a member is likely to function more effectively for a group if his experiences and value systems enable him to perceive and acknowledge the differential requirements defined by roles and positions.

Informal subgroups are formed by the same processes of interaction and reinforcement of expectation that operate to structure positions and roles in the larger, formal system. When closely observed, they are found to exhibit differentiated positions and roles. They differ from formal subgroups primarily in their relation to the purpose of the formal organization. Informal subgroups are formed to satisfy the interpersonal goals of the members without regard to the purpose of the larger group. Their legitimacy may be challenged if they are observed to work in opposition to the goals and structure of the larger group. However, since organization is an instrumentality rather than the end of human social purpose, informal subgroups are regarded (by most members) as legitimate aspects of group structure. They provide escape from unpleasant organization pressures, strengthen the confirmation of value systems, and often reinforce the identification of members with the larger group.

## Role Sanction and Legitimation

The right of a group to organize is derived from the social order in which it operates. This right impinges upon every member of the group, since it tends to legitimize the formal structure designed to accomplish a legitimate group purpose. Further, the members, in the process of differentiating and acknowledging the group role system, thereby tend to accord it a high degree of internal legitimation. Thus, when a member accepts a position in good faith, he expects to be able to exercise fully the obligations and rights attached to the position. Without this mutual recognition and legitimation of role definition, the group would have no basis for orderly operation, co-ordination of activities, or maintenance of its structural integrity.

The extent to which the group as an organized entity determines the function and status of a given position is related to its mode of initiation: whether by the mutual agreement of its members, by a legitimizing charter, by legislative action, or by the administrative decision of a parent body. Groups that are initiated by spontaneous agreement are likely to formulate a structure as a result of mutual interaction. Groups that are originated by the decision of a parent body are likely to be rather rigidly structured before any members are recruited to fill the positions. However, even under these conditions, the members, in interaction, tend to restructure the prescribed system in terms of their differential abilities and expectations. A member's conception of his position and of his role represents a set of differential expectations that is determined not only by his perception of the task to be performed but also by the expectations of other members and by the group as a whole.

A group, in defining the status and functions of different positions, sets bounds upon the effective responsibility and authority of the occupants of the positions. These bounds are determined by the interest of the group members in obtaining specified objectives. Each individual, as a group member, is expected to confine his activities to those performances and interactions that will further goal achievement and maintain the structure of positions in the group. The recognition and acknowledgment of the structure of positions and the structure of roles confirms expectations for the members relative to the status and function, the authority and responsibility, of each. The fact that the group operates on the basis of this mutual acknowledgment lends further reinforcement and legitimation to the system of expectations.

The role system is differentiated and defined in relation to the norm system of the group. The role and norm systems in combination define the ranges of permissible behavior available to a group member and specify also the rewards for conformity and the penalties for nonconformity to the group norm. The sanctions for conformity and nonconformity may be given formal definition in a set of rules and regulations or they may be mutually acknowledged without specific definition.

Lack of consensus in the definition of group goals, norms, and roles results either in operational inaction or in the division of the group into subgroups which compete with each other in their efforts to structure the group. The group cannot move toward a goal if its structure and operations are being determined simultaneously by two or more members or subgroups of members who differ in their goals for the group. Neither can a group operate effectively if its members challenge the legitimacy of the formal structure, disclaim the responsibilities defined for their roles, or refuse to acknowledge the authority of other roles. It is for reasons such as these that a group seeks to recruit members who are similar in value systems and then attempts to structure their expectations in accord with the group's normative range of values relative to group purpose, structure of positions, and structure of roles. Similar reasons operate in the definition of sanctions for conformity and nonconformity.

The definition of sanctions is not an unmitigated advantage to a group. Initiative in role enactment and conformity to norms is, for many individuals, highly related to their perceptions of the penalties attending error and nonconformity. For some members, the greater the penalty for nonconformity the greater the pressure toward nonconformity (even though they conform), and the greater the extent to which initiative is inhibited in resistance to pressure and avoidance of penalty. Since penalties as well as rewards become referents of expectation, the imposition of any penalty is certain to induce a certain amount of behavior with the penalty as a goal, even though a negatively valued one. The fewer penalties a group finds it necessary to define, the less deviant behavior it should induce in its members. However, since expectations and patterns of deviant behavior acquired by some members outside the group may be carried into the group, the imposition of penalties for behavior that is prejudicial to the group welfare may be necessary.

Those members who are granted the responsibility for initiating and co-ordinating group activities are accorded high status and high degrees of freedom in decision and action. These members are also likely to be given the responsibility of insuring that all members act according to the group plan and demand for co-ordination. The group itself may act to specify the penalties to be imposed upon members who fail to comply, or it may give its high status members a free hand in imposing such penalties as they think may be effective. The group may isolate, reject, or exclude a member who fails to respond to less severe penalties.

Both roles and norms represent ranges of behavior permitted the group members. Certain of the group norms may apply to all members equally. Other norms may vary for different status levels as well as for different subgroups within the same status level. Each member is expected to comply with the norms defined by his status level and subgroup. A member who identifies himself with a status level or subgroup to which he does not belong may find himself in difficulty when he attempts to act in accord with the norms of his reference subgroup rather than with those of the subgroup in which he is a member.

In addition to the norms defined by the members of a specific subgroup for the regulation of their own behavior, normative expectations may be formed in other subgroups which bear on the occupant of a position. An individual may find that members of subgroups in status levels above and below his own hold firmly defined expectations relative to proper conduct in his position. Although a position of high status may allow a member greater freedom in acting on behalf of the group, it may also be hedged in by expectations which deny its occupant certain privileges of self-expression and self-indulgence in role performance that are granted to members in positions of lower status. The feelings of security that members of low status positions experience in a group may depend upon their perceptions of the integrity and role conformity of a member in a position of higher status.

The normative expectations bearing upon different positions serve to formalize the patterns of interaction between status levels, thus protecting the legitimacy of the formal structure. The process of formalizing interaction in role performance acts as a differential barrier to the initiation of communication between status levels. It also acts at times as a differential barrier to the imposition of sanctions (rewards and penalties). It is at points where these barriers operate that the status structure is likely to create the most serious problems for a group.

The formalized status structure permits free access to the upward flow of information necessary for the co-ordination and control of group operations. It provides readily for the downward flow of information which defines objectives, initiates operations, corrects deviations from performance specifications, and imposes sanctions. It offers resistance to the upward flow of criticism. These effects are observed in experimental groups of short duration as well as in established groups.

Various students of social action have observed that the differentiation of authority creates differences in the power available to members in different status levels. Differences in interpersonal power are made possible by the differentiation of authority for initiating control and by the greater access of members in high status positions to information for the control of operations. The concept of power usually carries an unfavorable connotation in that it implies the use of freedom of action and access to information for purposes other than the control of group operations. The concept as employed in the social sciences suggests that the values created by a group may be regarded by some individuals as exploitable, and that the status and authority of a high level position may be used for exploitive purposes. Evidences of the use of power are many and varied. The most obvious are the use of power by a group member for the enhancement of his own wealth, prestige, position, and range of interaction. Less obvious, but no less real, is the use of power to control the behavior of other group members. The member who occupies a position of power can give or withhold financial and material rewards, punishment and penalties, commendation and recognition, promotion and advancement, responsibility and freedom of action, and can influence all aspects of group life that determine success or failure, satisfaction or despair. It seems reasonable to conclude that power resides in the hands of those group members who are able to control reinforcement.

The concern in this analysis is with factors that determine the strength and weakness of groups rather than with the activities of the power seeker. Nevertheless, it seems useful to note several differences between the opportunist who uses his formal position for the exercise of power and the professional invader who seeks to capture the power structure of a group. The latter appears to have a clearer perception of the vulnerability of human expectation. He is more highly skilled in the art of structuring the expectations of dissatisfied and frustrated individuals. He is less inhibited and more adept in the use of threat and physical violence in gaining and keeping power. After attaining control of a group he is more willing to use threat and violence in forcing the members to remain in the group and to exploit themselves in his behalf.

It was noted in an earlier chapter that desirability estimates are more readily confirmed than probability estimates. Appeals to value systems may structure member expectations independently of any objective outcome which permits a test of the validity of expectations. The more highly a member values the outcomes he expects to experience in a group and the lower the perceived availability of the outcomes outside the group, the greater the power of the group to control his behavior. Thus, a member may remain in a group even though his expectations have not been confirmed. The continued failure to confirm probability estimates reduces his freedom of action. Perceived inability to escape the situation renders a member increasingly vulnerable to the reinforcement of value systems at the expense of validating experiences. Under these conditions, he is likely to see merit in the argument that any change would be a change for the better. He may perceive no valid reason for refusing to support an individual who challenges the legitimacy of a role system that is perceived to be capable of satisfying his expectations, but refuses to do so.

A group derives its strength from the mutually reinforced expectations of its members. But it becomes increasingly vulnerable when it fails to satisfy the members' expectations. Granted that a group is likely to have among its members a few who are incapable of being satisfied by any outcomes that the group or its members can provide, these persons are likely to be in the minority. Their tendencies toward deviant behavior will be controlled by the norms of the group or subgroup if the majority of members are experiencing sufficiently satisfying outcomes to care what happens to the group. However, as dissatisfaction spreads to include a majority of the members, the group becomes increasingly vulnerable to the appeals of persons who are able to restructure the expectations of the members. It is apparent that a group is capable of generating power and that its power can be reduced, fragmented, and used to the disadvantage of the group members. The continued legitimation of a role in a group is dependent upon the conformity of role performance with the expectations of the members who define the role. Lacking legitimation of responsibility and authority or positive sanction of role performance, the role becomes subject to challenge. It is necessary to conclude that, although the status and function of a position may remain unchanged, the role of its occupant must be justified continuously in performance and interaction.


## Role Conflict

The advantage of role definition is that it provides the individual with a reference model in terms of which he can determine what he is expected to do and what he is expected to refrain from doing. At least two conditions operate to create role confusion and role conflict. First, roles are not always clearly defined. Second, various persons and subgroups may entertain different expectations relative to the same role. Either condition places the individual in a position where he is subject to uncertainty and strain.

Hartley and Hartley [302] identify five factors related to group functioning which interfere with role perception and enactment. These include the imposed nature of roles, limitations on the individual choice of roles, variations in the definitions of a role by different groups, the simultaneous imposition of different roles upon the individual, and discontinuity in the role behavior demanded at different developmental stages in the life of the individual. These are factors which affect all members of a society in some degree.

As the member of a subgroup, a member may find that he has acquired a role that differs somewhat from his role as defined by the larger group. In these circumstances, his effectiveness as a group member is likely to be judged in terms of his ability to reconcile the conflicting demands made upon him and to satisfy the expectations of the subgroup as well as of the larger group. A member may also define his role in terms of personal values and preconceptions which have little reference to the purpose or norm structure of the group. When this deviation from the established norm becomes visible, the group members may present information or persuasive arguments designed to enable the member to restructure his role perception. According to Stouffer and Toby [689], individuals differ in the extent to which they are dominated by personal and impersonal considerations in determining their values relative to social obligations. Group members are encountered who are so clearly dominated by personal values or external reference group identifications that they are little influenced by appeals for loyalty to a particular group. Some members appear to exhibit role conflict under the pressures exerted by the group to reduce discrepancies between personal goals and group purpose.

Roethlisberger [569] points out the fact that the foreman in industry, because of his intermediate position in the organization structure, is required to represent both management and the worker. He is expected to be loyal to both, to understand both, and to communicate to each in behalf of the other. The interests and demands of the two groups do not always coincide. As a result, the foreman is required to play a painful role, that of the "man in the middle." Stouffer [687] reports that the noncommissioned officer in the military services occupies a middle man position which subjects him to frequent role conflicts. Copeland [156] finds that the department head in industry, as the lieutenant of the executive and as the representative of his subordinates, occupies a similar position.

Role confusion and conflict, then, grow out of the lack of clarity in role definition, differences in the perception of a role by self and others, and differences in the expectations and demands made upon a role by various persons and subgroups in the system. The higher the status of an individual in a group, the greater the number of persons and subgroups he must represent and the greater the burden of conflicting demands made upon him. Thus, the amount of role conflict to which a member may be subjected tends to be related to his position in the status structure of the group.

Gross, Mason, and McEachern [271] have advanced a theory of role conflict based on the concepts of sanction and legitimation. Role conflict arises not only from the perception of incompatible expectations bearing upon the role but also from the individual's estimate of the legitimacy or illegitimacy of the expectations and from his perception of the nature of the sanctions (positive or negative) which will be imposed if he fails to comply with the incompatible expectations. When expectations bearing upon the individual are contradictory, he will tend to conform with those which are perceived to be legitimate and (or) attended by strong negative sanctions, thus providing a resolution of role conflict.

Other factors which appear to operate in role conflict arise from differences in the values placed upon different positions in the system and from differences in the demands made by formal structure and role structure. Some functions of positions in the same status level are more highly valued than others. High status is valued by many, but not by all, members of a group. Some members refuse advancement to higher positions. Many individuals feel insecure when required to initiate structure, reward performance, or impose penalties for deviant behavior. Movement into a higher status level not only imposes a different order of responsibilities but also may require new reference group identifications, changes in value systems, and marked changes in social activity and way of life. Not all individuals are willing to pay these costs of status mobility.

If a member accepts a position which imposes functions, status, or role requirements that are incompatible with his value systems and reference group identifications, he may experience guilt or conflict.

Another aspect of conflict is that arising from perceived discrepancy between the demands of formal organization (as defined by function, status, and group purpose) and the demands for role performance. A member may find that he has a difficult decision to make when powerful subgroups challenge the legitimacy of his role as a reaction against his refusal to support them in a course of action which he believes to be contrary to the group purpose. Even more acute conflict may be experienced when a member feels that strong authoritative demands are being made upon him to act in violation of the group rules, norms, and regulations.

A member's perception of his role is determined not only by his own expectations but also by the reactions of other members toward him. Consistency of responses toward his initiative tends to validate his estimates of the probable courses of action available to him in the group. Such consistency also tends to confirm his estimates of the desirability of the outcomes produced by his pattern of role performance.

It is apparent that the attempt made by a group to induce consensus is not a meaningless pastime. Consensus in member expectations legitimizes the role system, defines the normative range of behavior allowed each member in performing his role, and sanctions a defined area of freedom for initiating performance and interaction. The members, performing their roles singly and in interaction, carry out the operations of the group.

## Structure, Motivation and Operations Control

Differences between status, function, responsibility, authority, group norms, and group purpose can be detected in very small groups that are formed in the process of mutual interaction and have only a single task to perform. We may wonder whether this elaboration of structure is really necessary. We have noted that there are contradictory and diverse, as well as conformative and integrative, processes at work in a group. Action and interaction are necessary for the initiation and continuance of group operations, but such action and interaction must be limited to boundaries which define normative ranges of behavior.

It is not necessary to specify the amount of deliberate intent that goes into the structuring of a group. It is sufficient for theoretical purposes to note that the structure of a group bears a close instrumental relationship to the operations initiated for the accomplishment of group purpose.

In order to accomplish a group purpose, it is necessary for all members to operate upon the same goal objective or upon instrumental sub-objectives. The greater the complexity of the task, and the more numerous the instrumental objectives which must be operated upon, the more difficult it becomes for all members to perceive the relationship between individual role performance and the ultimate purpose of the group.

Status levels define differences in the extent to which the members of various positions are held accountable for the total group achievement and for subgroups of tasks which contribute to the total group effort. The fact that different individuals and subgroups are made accountable for different aspects of the task creates a demand for co-ordination and control both within subgroups and within the group as a whole. The status structure describes these different levels of accountability.

The ability of the members to act in behalf of the group is dependent upon the area of freedom available to them for initiating action and interaction. The members tend to act when permitted to do so. For this reason, the scope of action available to the members is to be regarded as an important element in group motivation. However, individuals and subgroups differ in the strength of motivation they exhibit. The necessity of regulating the rate of performance and of insuring the conformity of performance with specifications for goal achievement imposes the demand for control of operations.

The larger the group, and the more complex its activities, the more important the control function becomes. This is especially true when the group formulates a set of clearly defined goals and assigns specific tasks to different subgroups in order to achieve the goals. Both the definition of goals and the assigning of tasks have the effect of establishing performance criteria for the subgroups and for the group as a whole. The control function is directly concerned with the conformity of performance with these criteria. It is also concerned with the balance or approximate equality of performance among the various subgroups. If one subgroup continues over a long period of time to produce more than can be used, or less than is needed in relation to the productivity of other subgroups, the survival of the entire group may be jeopardized.

The factor of operational balance is of critical importance when the group has access to limited financial or physical resources which must be used with economy. Each subgroup must then perform according to expectation or specification. Further, the performance of the different subgroups must be co-ordinated and balanced. It is the function of control to see that the group operations are maintained in balance. This means that the performances of the different subgroups must be geared to a common pace.

The pacing of operations affects both individuals and subgroups. It tends to depress the performance of the most capable and to put a strain on the least capable. Mayo [477], Roethlisberger [569], and others have shown that inequalities in performance, pay, recognition, and the like, among subgroup peers tend to result in further stresses and strains. However, the subgroups are not without resources to cope with operational pressures and inequalities among peers. They develop their own standards or norms relative to a reasonable rate of continued performance and, with some exceptions, tend to enforce conformity to these norms. They may speed up under emergencies or slow down under pressures that are perceived to be unreasonable or unnecessary, but, in general, the subgroups tend to pace their own performance. This pacing tends to conform to the pace of other related and interdependent subgroups. Overperformance or underperformance in one subgroup tends to throw the whole system out of balance.

The higher the level of control over first line operations, the less able is the organization to tolerate deviations and exceptions to the system of control. The amount of slippage that can be tolerated diminishes rapidly as control is pushed higher and higher up the line. Control must be exercised actively and continuously, with provision for the immediate determination of deviation from the prescribed course of action. In addition, the bypassing of intermediate levels of supervision tends to fragment the authority structure of the organization, producing role conflict, indecision, and dissatisfaction. Increased effectiveness under such conditions is achieved at a heavy psychological cost to all members of the organization.

Historical records from ancient times to the present day testify to the fact that even very small groups, when highly motivated and closely integrated and co-ordinated, are capable of generating tremendous amounts of power. The power of a group is dependent upon the unity of its goal direction, the strength of its efforts to attain the goal, the integration of its structure, and the co-ordination and control of its operations. The disruption or fragmentation of any one of these factors tends to diminish the power of the group.

## Structure Within Structure

Students of organization theory have been interested primarily in the formal structure of groups. Organization charts have been used to show the structure of positions, divided into status levels and subgroups of related functions. The formal organization chart takes no account of any informal or covert subgroups that may be operating within the group. The author has encountered persons who argue that a group has no legitimate right to concern itself with the structure or membership of its informal and covert subgroups. This is to argue, of course, that a group has no right to act for the preservation of its own integration and survival. Whatever the merits of this opinion insofar as the ethics of group conduct are concerned, they need not concern the scientist. It is his right to inquire into any matter whatsoever. Beginning with the work of Mayo [477] and Roethlisberger and Dickson [571], a convincing body of evidence has been accumulated which indicates that the behavior of a complex group cannot be understood without an accurate knowledge of the structure, norms, and operations of its informal subgroups.

*Formal organization* and *role system* may, under certain conditions, be used as synonymous terms for describing the structure of differentiated positions. It is worth noting, however, that *formal organization* is usually conceived as a set of expectations which is defined by the group on the basis of rational considerations. The *role system* is often regarded as a set of expectations arrived at through the mutual interaction of the members. These differences reflect considerable variance in the theoretical approaches of the organization theorist and the behavior scientist. They also reflect differences which arise from the types of groups studied. The organization theorist is interested in large, structured groups. The behavior scientist is more often interested in small, experimentally created groups. Whether the positions in a system are structured according to an externally imposed model or as a result of mutual interaction, they specify sets of expectations relative to performance and interaction, and they define each member's function and status in the group. However, it is only when the formal structure and the role system are defined by the members in interaction, that the two structures are found to be identical. Even under these circumstances, the formal structure as initially defined by the group, and the role system as modified by continued interaction, tend to diverge as operations continue.

A number of systems interact to describe the structure and operations of a large organized group. Among the systems which can be clearly differentiated are the following:

1. The structure of positions which is given formal definition and sanction by the differentiation of function and status.

2. The operative role system which is defined by the different degrees of responsibility, authority, and delegation exhibited by the occupants of various positions.

3. The formal interaction system which tends to parallel the formal structure of positions but is subject to deviation in response to the changing demands for co-ordination of individual performance and subgroup operations.

4. The norm system of the group and of its subgroups which, through sanction and prescription, defines acceptable conduct for group members and subgroup members.

5. The system of member performances which describes the

operations of the group and changes in response to variations in the group task.

6. The system of informal interactions which brings together group members on the basis of propinquity, mutual liking, and similarity of interests.

7. The system of covert interactions, if present, which brings together persons who challenge the legitimacy of the operative role structure and the differential sanctions associated with it.

All of these structures are derived from the performances, interactions, and expectations of the group members. Since they are based on a common set of input variables, they exhibit considerable overlap and interdependence. However, they differ both in visibility and stability. The formal structure of positions is the most stable and one of the most easily recognized structures in an organized group. Most easily recognized is the system of performances and operations, but this system is also most subject to change. Ordinarily, little attention is paid to informal subgroup structures unless they absorb excessive amounts of time that should be devoted to task performance or unless they develop into cliques with conflicting interests so as to threaten the integration of the group.

The operative role structure is seldom differentiated from the formal group structure. However, this differentiation seems necessary in order to account for deviations between function and responsibility, and between status and authority. A member may find that he is not inclined, able, or expected to fulfill all the expectations which at one time or another were attached to his position and which defined its functions. The moment to moment and day to day redefinitions of function which take place in response to task changes, interaction, and the expectations of other group members, define the member's responsibilities in the position. Authority represents a similar practical redefinition of the degree of freedom of action attached to the status level of the position.

Interaction structures cut across all other systems in the group and constitute the basic substructures on which all are based. It is for this reason that a group is defined as an interaction system.

Few members of a group are aware of the number and complexity of structures that are present in a group. Guetzkow [278] has observed that only those members who succeed in achieving high status exhibit a realistic understanding of the structure of a group, even though it be very small. The author has observed that experienced administrators require on the average, about eight or nine months to become sufficiently acquainted with the structure and operations of a new group to make a measurable difference in its effectiveness.

Although the members of a group may not comprehend all the complexities of its structure, they do exhibit a keen awareness of the presence of individuals and subgroups that threaten the integration or achievement of the group. They tend to exert pressure upon deviant members or subgroups to bring them into conformity to the norms of the group.

However, groups can be observed which rely heavily upon the formal role system to maintain integration without any effort on the part of the members. New members are introduced to their positions without any effort made to define responsibility and authority. Mistakes are reprimanded or ignored without explaining the normative system of roles and regulations. The structuring of a group, while it solves certain problems, does not necessarily solve all of them. Differences between individual values and group purpose, and differences in the interests of various subgroups, are not likely to remain permanently solved by the initial structuring of the group. Expectations change in response to various outcomes experienced by individuals, by subgroups, and by the group as a whole. Since the primary purpose and the role structure of the group tend to remain relatively stable, there is a tendency for the group to rely upon these factors to maintain stability in the expectations of the individual members. That this reliance may be unwarranted is evidenced by the rude awakenings experienced by a group when it finds that various subgroups of its members have rebelled against the continued disregard of their expectations. In order to maintain the sound integration of a group, it is necessary to pay continuous attention to those expectations which determine group structure and member satisfaction.


## RESEARCH ON STRUCTURE AND OPERATIONS

Much of the literature on group structure, role systems, function, status, responsibility, authority, and operations is of a highly theoretical nature. The research on these variables tends to be related either to behavior variables (performance, expectation, interaction) or to group achievement variables (productivity, morale, integration). As a result, some of the data relative to the differentiation of role structures have been discussed in preceding chapters. Other pertinent studies can be discussed most appropriately in relation to group achievement.

Sociological studies of class and caste structures provided not only impetus but also essential concepts for the investigation of group structures. The class structure of a society exerts important effects upon the structure of organizations and institutions that develop in the system. However, a decision was made to disregard these effects in developing the present theory. The decision, while arbitrary, permits us to concentrate attention upon effects which arise within the group. Kahl [370] has made an excellent analysis of the literature on social class structure. Davis [171], Warner, Meeker and Eells [748], Hollingshead [330], Centers [121], and others have conducted intensive studies of the social class structure in American society.

Experimental studies of small groups have produced the most rewarding insight into the processes at work in the structuring of groups. The studies of Shartle, Stogdill, and associates may be regarded as unique in that they were designed to determine the relationships between formal structure (status and function), role structure (responsibility and authority), interaction structure, performance, and expectation.

## The Differentiation of Structure

According to Barnard [36], formal status systems serve several useful functions in organized groups. They protect the members from the unpleasantness involved in competing with other members who differ greatly from them in ability. They present visible evidence of the difficulty and relative importance of different kinds of work. They provide visible evidence of differences in power to act for the group and so facilitate the acceptance of authority and the initiation of co-ordinative control. They protect the integrity of the individual. Individuals of superior ability and those of inferior ability can co-ordinate their efforts and work together in harmony under conditions of formal differentiation which do not bring them into direct competition or unfavorable comparison with each other. If the group is not structured to begin with, the members tend informally to separate themselves into subgroups in which they can be comfortable and in which their contributions can be recognized.

Moreno [501] has demonstrated that in any group situation, when the members express a preference for each other they direct their choices toward a few. These choices are not extorted by the "overchosen," but are freely given. Jennings [364] finds that the overchosen tend to choose each other, thus forming a mutually reinforced subgroup of high preference status in the group. These same members are the ones most likely to be preferred by the members of other groups. Moreover, those who are preferred on one criterion of choice tend to be preferred on other criteria. However, when ability, technical skill, or leadership are involved, a more rigorous standard of choice appears to operate than when informal companionship is involved.

Sherif [631] reports that judgments of performance tend to be related to group structure. In experimental groups which develop stable structure, performance tends to be judged in terms of the status of the members. In groups of less stable structure, performance is overestimated but tends to be judged in terms of actual skill rather than status. Harvey [304] also reports that the higher a member's status in the group the more his performance is overestimated by other members and the greater the expectational demands made upon him.

Schiff [605] found that those members of a group who underestimate their own status tend to have relatively low self-expectations, while overestimators tend to have high self-expectations. Those who underestimate their own status tend to perceive other members as more generous than themselves, overestimators, as less generous. However, those who underestimate the status of others tend to see the group as less generous than themselves; overestimators, as less generous in attributing status to others. Those members who anticipate low ratings for themselves tend to overestimate the sociometric status of others; those with high self-expectations underestimate the status of others. Underestimators of self and others are more accurate than overestimators in estimating the status of self and others. Greer, Galanter, and Nordlie [265], studying sociometric status in infantry rifle squads, found that high status members were more accurate than low status members in judging the preference structure of the squad.

Hovland, Janis, and Kelley [339] and Katz and Lazarsfeld [378] have observed that communications attributed to high prestige persons are more readily accepted than those attributed to low prestige persons. These studies suggest that an individual's perception of the status structure is related not only to his own status and expectations but also to other members' perceptions of his status.

Thibaut and Riecken [707] studied the reactions of group members toward aggressors who differed in attributed status. Subjects confronted by a high status aggressor changed toward a lesser rejection of him, while low status aggressors received greater rejection. Less intense rejection in overt communication was directed toward high than toward low status aggressors.

The effects upon the group of bargaining for limited group resources were investigated by Hoffman, Festinger, and Lawrence [328]. The materials required for task completion were divided among the different members, and the total distributable reward was limited. It was found that when one member is given an initial advantage, the remaining members tend to form coalitions in order to improve their position in bargaining with him for materials and in order to increase their chances of task completion and resultant reward. The member who held an initial advantage was unable to form a fair share of coalitions, even though he was willing to pay a higher price than his competitors. When he was able to form coalitions, he was unable to obtain a fair price for his collaboration. When the members of the group were perceived as equal in ability, those who held an initial disadvantage tended to compete primarily with the member holding the advantage. When the members were perceived as unequal in ability, those members holding an initial disadvantage tended to compete with each other. The authors conclude that coalition between low status members tends to maintain their comparability with each other, while reducing the difference between them and the high status member.

Kelley [379] studied the communication output of members in positions of high and low status in experimental groups, with and without the possibility of locomotion between different status levels. High status members offered more negative comments when downgrading was possible than when it was not possible. Low status members made fewer negative comments about the group task when upward mobility was possible than when it was not possible. Low status members tend to address these communications to persons of high status. The highs, when dissatisfied, tended to communicate with others at their own level. These findings suggest that the attractiveness of a position depends not only on how it is evaluated by self and peers but also by other status levels. Members in high status positions exhibited a greater degree of freedom in criticizing members of other status levels but tended to communicate criticisms of superiors to other members of their own status subgroups. The role structure appears to impose barriers to the upward communication of criticism and negative evaluations. Members who are secure in high status positions, and members in lower positions with the possibility of upward mobility, are less deferent to other members.

Results attained by Willerman and Swanson [770] in a study of campus sororities indicate that the members prefer, when possible, to belong to a high prestige organization. The members of high prestige groups tend to be better satisfied with their groups, but membership in a group of lower prestige can also be satisfying. Thibaut [705] studied experimental groups which differed in status and in the opportunity to improve the status of the group. It was found that the volume of communication among the members increases rapidly with failure and decreases with success in improving the status of the group. Low status groups, upon becoming successful in improving their status, exhibit more hostility toward high status groups than to unsuccessful low status groups, suggesting that an improvement in the status of the group enlarges the area of freedom of action for its members.

Pepitone and Reichling [536] report that highly cohesive groups are able to express more hostility and to express it more directly toward an aggressor than are less cohesive groups. The high cohesive groups were less restrained in their actions and, having once expressed hostility, were better able than the low cohesive groups to accept the aggressor. Festinger, Pepitone, and Newcomb [204] observed that a condition of deindividuation, in which the members of a group regard each other impersonally, permits the members to interact more freely than in a situation where they are singled out as individuals. These results are in line with the report by French [225] that the members of organized groups experience a greater degree of social freedom than do those of unorganized groups.

The prestige of a group to which a member belongs and his status in the group are matters of importance to him. These factors exert a direct influence on a member's personal pride, self-respect, and satisfaction with the group. However, a group as structured by the members themselves does not grant equal status to all its members. Those who do not succeed in achieving high status may nevertheless derive certain advantages from their membership in the group. Among the advantages yielded is a greater area of freedom for action as compared with that obtainable through direct contention in competitive interaction.

The depersonalization of the formalized structure defines an area of expectation for each member relative to his freedom for action on behalf of the group. Any other member who acts to restrict this area of freedom will eventually be made to feel the disapproval of the group. It is true that high status members possess greater power to limit action and interaction than do low status members. If there is any advantage to be gained from having high status members chosen by subordinates rather than superiors, it would appear to lie in the fact that the former tend to choose members who are capable of enlarging the area of freedom of action available to the group.

Moreno [502] and Jennings [364] have demonstrated that the members of a group who receive the greatest number of sociometric choices from their fellows are those characterized by a comparatively high degree of spontaneity in interaction. Similar results have been reported by Polansky, Lippitt, and Redl [541], who studied the effects of behavioral contagion, or conduct which is a spontaneous reaction to the behavior of another person. Those members who were accorded high status by their fellows were observed to be more active and more successful in initiating contagion. Those members who made a high number of influence attempts with a low degree of success were observed to be more impulsive and to act in terms of their own needs without considering the situation. The findings indicate that members who occupy positions of high status are more able to act spontaneously in their groups and to facilitate spontaneity in others. Their readiness to act spontaneously results in their being more susceptible to contagion than are those members in lower status positions, but they also appear to feel secure enough in their positions that they are more able to resist direct attempts to influence them. The member who perceives his own status to be low is able to react to contagion more readily when it is initiated by another member.

Results of the latter study confirm findings reported by Jennings [364] that the members of a group are quite capable of distinguishing between spontaneity and impulsive forms of behavior. They value the high status member, and grant him high status, because his spontaneity stimulates and legitimizes spontaneity in others. In doing so, he enlarges the sphere of action and interaction for the group as a whole.

The status system is important not only to the individual but also to the group as a whole. Morse [505] varied the structure of operating groups in a business office. In some groups, the formal structure was reinforced by increasing the decision-making performances of the high status members. In other groups, the differentiation of the formal structure was decreased by increasing the decision-making performances of low status members. Group effectiveness increased in the more highly structured groups and decreased in the less highly structured groups. The trend for morale was reversed. Morale was lowered when the differentiation of structure was increased, and improved when role differentiation was decreased. These results suggest that changes in the role structure may exert differential effects upon the group. Overstructuring or understructuring may produce gains in one area which are offset by losses in another area.

Barnard [36] maintains that the status system, while it presents many initial advantages to the members and to the group, tends in time to develop features which are disadvantageous. The status system tends eventually to distort the value of the contributions of the individual members and also tends to limit the upward mobility of members who are capable of filling high level positions. It distorts the system of distributive justice so that high status rather than personal contribution to the group is rewarded. It exalts the symbolic function beyond the level of sustainment, so that members in high status positions become figureheads rather than contributors to the progress of the group. A rigid status system may limit the adaptability of the organization through limiting the freedom of action of the members. Sherif [631], Torrance [725], and Merton [483] present evidence which supports these observations. Chapin and Tsouderos [130] report that, as groups increase in size and complexity the rank and file members become more passive and further dissociated from the central purpose of the organization. The high status member becomes further removed from the activities which he plans and initiates, and long lines of command impose communication problems which intensify the separation between members in different status levels.

The status system may make both positive and negative contributions to the group. This is true no matter what the origin of the status system. If the group is not organized in reference to an external model, it tends to develop a status system through the process of mutual interaction. Those members who achieve high status are better liked than members in positions of lower status, and their contributions are more highly evaluated. Those in high status positions appear better able than those in low status positions to support their fellow members. However, when the role system comes increasingly to serve the purpose of symbolizing fixed differentials in prestige and power, it functions decreasingly to provide support for members in low status positions. The problem of preventing structural sclerosis and functional senility is one that involves the constant balancing of the expectations among the individual members in all status levels and balancing these expectations against the requirements of the group as a whole.

The co-ordinative demands of a group impose severe restrictions on the proportion of members who can occupy high status positions, and the members are highly selective in ascribing status to their members. However, once the high status of a member has been acknowledged, he is allowed greater initiative, aggressiveness, and power than other members. More members of a group value high status than are able to achieve it, and the possibility of losing status constitutes a severe threat. When the role system is being developed in a new group, or if it is under contest, peer tends to compete with peer or else to form peer coalitions for the purpose of competing against those with higher status. The status system imposes barriers against the upward communication of criticism. However, the high status member is comparatively free to criticize members in lower status positions.

These findings, obtained in experimental groups, appear to apply equally well to formally structured organizations.

Results from a variety of studies indicate that the high status members of a group tend to communicate most with other high status members, that their high status is recognized by other group members, that they make more attempts to initiate influence than do low status members and their attempts in this direction are better accepted, that they are less likely to be rejected when they criticize or initiate aggression against low status members, and, along with all these factors, that they are better liked than low status members. It is apparent that high status is not a cause in itself for rejection. In fact, many organizations recruit high status members in order to lend prestige to the group.

## The Role System: Responsibility and Authority

Organization theorists differ to some extent in their conceptions of the details of role differentiation. Benne and Sheats [56], for example, see three kinds of roles that are played by the members of a group. One type of role facilitates the accomplishment of the group task. Another type of role serves the function of building and maintaining the group. A third type serves to satisfy the needs of the individual members without regard to the group purpose or task. Different members play these roles in differing degrees as the types of problems and stages of the group task undergo change. According to the point of view being developed, these three types of member performance represent differentiations of function. That is, the members of a group tend to differ in the functions they perform, and the functions performed by any one member may be expected to change from time to time.

Bales' [28] observations of experimental groups have led him to propose a different conception of role differentiation. He finds that the role of a group member tends to become differentiated in relation to the degree of access to group resources, the degree of control exercised over persons, the status of the position occupied, and the degree of identification and co-operation with the group task and purpose. These variants of role differentiation may be regarded as aspects of status. According to the point of view being developed, a position of high status in a group provides a member with a greater area of freedom to utilize the group resources and to exercise control over other persons, as well as with greater motivation to identify himself with the group than does a position of low status. The research on role differentiation is more frequently concerned with differences between status levels than with differences between functions.

Jaques [361], confronted by the problem of developing a method for determining wage and salary differentials, concluded that amount of responsibility was the most satisfactory criterion. He found that the effects upon the organization of decisions made in some positions last for only a few minutes. The effects of decisions made in other positions may commit the resources of the organization for a period of several years. Work, according to Jaques, is a kind of investment behavior. A member invests the ability to foresee the consequences of his behavior. The longer the periods of foresight required, the greater the tolerance of uncertainty required and the greater one's responsibility for discretion. Martin [469] presents evidence in support of this hypothesis. He studied the time span for decision in four status levels of an industrial plant. Significant differences were found between works manager, division superintendent, department foremen, and shift foremen. The time limits within which effective action could be taken were found to be much shorter in the lower levels, where immediate decisions were required. In the top levels, the decision situation was often ambiguous and elastic, with a wide interval of time separating inquiry, decision, and final report of action. The effects of 98 per cent of the decisions made by shift foremen became apparent within a period of two weeks. The works manager was required to wait at least a year to determine the effects of 50 per cent of the decisions he made. These results clearly support the view that the level of responsibility defined for the occupants of positions in different status levels differs in the extent to which it commits the organization as a total system.

Gibb [245] has reviewed a variety of studies on the differentiation of the leadership role. Bass [40], Bales [28], Hemphill [313], Homans [331], and others have shown that variance between members in the initiation of interaction is the basic condition which underlies the emergence of differentiated roles. Carter [109] found that functional differentiation is related to differences in the group task and to differences among the members in task related skills. Jennings [364] and Lippitt [428] report that the emergence of status differences is related to personality differences among the group members, particularly in reference to spontaneity and personal security.

Swanson [694] studied groups that differed in knowledge of task and amount of prior experience in working together. Groups that had worked together previously on a task exceeded other groups in success of task performance, mutual satisfaction, and expression of self-oriented need. Newly formed groups exceeded previously organized groups in amount of communication, clarity of role definition, and fixity of role specialization. These results suggest the importance of role differentiation in the early stages of group formation.

Borgatta and Bales [75], Heinicke and Bales [308], French [225], Bales and Strodtbeck [30], and others have observed that newly assembled groups are able to make only abortive attempts at task performance so long as the role structure remains undefined. The members seem compelled to direct their efforts toward the differentiation of function and status. Once they have developed and acknowledged a role structure, the members are able to go ahead with the group task.

Bavelas [50] has invented designs which impose strictly controlled communication channels upon experimental groups. A "circular" design permits each member to communicate only with one member immediately to his right and another immediately to his left. An "all channels" design permits each member to communicate with every other member. A "wheel" design makes one member a co-ordination center, and all other members are able to communicate only with the central, co-ordinative member. Groups with wheel designs quickly develop clearly defined role structures with the co-ordinative member occupying the high status position in the group. Leavitt [407] and Shaw [626], using Bavelas designs, have shown that a position of centrality is an important determiner of a member's success in achieving status in a group. Shaw and Rothschild [628] found that groups with positions of centrality are more efficient than those that provide no such position. However, the latter groups were found to be more effective than those that provided two positions in which their occupants could compete for authority.

Lanzetta and Roby [403] studied experimental groups working on an information processing task. It was found that the average number of messages transmitted, the average length of messages, and the proportion of trial interval spent in communication varied with changes in the communication structure. Practice enabled a group to transmit more information during a fixed time interval. Lack of discontinuities in the learning curves suggested that insightful reorganization did not account for the improved performance with practice.

Guetzkow and Dill [279] have subjected the Bavelas design to a searching analysis. The group's handling of its operations was studied separately from its handling of organizational problems. Construction problems were solved by 56 groups of five men each. Each group solved 20 problems and was allowed two minutes between tasks to solve organizational problems. Within three to six trials, the wheel, or central, type of arrangement permitted the members to achieve organization in such a way that they did not require the full two minutes of intertrial time to solve the organizational problems involved in receiving and sending messages. There was a greater tendency for the circle and all-channel arrangements to impose restrictions which required the full two minutes of intertrial time for organization, and to prevent the differentiation of role structure. Whereas the wheel arrangement used the same structure for receiving and sending messages, the circle and all-channel groups tended to develop different structures for receiving and sending messages. Guetzkow and Dill found that those members who were the most active in providing solutions were the most frequent recipients of messages containing information relevant to problem solving. They interpret these results as supporting a learning or reinforcement theory of role differentiation. The member who provides solutions rewards the other group members and thereby reinforces the expectation that he will be able to supply future solutions. Although reinforcement appeared to explain role differentiation during task operations, it did not seem to account for differences in the types of structure achieved. All the wheel groups with a co-ordinative member developed two-level hierarchies. The circle and all-channel groups that were able to organize developed two-level or three-level hierarchies. An analysis of the content of messages sent during the intertrial periods suggested that planning might be an important factor in the development of structure. The percentage of messages that proposed plans for group structure was 14 for wheel nets, 30 for circle nets, and 39 for all-channel nets. Messages concerned with the perception of structure accounted for 86 per cent of the intertrial communications for wheel nets, 70 per cent for circle nets, and 35 per cent for all-channel nets. Thus, although the achievement of structure was most difficult for circle designs, these groups made less use of intertrial sessions for the perception and planning of structure than did the all-channel nets. These results suggested that the communication restrictions imposed during task periods prevented the circle groups from using the intertrial periods for improving organization. Restrictions in communication which require the members to organize in order to communicate tend to reduce the amount of effort devoted to planning for organization. Although insight and planning facilitate the understanding of organization structure, this facilitation is dependent upon the development of structure for the communication of insight and planning.

There is clear evidence in the studies described above that the members of experimental groups find it necessary to develop a recognized role structure before they can devote their efforts to effective task achievement. The nature of the group task and differences in task ability are found to be determinants of functional differentiation. Status differentiations are related not only to task ability but also to personality variables, such as spontaneity of behavior and personal security. The high status member of a group occupies a position of centrality in that he acts as a co-ordination center and is able to control the flow of information. His ability to control reinforcement is an important factor in the development of the role structure. Since the differentiation of role structures is facilitated by reinforcement, the development of organization may be regarded as a learning process. However, such reinforcement is dependent upon adequate channels of communication and tends to be ineffective when the group must develop structure in order to communicate for the purpose of reinforcing structure.

In a study of 105 superintendents and school boards, Gross, Mason, and McEachern [271] found that the degree of consensus within each sample relative to the attributes required for potential occupants of a position was significantly greater than that relative to the performances required after occupancy of the position. The degree of board members' motivation to achieve the formal goals of the educational system was found to be related highly to the degree of their conformity to superintendent's expectations relative to their roles. These results appear to lend direct support to the hypothesis that those expectations which define positions exhibit a higher degree of mutual confirmation and stability than do those that define roles.

Results from a variety of studies conducted by Shartle and Stogdill [624] indicate that formal organization structure (status and function) is related to operative role structure (authority and responsibility). These structures are also related to the interaction structure. However, none of the relationships are high enough to suggest that either the status structure or the effective authority of individual members is dominant enough to explain all the important variance within a single group or between different groups. The results do suggest that delegation bears an important relationship to the status structure.

Stogdill and Scott [678] found that responsibility and authority were positively related to status in six different naval organizations. The status level of the positions was correlated about .25 with responsibility and authority, and about .35 with delegation.

The average correlation between estimates of authority and estimates of responsibility was found to be about .55. Those members occupying high status positions tended to exhibit wider areas of responsibility and authority and to delegate more fully to their subordinates than did members in lower status positions.

Studies by Stogdill and Shartle [680] indicate that variance in responsibility and authority is also related to differences in function. Members occupying positions of command and co-ordination were found to rate themselves higher in responsibility, authority, and delegation than members occupying supervisory positions. Although these results can be attributed largely to differences in status, marked differences were found between different functional specialties in the same status level. Homans [331] reports that the status of a position and the range of interaction of its occupant tend to decline as the functions of the position become more highly specialized.

Stogdill, Shartle, Wherry, and Jaynes [683] found that authority and delegation, but not responsibility, are related to differences in function. They divided 470 officers into 120 groups according to similarity of function. A factor analysis of the intercorrelations among the 120 specialties yielded eight factors. The members whose status and performances were described by two factors, identified as Personnel Administrators and Schedule-Procedure Makers, made outstandingly high scores on authority. Both factors describe members who occupy positions that are intermediate in status. Delegation was related to two factors identified as Technical Supervisors and Decision Makers. The former made very low scores, while the latter made very high scores, on delegation. These two factors represent subgroups of members who occupy the bottom and top positions in the leadership hierarchy. The results suggest that status is more highly related to degree of delegation than to degree of effective responsibility and authority.

Studies by Stogdill and Scott [678] indicate that the relationship of responsibility and authority to interaction structures varies markedly from one organization to another. The only consistent finding across organizations was that those members who initiate more interaction with subordinates and are the objects of inter-actions initiated by subordinates tend to make higher scores in re-sponsibility, authority, and delegation.

Stogdill and Haase [676] found that members who occupy high status positions tend to initiate more interactions, and to be the recipients of interactions initiated by others, to a greater extent than members in low status positions. Interaction tends to be related also to functional differentiation, with those members who occupy positions that are focal centers of ongoing operations at a particular period of time being the recipients of a high rate of initiated interaction. Interaction structures are found to be related to function as well as to status.

A number of interconnected studies conducted by Shartle, Stogdill, and associates indicate that role structures and inter-action structures are related to the formal structure of positions and that the relationship between interaction and role structure changes in response to changes in operations. However, each of these structures is found to exhibit a high degree of essential stability despite changes in group operations.

There is a mass of literature which indicates that role systems and formal group structures tend in time to become so rigid as to restrict the upward mobility of their members and to limit the adaptive capacity of the group or society. Bendix and Lipset [54] and Merton and associates [485] have edited volumes of selected readings on bureaucracy, class, status, and power. That social systems tend toward structural rigidity and functional conserv-ancy is well documented.

In large organizations, the problem of mobility is of importance not only to the individual but also to the group. The success of the group may depend upon its ability to recruit, select, and pro-mote capable members for positions of leadership. Even in groups with a large number of members to select from, this problem is not as easy as might be expected. The members them-selves appear to be aware of this fact in that they do not nominate for leadership many of their fellow members whom they regard as technically competent and socially desirable.

Group structures impose barriers to upward and downward

mobility. A member may find that he is not accepted if he moves so far up or down in the organization scale that he is thrown into the company of members whose values, patterns of behavior, and reference group identifications differ markedly from his own. The barrier is not always imposed by the group. It may be imposed by the member himself. Both military and industrial organizations find that many technically competent members, after reaching a particular level in the status or economic hierarchy, refuse further promotions, even when invited and encouraged to do so. Reider [558], studying the emotional breakdown of medical officers in World War II, found that promotion to a higher level of responsibility and status was one of the factors involved. If an individual is dependent upon his superiors for psychological support, this support is removed when his promotion elevates him to the status of peer rather than to that of dependent subordinate. He not only loses his source of emotional support, but he is expected to act as a source of such support to his own subordinates, thus subjecting him to redoubled stress. Livingstone [432] and Hall and Locke [289] found that women in industry are often reluctant to assume supervisory responsibilities. In 35 per cent of the organizations sampled by Waddell [743], some workers were found who refused promotion to position of foreman.

As a member rises in the organization hierarchy, the complexity of the factors with which he has to deal increases at an extremely rapid rate. Many technically competent members reach a stage beyond which they appear unable to perceive, conceptualize, and understand all the diverse structural, operational, personal, and environmental factors that are at work in the organization. As a result, they are unable to cope with all the demands made upon them. It is for this reason that it is more difficult to fill high status than low status positions with competent and adequate persons. Not only does the group structure impose barriers to mobility, but individuals appear to exhibit upper limits of ability, comprehension, and capacity to interact which further restrict their upward mobility. The group members, in according high status to only a few of their associates, appear to recognize the differential abilities among the members. The extent to which a given member will be satisfied with the function and status accorded him appears to be related to his personal values, level of aspiration, and reference group identifications.

## Role Sanction and Legitimation

The hypothesis has been advanced that norms and roles represent different systems within a group, but that both must be regarded as mutually confirmed sets of member expectations. Gross, Mason, and McEachern [271] have provided evidence which supports this point of view. These authors found that the longer the period of time in which school board members had served together the greater their consensus in defining the board member role. Only weak support was found for the hypothesis that homogeneity of value systems between board members and superintendents would be related to greater consensus in own and other roles. In other words, role definition could not be explained in terms of normative value systems.

It was further observed by Gross, Mason, and McEachern that the greater the degree of conformity between school board action and superintendent expectation the greater the satisfaction of the superintendent with his position and the more highly he rated the board. Conformity of board members with superintendent expectations, but not consensus between them in role definition, was related to the board's evaluation of superintendent performance. Consensus between superintendent and board in defining their roles was associated with high ratings of the board by the superintendent, but not with high ratings of the superintendent by the board. These results suggest that the high status member of a group may be allowed a high degree of freedom, not only by his subordinates but also by a higher echelon organization which determines policy for the group in which the high status position is located.

Shibutani [637] maintains that a reference group should be defined as a group whose perspective constitutes a frame of reference for the individual. It seems likely that each group of which an individual is a member will serve as a reference group, since it provides a frame of reference for estimating comparative status, function, and experienced outcomes. But an individual's values, satisfactions, and loyalties in a membership group may be more highly determined by external reference groups than by the membership group. Gross, Mason, and McEachern [271] found that among superintendents and board members, each tended to estimate the importance of the functions of his position in relation to his own reference groups. Superintendents tended to identify with members of their profession, while board members identified with interest groups in the community.

Hyman [348] reports that an individual's judgment of his status shifts when his reference groups are changed. Individuals were found to use different criteria in estimating economic, intellectual, social, and other variants of status. Satisfaction with a particular status is dependent upon the reference groups (family, friends, work associates, people with more or less, etc.) with which an individual compares himself. A person's level of aspiration and his evaluation of his own worth appear to be important factors in determining the reference groups with which he will compare himself.

Shils [639] found that 90 per cent of the soldiers interviewed at the close of World War II expressed the opinion that men are greatly concerned about the respect in which they are held by other members of their units. Men who felt the acceptance and support of their peers stood up better under stress and exhibited less fear in combat. The generalized group norms relative to mutual support and getting the job done were found to strengthen the acceptance of instrumental commands issued by official agents of the group. New men tended to follow the pattern of behavior set by veterans.

Merton and Kitt [486] found that soldiers tend to compare themselves not only with groups in combat and groups that have not been in combat, but with civilian groups as well. Thus, the soldier finds himself well off in comparison with some groups and not so well off in comparison with others. His satisfaction with the army is related to the condition of the dominant reference group with which he compares his own condition. Green troops were found to be less reluctant to go into combat than veterans. The new troops appeared to be identifying themselves with the idealized norms of the civilian population, while the veterans had developed a common norm that combat is something that one can take or leave alone, but preferably the latter. Replacements mixed with veterans tended to adopt the normative values of the veterans. Enlisted men who expressed attitudes most in conformity with the army norm were more rapidly promoted. This fact is attributed to the anticipatory preparation for membership in a higher status reference group. Merton and Kitt observed that when the individual accepts the status structure of the larger group as legitimate, he tends to compare himself with others in the same or in a neighboring status level. If the structure is under dispute, the situation is open for comparison with a wider range of statuses. The range of status groups taken as effective bases for comparison may be closely associated with the degree with which legitimacy is ascribed to the group structure. Thus the individual's aspirations for increased status in a group are likely to be related to his perception of the legitimacy of the status structure. His chances for advancement in a stable structure are better if he conforms to the norms of the group.

Clark [141] found that the effect of group norms tends to be precarious when they are not clearly defined, when the positions of high status members are not fully legitimized, and when the norms are not acceptable to the group members.

Fenchel, Monderer, and Hartley [195] found that college students identify themselves with different reference groups in the following order of importance: campus residence groups, campus activity groups, the general student body, friends and acquaintances, and family. When asked to indicate their actual and desired status in each group, it was found that they aspire to higher status in those groups in which their status is lowest. Negative status strivings were observed in 20 per cent of the ratings. The attempt to raise reference groups to own status was interpreted as an evidence of status insecurity. Higgin [324] studied the estimates made by military personnel of their status positions in military and civilian organizations. Those who exaggerated their upward mobility in moving from civilian to military positions were found to be better satisfied with their military positions. Those who exaggerated their downward mobility were found to value civilian organizations as reference groups. Bettelheim, Janowitz, and Shils [65] found that veterans who had experienced downward mobility from prewar to postwar positions exhibited more intolerance toward minority groups.

The studies discussed above indicate that reference group identifications may determine to a large degree an individual's satisfaction with a group, his support of its activities, his acceptance of the group norms, his perception of the legitimacy of the role system, his aspirations for status, and his chances for upward mobility in the group. Acceptance of the norms of a group and integration into the normative system provides emotional support for the individual and also tends to legitimize the systems of status and authority within the group. The contradictory expectations derived from identification with different reference groups may result in role conflict.

Gross, Mason, and McEachern [271] found strong evidence to support the hypothesis that role conflict is related to the perceived degree of legitimacy of contradictory expectations made upon the occupant of a position and the nature of the perceived sanctions likely to be applied in case of failure to conform with the incompatible expectations.

Slater [649] studied role differentiation in small, experimental groups. The "best liked man" held the top position in that category through 30 sessions. The man who talked the most, received the most interaction, contributed the best ideas, and gave the best guidance held the top position in that category in 10 to 12 sessions only. In groups with high consensus in role definition, high participation (talking and receiving interaction) is associated with high rated task ability (ideas and guidance), but neither is strongly related to liking. In the low consensus group, the relation of task ability to popularity is even less. All the characteristics of role behavior are more highly interrelated in high consensus than in low consensus groups. These findings suggest that the role of the "task specialist" is more highly subject to redefinition in response to group operations than is the role of the "best liked man."

Scott [610] made an intensive study of errors in the perception of status in ten highly structured organizations. The status of peers was perceived less accurately than that of superiors and subordinates. The most frequent status error consisted of naming superiors as peers or peers as subordinates. Subordinates were less frequently named as peers. Occupants of high status positions made fewer errors than their subordinates in the perception of superiors and peers. The more extensively a superior interacted with other members throughout the organization the greater the perceptual error of his subordinates. Organizational relationships were perceived more accurately by subordinates when their superior held more authority in his own hands and delegated less. Those members whose expectations were confused tended to have many of their expectations unrealized in that other members failed to acknowledge the mutual relationships between their positions.

Scott's findings suggest that the legitimation of a role may depend upon the degree of accuracy with which the members perceive the status of the role and the degree of consensus among them in defining the role. The function of the high status member in maintaining stability in the definition of structure is clearly revealed.

The evidence reviewed in this section indicates that roles and norms must be regarded as separate systems. However, a member tends to interpret the functions of role and the legitimacy of the group norms in relation to the reference groups with which he identifies himself. Greater consensus is found in definitions of the formal system of positions than in definitions of the role system. Role definition related to task performance is found to be less stable than role definition that is not task related. The function of the high status member in maintaining definition of structure is clearly revealed.

The hypothesized relation of interpersonal power to the perceived legitimacy of group structures is substantiated in numerous empirical studies. Dubin [185] maintains that power implies a relationship of interdependence relative to identical functions. He interprets industrial conflict as a continued struggle for the exclusive right to exercise essential functions in the organization. Chamberlain's [126] study of union challenge to management control confirms the view that labor leaders have made strong and successful efforts in the direction of gaining legal definition of the right to exercise functions which formerly were regarded as exclusive prerogatives of management. Further support of this point of view may be derived from the work of Slichter [650], Teller [703], and Harbison and Dubin [295].

Numerous investigators, including Stagner [666] and the authors of various papers edited by Hartmann and Newcomb [303] and Kornhauser, Dubin, and Ross [397], indicate that the conflict between managers and union officials tends to center upon the right to determine wage levels, supplementary rewards, and penalties. Workers, however, tend to be more deeply concerned with the neglect of their rights and interests in the workplace than with the wages they are receiving. The greater the perpetuation of disappointment in the workplace the greater the likelihood that workers will ally themselves against management.

The characteristics of the professional agitator and the methods he uses to gain control of power structures have been described by Selznick [619], Gilbert [249], and Lowenthal and Guterman [438].

Individuals who seek power in a group tend to challenge the differential reward structure. The group members, however, tend to support a differentiated system of rewards. Rohde [573] studied experimental groups under four different conditions of reward and punishment: (A) the entire group rewarded for good performance, (B) only the supervisor rewarded for good performance, (C) entire group rewarded for good performance, and only the followers punished for poor performance, (D) entire group rewarded for good performance, and the prestige of the supervisor reduced for poor performance. Satisfaction with the group was highest under Condition B, while satisfaction with group performance was highest under Condition C. Willingness to work with each other again was significantly higher under Conditions B and C than under Conditions A and D. Both supervisors and followers rated their own performances as poorest under Condition D. It is evident in Rohde's experiment that the members support a system which differentiates between status levels in the distribution of punishment and reward. They perceive the group to be more pleasant and more effective when the high status member is favored in the receipt of reward and when they alone are the recipients of punishment. They value the prestige of their high status member and suffer a decline in their willingness to support the group when the prestige of the high status member is challenged or reduced.

Weiss [754] studied the allocation and acceptance of responsibility in a government research agency. The characteristics of individuals which tend to legitimize the exercise of policy making responsibilities were education, experience, and length of service. Being a woman was found to be a legitimizing characteristic for the allocation of service responsibilities. These findings suggest that the legitimation of roles is determined to a rather high degree by the kind of person a member is perceived to be.

Adams [2] found that member satisfaction is directly related to the degree of status congruency in a group. That is, member satisfaction is greater when high level positions are occupied by persons who rank high in age, education, experience, military rank, and other indicators of status. Group productivity was found to be highest under medium degrees of status congruency. Supporting evidence has been reported by Shepherd and Weschler [630].

Evidence that the perceived legitimacy of a role influences the behavior of group members is presented by Raven and French [556]. Members of experimental groups elected one of their number as a supervisor. In half of the groups, the elected member was replaced as supervisor by a member not elected. Some of the members under both supervisory conditions were fined for poor performance. Election was perceived to establish the supervisor's right to his position. Election also tended to establish the legitimacy of his conduct as a supervisor, increased his personal attractiveness, and resulted in his suggestions being adhered to and privately accepted. Coercion (imposing a fine) reduced perceived group support and personal attraction. Using an adaptation of the same method, Levinger, Morrison, and French [410] found that the threat of punishment induced conforming behavior before punishment. However, conforming behavior before punishment was not related significantly to conformity after punishment. The perceived threat of punishment increased productivity, but the effect was reduced following punishment. The perceived legitimacy of punishment reduced resistance to conformity. These results give support to the view that the legitimacy of a member's role is related to the manner in which he acquires his position. If the members acknowledge the right of an individual to occupy a position, this acknowledgment tends to legitimize his role in the group. However, the continued legitimation of the role is dependent upon the pattern of behavior exhibited by the occupant of a position.

The members of a group develop formal structures, role structures, and systems of sanctions in the process of mutual interaction. The continued legitimation and support of these structures and systems by the members is closely related to the extent to which the group continues to confirm the expectations of its members.

## Role Conflict

In view of the strong pressures exerted by groups to induce conformity to norms, it may be expected that conformity would reduce role conflict. There is experimental evidence which lends some support to this point of view. Bates and Cloyd [46] regard roles as patterns of anticipated behavior which group members associate with a particular person, while norms are defined as evaluations of anticipated behavior which are shared by the group members. These authors recorded the behaviors and opinions exhibited by the members of discussion groups. Each mem-

ber of a group was then given a list of the items and was asked
to identify the persons who might exhibit the behaviors or opinions. A role description, consisting of the behaviors ascribed to
him, was prepared for each subject. Approximately 70 per cent of
the identifications were correct. The opinion items of the list were
rated to determine the extent to which the opinions were shared
by all and the extent to which individuals lived up to each opinion norm. Role description and norm conformity on the same
items of behavior were highly related.

Cohen [148] asked pairs of subjects to rate items together,
then apart. He found that a social norm found jointly in the first
two sessions caused partners to rate items similarly when apart.
Raven [555] informed experimental groups of a fictitious group
norm while rating opinion items. Deviates changed more toward
the norm than non-deviates. Change toward the norm was greater
in groups in which the subjects were required to make public an-
nouncements of their opinions than in groups where no such an-
nouncements were required.

Dittes and Kelley [180] asked participants of experimental
groups to make successive ratings of each other relative to desirability as group members. Each subject was then informed of a
fictitious group rating. Those supposedly rated low decreased in
participation by about 50 per cent. Those rated average in
desirability increased in participation, while those rated high
did not change. Those rated average tended to conform to the
group norms, while the highs tended to deviate from the norms.
Those rated low deviated more than the average members, but
less than the highs. These results suggest that conformity to norms
is related to the acceptance of status in the group.

Kelley and Volkart [382] found that resistance to contra-norm
arguments is greater on the part of members who value their
membership in the group, and under conditions in which no public announcement of attitudes is required. Cervin [123, 124] reports that emotionally unstable subjects exhibit greater resistance to opinion change under stress and opposition than do emotionally stable subjects, but that the two groups of subjects do not
differ under conditions of group solidarity.

Siegel and Siegel [640] observed greater change of attitude in the direction of conformity to the norm of a membership group among members who came to regard it as a preferred reference group than among those who continued to regard it as a non-preferred reference group.

Results from a number of studies suggest that expectation is more important than accuracy of perception in conforming behavior. Weiner, Carpenter, and Carpenter [753], studying judgments of perceptual designs, found greater change in the direction of conforming behavior in ambiguous than in non-ambiguous stimulus situations. Crow and Hammond [165] were unable to confirm the hypothesis of a generalized ability to predict interpersonal responses when subjects were asked to judge the responses of other persons to personality and attitude tests. Response set (expectation) was found to be more consistent over time than predictive accuracy. Grossack [272] found that regardless of the experimental instructions given to structure the expectations of his subjects they tended to judge other members of the group in terms of observed behavior. However, subjects' preferences for other members were related to their own prestructured expectations. These findings led to the conclusion that the behavior of a group member is a function of his own expectations and the stimuli provided by the behavior of other members. Results reported by Exline [194] indicate that members of congenial groups are more accurate than members of uncongenial groups in perceiving task oriented behavior, but not social behavior. The various findings described above suggest that the perception and evaluation of role behavior may be determined more highly by the confirmation of desirability estimates than by the confirmation of probability estimates.

Berg [59] presented groups with a complex perceptual task but prevented the development of group norms by prohibiting communication. He found that the subjects responded on the basis of their presuppositions as to what the other group members would do. Weiner [752] has demonstrated that it is uncertainty of judgment rather than stimulus ambiguity which induces conformity to group norms. He found no relationship between conformity and degree of ambiguity when the amount of disagreement and certainty were held constant. However, with certainty and ambiguity held constant, a relationship was found between conformity and amount of disagreement with the norm. Conformity acts to reduce the discomfort and pressure associated with uncertainty.

According to Getzels and Guba [243] role conflict varies as a function of the incompatibility of expectations made upon a role. Jambor [358] found that role conflict differs in relation to the status levels from which varying expectations bear upon a role. When a supervisor who occupies a position of middle status in a group finds that his superior's perception of the role differs from his own perception of it, he experiences more conflict and anxiety than when his perception of his role differs from his subordinates' perceptions of the role. Weitz [755] reports that new members remain longer with the group when their expectations relative to role requirements and group norms are carefully structured before entrance into the group.

Gardner and Whyte [234], Stouffer and associates [688], and Wray [784] point out the fact that the leader often occupies a middleman position. He is confronted by conflicting demands from superiors and subordinates. In a direct test of this hypothesis, Brooks [87] found that superiors and subordinates in a business firm differ in their expectations relative to the role performance of supervisors. Superiors expect results, initiative, planning, firmness, and structure. Subordinates expect recognition, opportunity, consideration, approachability, encouragement, and representation. Both superiors and subordinates expect communication, development, delegation, understanding, know-how, and teamwork. Effective, as compared with ineffective, leaders perceive themselves as letting subordinates know what is expected of them, informing subordinates on policy changes, explaining the reason for decisions, and getting member reactions before going ahead with a new plan.

Wispé and Thayer [776], in the study of an insurance agency, found greater consensus in definitions of function for the agent and manager than for the assistant manager. The latter was confronted by both vertical and horizontal role ambiguity in that both he and the manager were expected to exercise the same functions, but he could not determine whether a given function was compulsory or optional.

Not only do supervisors and subordinates differ in their perceptions of the role of middle echelon leaders, but effective and ineffective leaders are found to differ in the perception of their own roles. In addition, members at the same echelon or in the same subgroup may differ among themselves in the demands they make upon their leader. Seeman [616], in a study of teachers and principals in 26 communities, found that teachers divide about six to four among themselves in answer to questions relative to whether the principal should act as chairman of staff meetings, discuss his personal problems with teachers, and invite teachers to his home. The higher the degree of separation between principal and teachers as perceived by the teachers, the greater the salary increases obtained for the teachers. Although the teachers expected the principal to attend to matters within the school, his success in improving the school situation was dependent upon his devoting time to public relations matters outside the school. When principal and teachers disagree relative to the role enacted by the principal, the latter reported less indecision than did the teachers. Seeman concluded that the necessity for action may resolve some conflict for leaders, while followers have comparatively little opportunity for such action.

In a study of role conflict among school superintendents, Gross, Mason, and McEachern [271] found that perceived differences in the expectations made upon the superintendent vary in relation to such matters as hiring personnel, teacher salary recommendations, budget recommendations, and use of time. Worry, reduced job satisfaction, and reduced career satisfaction were associated with role conflict. Role conflict solution, as a function of the superintendent's perception of the legitimacy of the conflicting expectations to be satisfied and the nature of the sanctions which might be applied in case of nonconformity, was correctly predicted in 91 per cent of the conflict cases. These results lend strong support to the legitimacy-sanction hypothesis. In explaining those cases which were not correctly predicted, it was suggested that formal definitions of the superintendent's position, rather than perceptions of legitimacy and sanction, may have operated to influence the superintendent's final decision. It was also suggested that the superintendent may have been guided by his own expectations rather than by the perceived expectations of others in the performance of his role.

Halpin [291] found that school board members and members of the superintendent's staff differ in their perceptions of the leader behavior of superintendents. Staff members perceived the superintendent to be less considerate than he was described by board members or by himself. Board members described him as initiating structure to a greater degree than did the superintendent or his staff members. Superintendents felt that they should be more considerate than did board or staff members. Board members expected the ideal superintendent to be more considerate than staff members consider ideal. Discrepancies between the expectations of different reference groups, as well as discrepancies between perceived behavior and expected behavior, were found to influence the superintendent's perception of the difficulty of his role.

Kanareff and Lanzetta [374] have produced experimental evidence which indicates that conformity to a norm is greatest under high probabilities of reinforcement and least under low probabilities, but the expectation of negative sanctions tends to lower the effects of reinforcement on conformity under high probabilities of reinforcement. The expectation of negative sanctions tends to weaken the effects of reinforcement on nonconformity under low probabilities of reinforcement. These results are of importance in indicating that the expectation of sanctions may operate to reduce the effects of intermember reinforcement upon conformity and nonconformity when sanctions and norms are in conflict.

Browne [91], Willerman [769], and others have shown that the higher the status of a member the greater the number of external groups in which he holds membership. Each member of a large organization holds membership in overlapping sub-groups. This is particularly true of members who occupy intermediate status positions. Pelz [529], Mann and Dent [465], Likert [422], and Jacobson and Seashore [357] present evidence which indicates that the effective mid-status supervisor is one who has influence with his superiors and also identifies with his subordinates. His skill in both leadership and membership roles enables him to link the subgroups on the status level below him with those on the status level above him. Eisenstadt [190] also reports that the occupant of a leadership position, because of his wider range of membership groups, is able to serve as an agent for consolidating subgroups and integrating them into the larger system. Walker, Guest, and Turner [744] have shown that group members value the superior who is able to absorb the pressures passed down from higher status levels.

A member, regardless of his status, is confronted by conflicting demands arising from persons, group operations, group structure, and the external environment. The occupant of a high status position may have to pay a rather heavy cost for the privilege of status elevation. If he is effective in his position, he is valued for the diverse functions he fulfills in serving the interests of the members and the group.

A variety of studies has been described that indicates that the members of a group develop and perceive individual roles and common norms. Values and opinions that are publicly expressed in the group tend to conform more closely to the common norm than values that are held in private. Those members who perceive themselves to be about average in acceptance by the group participate more actively and conform more closely to the norm than do members who feel rejected or highly accepted. Those members whose acceptance status is high conform less closely to the norms than do other members. Despite the fact that high status members are less dominated by the group norm, the expectations of superiors are more likely than those of subordinates to produce role conflict when self-expectations deviate from the expectations of others. Conformity is higher when the membership group is also a highly valued reference group.

The importance of norms to role enactment is evidenced in the fact that, when communicative restrictions prevent the development of norms, the members act on the basis of their suppositions relative to the nature of a possible norm. Although the group situation creates conditions which stimulate role conflict, such conflict is an attribute of individuals, not of the stimulus situation. Conformity to the group norms tends to reduce uncertainty and role conflict.

Role conflict appears to arise primarily from the perception of discrepancy between the demands made by different individuals, subgroups, and status levels. Factors which serve to resolve conflict are the possibility of overt action, perception of the differential legitimacy of contradictory expectations and the nature of possible sanctions, and support provided by the formal definition of function and status.

## Structure, Power, and Operations Control

The hypothesis has been advanced that interpersonal power is a function of the differential abilities of the group members to control the reinforcement of expectation. If this supposition is valid, the high status members should be able to exert more power because of their greater access to group resources and because of their greater freedom to initiate behavior which reinforces their own expectations and those of other members. Studies of the power structures of large societal systems edited by Bendix and Lipset [54] and Kornhauser [396] do not contradict the hypothesis.

Studies of both experimentally created and operating groups indicate that the functioning of status systems is a complicated matter indeed. Zander [788] introduced two newcomers to various groups. One newcomer was introduced as a person high in prestige, the other as a person low in prestige. The person playing a high prestige role reported feeling comfortable and accepted. The low prestige newcomer reported feeling uncomfortable and unwanted or ignored. Zander concludes that the prestige or power attributed to another member may determine to a large extent his satisfaction in the group.

Veroff [739] found that those group members who exhibited strong motivation for power scored high on the satisfaction of being a leader and were rated high in argumentation and attempts to control others. They did not score higher than other group members in the satisfaction of being boss or in political and economic values. The different relationship of power motivation to the satisfaction of being a leader and the satisfaction of being a boss was interpreted as indicating that the need for recognition may be more important than the need for power.

Evidence presented by Berkowitz [62] indicates that group members are by no means motivated universally by the desire to gain at the expense of others. It was found that a subject working in an experimental group in which self only or others only could win a prize exhibited increased task motivation when he perceived that other members were dependent upon him for the attainment of their valued goals. The subjects were highly motivated to perform when their partners could receive a reward even though the subjects themselves were not eligible.

Leavitt [407] found that the member of a highly structured experimental group who occupies a position of centrality is better satisfied than are members who occupy peripheral positions. A position of centrality is one into which information is channeled and from which it may be dispatched to other positions. The member in a position of centrality is able to control the flow of information to members in other positions. In doing so, he is able to control the reinforcements they experience. Trow [730] repeated Leavitt's experiment, but with varied autonomy as well as centrality. Autonomy was controlled by varying the extent to which a member was enabled to solve translation problems with or without access to decoding information possessed by another member. Autonomy, but not centrality of position, was related significantly to job satisfaction. Those members who exhibited a strong need for autonomy were better satisfied in autonomous than in dependent positions. Estimates of member status were significantly related to centrality but not to autonomy. Subjects expressed the opinion that the central member should receive significantly higher pay than members in autonomous, dependent, or peripheral positions. These results suggest that satisfaction is more highly related to the ability to complete an assigned task than to the status level of a member's position. Differential reward is associated with differences in status and control. Shaw, Rothschild, and Strickland [629] observed that members in positions of centrality made stronger efforts than peripheral members to change the opinions of those who disagree, but they themselves changed more than peripheral members when they failed to influence divergent opinions. Member satisfaction was found to be a function of centrality and amount of support received from other members.

The results of the various studies considered above indicate that a position of high status carries with it certain potentialities for satisfying the expectations of its occupant. The high status member tends to be better liked and better accepted than other group members. In addition, a position of high status endows its occupant with power to influence others. Torrance [725] found that having high status was more effective than knowing the correct answer in influencing other members to accept the correct answer. This effect was particularly noted in permanent groups where the established position of high status members enabled them to exert influence without much effort. Low status members in permanent groups appeared more resistant to influence, probably because of their restricted participation in the decision making process. Members at all status levels in temporary groups were able to exert more influence than in established groups.

Mills [495] studied the power relations among the members of three-person groups. The power position of a member was defined in terms of the relative number of his contributions and the relative frequency of support given him by other members. It was found that members who occupy the high and middle positions of power support each other in about equal degrees. They also support the low status member much more than he supports them. These results suggest that a position of low status in a group tends to disable or handicap a member in supporting other members, particularly those in higher status positions. Mills also found that some of the groups did not develop stable power structures during short periods of interaction but exhibited continued role conflict.

Wolman [778] conducted experiments to test the hypothesis that status is a function of power and acceptance. He found that among the members instructed to play various roles the one who played the role of a "strong, hostile person" received a negative acceptance score. However, his scores for power and leadership were the highest in the group. It was concluded that leadership is a function of power rather than of acceptance. Results of experiments conducted by Hemphill, Pepinsky, Shevitz, and Jaynes [316] and Shevitz [636] indicate that the exclusive possession of task relevant information has the effect of differentiating a member from other members and of enhancing his status in the group.

Hurwitz, Zander, and Hymovitch [347] asked the members of adult groups to rate each other as to the degree of perceived power. Those rated high in power were better liked than those low in power. Those high in power initiated more communication and had more communication addressed to them than to those low in power. The highs, because of their high status, appeared secure enough to underestimate the extent to which they were liked. The lows, because of their need to be liked, tended to overestimate the extent to which they were liked. Here again, the results suggest that the low status members of a group, because of their insecurity and need to be liked, are less able than high status members to support others.

Lippitt, Polansky, and Rosen [429] have defined power as the potentiality for inducing forces in other group members toward acting or changing in a given direction. Among groups of boys at summer camp, their estimates of the power of another boy "to get other boys to do what he wants them to do" were found to be highly related to the number of influence attempts observed. In the formative stages of a group, the subjects did not accept influence attempts much more frequently from those they rated high in power but, after a period of four weeks, influence attempts were much more frequently accepted when initiated by high power members. A significant tendency was observed for the average member of a group to initiate deferential, approval seeking behavior toward persons high in power. Self-rankings of influence were highly related to power rankings by others. Those rated high in power not only initiated more influence attempts but were more successful in their attempts and were better liked by other members of the group.

Hollander and Bair [329] found that members of formal organizations who are strongly motivated toward task completion tend to identify themselves with the high status (more powerful) members of a group. Stotland [685] observed that group members who were required to work with domineering supervisors tended to identify themselves with the supervisor. However, when able to interact with peers from other subgroups the members were able to express more hostility toward their domineering supervisors and to complete their tasks despite hindrance. These findings suggest that identification with high status members facilitates group cohesion necessary for task completion. In a study of life insurance agents, Wispé and Lloyd [775] found that high producers preferred a permissive group while low producers preferred a structured group, and high producers perceived their superiors as less threatening than did low producers. The desire for structured personal interactions in this situation was interpreted as a defense against the behavior of those persons in the interaction system who have the power to initiate negative sanctions.

French [227] has used graph theory to test the logical consistency of a system of hypotheses relating to social power. He is able to demonstrate that the power of a group is a function of the cohesiveness of its structure. A group has power when it is able to exert pressures toward conformity upon its members without driving them away from the group or splitting them into independent subgroups.

The results of these various studies suggest that the power of a group is related to its cohesiveness or integration. The power of an individual member appears to be related to his ability to control reinforcement for himself and for other group members. There is clear evidence that interpersonal power is related to the determination and maintenance of group structure. It can be inferred from a number of the experiments analyzed in this section that the exercise of interpersonal power is related to the control of group operations. Research conducted by Tannenbaum [698] suggests that the amount of control a leader will be able to exercise in a group is related to the degree of integration of the group structure and the support of its goals by the members. The control of operations is a concern in groups of all types. Bales and Strodtbeck [30] have shown that experimental groups exhibit well-defined sequences of operational problems as they continue with a task. They tend to move from emphasis upon problems of orientation to problems of evaluation, then to problems of control.

Operations research is a rapidly developing methodology for the evaluation and control of group operations. Developments in this field are ably described by Churchman, Ackoff, and Arnoff [140] and in a collection of papers edited by McCloskey and Trefethen [447]. The problem defined for operations research is not related to the performances and interactions of group members but is concerned with large segments of organizational activities. The method has been used for the reduction of waiting lines at highway toll stations; the determination of optimum docking schedules for ships; the optimum assignment of men, materials, and machines in order to obtain a given product at minimum cost; and for the solution of a host of similar problems. Although the problems defined by operations research are not irrelevant to the present theory, neither are they phrased in terms of the interpersonal effects with which the theory is concerned. For this reason, no attempt will be made to examine in detail the data provided by operations research.

The operations of a group involve not only member performances but also interactions. The stratification of the group structure in large organizations is made necessary by the fact that one leader cannot possibly interact with all the members simultaneously. Graicunas [263] has attempted to show that the high level executive can supervise effectively the work of from three to six subordinates. Beyond this number, the executive is likely to become overburdened and unable to maintain the co-ordinative contacts with his subordinates that are necessary for successful administration. Davis [174] has shown that the number of major service levels required in an organization increases sharply when the average span of control drops below five subordinates. It is affected but slightly after the average span is increased beyond seven subordinates. Variations in the number of subordinates supervised have their greatest effects on the number of first line supervisors required. Rudduck [595] has reviewed the various theories of administrative control.

Stogdill and Haase [676] report stable, underlying substructures of performance and interaction which maintain a group under varying conditions of operations. These substructures become routinized and habituated in the performances of the members, so that they operate without a great deal of conscious attention. Thus, the members are freed to devote particular attention to emergencies and changing operational demands. Stogdill, Shartle, and associates [681] studied fourteen different aspects of role enactment, including the performance of such responsibilities as inspection, planning, evaluation, co-ordination, supervision, and scheduling. It was found that patterns of performance differ not only with the function but also with the status of a position. The same performance may be exhibited in differing degrees by members whose positions differ not only in status but in function. Some performances are exhibited primarily by persons in high level positions while others are exhibited almost exclusively by members in lower level positions. Performance in the same position tends to vary in correspondence with changes in group operations. When the same type of position is found in different organizations, the performance of the occupants of the similar positions is found to vary less when the groups are similar in size, structure, and operations than when the groups differ in these respects. However, when closely matched organizations are studied, Jaynes [362] found less variance in performance between organizations than between the different status levels within the organizations. When the performances of all the members of a group are considered, Fleishman [216] observed as many similarities as differences in comparing the operations of four military and four business organizations.

Stogdill, Scott, and Jaynes [679] studied the behavior and expectations of superiors and subordinates in a large naval organization. Each member described his performance in relation to 45 items descriptive of responsibility, authority, work performance, and leadership. Each described what he felt he ought to do in relation to the same items. In addition, each member described what his superior was observed to do and "ought to do." The findings indicate that the higher the status level of a member the greater his degree of responsibility and authority and the greater the extent to which he feels that his responsibilities are heavier than they should be. The subordinates of high status members describe themselves as having heavy responsibilities and as delegating extensively to their own subordinates. Superiors do not spend much time in supervision or feel that they should, although their subordinates expect them to spend more time in supervision than they are observed to do. Both high status members and their subordinates report that they spend large amounts of time in planning, reading and answering mail, and attending conferences. They spend more time in conferences than they think they should. The subordinates of high status members spend large amounts of time in co-ordination and examining reports, and such performances are in accord with their expectations. These results suggest that high status, as well as high degrees of responsibility and authority involve the functions of planning, co-ordination, and control of operations.

The act of delegation is a matter of prime significance to the group and its subgroups, for it determines to a large degree the area of freedom available to the members in carrying out their duties. Stogdill and Scott [678] show that the pattern of delegation set by superiors determines the pattern of delegation exhibited by subordinates. If superiors maintain tight control, it is necessary for subordinates to restrict delegation to their subordinates in order to maintain control. If superiors delegate more freely, subordinates are able to allow their subordinates a greater area of freedom. Campbell [101] and Stogdill and Scott [678] find that subordinates regard as better leaders those superiors who delegate more freely. Stogdill and Haase [676] find that subordinates tend to work more closely with superiors who delegate freely and to avoid interaction with superiors who fail to delegate. The refusal by a high status member to delegate tends to restrict both performance and interaction. These results pertain to large as well as to small organizations. However, certain exceptions are to be noted. A superior whose delegation is interpreted as evidence of negligence, irresponsibility, or a means of avoiding work is regarded as a poor leader by his subordinates. Also, in situations where a high degree of coordination is required, overdelegation may result in confusion and misdirected effort.

Strong evidence relative to the importance of control in group operations is provided by Hemphill [314] who used 14 scales for obtaining descriptions of different characteristics of groups. One sample consisted of 500 groups which differed in size, structure, purpose, and composition of membership. High and significantly positive intercorrelations were found between degree of member participation, importance of group to the members, unity of group goal direction, and group control of member behavior. In a second sample of 100 varied groups described by the group members, a different cluster of intercorrelated descriptions was obtained. This cluster consisted of member participation, unity of goal direction, group stability, and group viscidity (integration). In both samples, degree of member participation was positively and significantly related to degree of control, unity of goal direction, and importance of group to the members. Degree of control was positively related in both samples to participation and unity of goal direction, but was negatively related to group autonomy (independence of a parent body).

Hemphill's findings suggest that control is not inimical to member participation. The higher the rate of member participation and the greater the importance of the group to the members, the greater their acceptance of control.

An intensive case study made by Richardson and Walker [561] of operations in a manufacturing plant indicates that the higher the level of the positions in which co-ordination control is exercised the more frequent the delay and breakdown in operations. A change in procedure which gave first line supervisors greater responsibility and authority for the initiation of control procedures produced a marked reduction in the delay and disruption of operations and in worker frustration.

Operations control if overdone would be expected to restrict freedom of action. It can be observed to do so when co-ordination control over first line operations is centralized at such a high level that pressure is applied directly on the operative members from a strong power center. Under this condition, granting freedom for action does not increase satisfaction but produces confusion and frustration.

Evidence has been presented which suggests, at least indirectly, that the structure of a group may be regarded as an instrumentality for the initiation and control of group operations. Lacking structure and control of operations, the group is able to make little progress toward task achievement. Although structure creates differences among the members in their access to power and satisfaction, they find it necessary to accept structure in the interest of group achievement.

## Structure Within Structure

The predictability and controllability of an organization is derived from the fact that its role system is compounded in part of expectations which are anticipatory, predictive, reinforcible, and generalizable. The role system of a group is not only originated by but is maintained by the mutuality of expectation among its members. All of the members of a group contribute to some extent, either positively or negatively, toward the formation and maintenance of the role structure. This observation holds, even for subgroups that are organized after a model provided by the larger organization. Stogdill and Shartle [681], Campbell [101], and Jaynes [362] found that naval ships of the same class, age, and mission are never identical, even though all are organized in terms of the same standard organization chart which specifies the number and types of positions, as well as the duties of each position. These authors, in studying squadrons of submarines and landing ships, found no two ships which were identical in structure. In the process of organizing, each crew made some departures from the standard, specified structure of positions. The role expectations, although these were specified by "job specifications" for each position, differed for each ship. Each crew developed a distinctive role structure which differentiated it as clearly from other crews as the personality of one person differentiates him from other persons.

Despite the fact that each group develops a distinctive "personality" which differentiates it from other groups and is constantly undergoing operational change, in time it also develops structures which give it a high degree of stability. Stogdill and Haase [676], in a study of organization change, observed a high degree of similarity between the correlations among different measures of group structure and operations under different conditions of operation. The findings suggest that a large organization that has been operating over a period of years develops a massive degree of basic structural stability. This stability provides a basis for predictability which permits action without the necessity of regarding each act as a new and unique event requiring conscious search, deliberation, and decision.

A comparative analysis of studies conducted by Stogdill and Shartle [680], Campbell [101], Stogdill and Haase [676], and Stogdill, Shartle, Scott, Coons, and Jaynes [682], and Stodgill and Jaynes [677] permits us to make some rather tentative speculations relative to the stability of different structures in an organized group. The most stable system appears to be the formal structure of positions, differentiated as to function and status, which may be portrayed on an organization chart. Correlations ranging from .97 to 1.00 were found between the status rankings of positions occupied by the same members in Navy organizations studied and restudied over time intervals ranging from one to eight months. These correlations represent a very high degree of stability in the structure of positions in an organization.

If responsibility and authority may be regarded as adequate measures of role definition brought about by interaction and group operations, then the role system also exhibits a rather high degree of stability. In the study and restudy of eight organizations, responsibility in the first study was correlated .76 on the average with responsibility measures obtained in the restudy. The average correlation for authority was 81, and that for delegation was .34. Delegation was found to be more responsive than responsibility and authority to organization change. Although these variables must be regarded as very general measures of role definition, they appear to be relevant to the problem under consideration.

The next most stable structure is, perhaps, the interaction structure as measured by the interactions initiated toward the occupants of various positions rather than by the interactions initiated by them. In agreement with Jennings [364], it is found that, although an individual's initiation of interaction may undergo considerable change with time, the number of interactions initiated toward him remains highly constant. The same effect is observed in number of contacts initiated and received, both estimated and logged. Test-retest correlations between the number of contacts received from superiors, subordinates, and peers range from .57 (peers) to .97 (subordinates). Interaction structures are found to be fairly stable over time.

Another structure which exhibits a moderate degree of stability is that which describes the operative performances of the members. Test-retest correlations of 28 different work performance variables in eight organizations range from —.29 to .72. The average of these correlations is above .40. When a single organization was studied under different operating conditions, the test-retest correlations for 20 performance variables ranged from zero to .80, with an average correlation above .50. The structure of member performances also exhibits a fairly high degree of stability.

No empirical data are available in these studies relative to the stability of the norm system or the informal subgroup system.

Data derived from a number of related studies indicate that organized groups develop a variety of structures and that these structures differ in stability over time. The formal system of positions, although it does change, is the most stable of these structures. The role structure, insofar as it can be represented by general measures of responsibility and authority, also exhibits a rather high degree of stability. The interaction structure is somewhat less stable than the role system, since it is highly responsive to changes in the locus of group operations. The informal group structure and the norm systems of the subgroups probably rank next in degree of stability, but this speculation is not supported by empirical findings. The structure of interrelated member performances is less stable than the role structure or interaction structure, since it is rather highly responsive to changes in task conditions. Even so, each of these structures exhibits a rather high degree of stability under operational change. There is also evidence of considerable general stability in the interactions among these different structures.

Stogdill and Jaynes [677], who studied 22 organizations twice with approximately six months intervening between the two studies, present additional data on the stability of group structure and individual performance over time. In this analysis, 39 Navy officers were studied twice in the same job; 40 officers were studied twice, but in different jobs; and 40 jobs were studied twice, but with different officers occupying the jobs. The organizations considered were of two types: large establishments ashore and small landing ships. When the same job is studied twice with either the same or a different occupant, its level remains highly stable, as indicated by correlation coefficients ranging from .84 to 1.00. However, when the same man is studied twice in different jobs, the level or status of his two jobs does not correspond so closely. The correlations between the status level of the two jobs are .38 in large organizations and .51 in small ships. Although there is a tendency for persons to be assigned similar status in different groups, the status level of a position is determined by the group rather than by the occupant.

As would be expected, an individual's position in the interaction structure is more highly determined by the group than by the individual. When the same man is studied twice on the same job, the number of persons who mention him as a work partner tends to remain fairly constant. The correlations between first and second sociometric score are .76 for large organizations and .71 for small ships. However, when the same individual is studied twice, but in different jobs, the correlations drop to —.01 and —.40, indicating that different interaction structures are involved in the different jobs. When two different individuals are studied in the same job, the correlations between the first and second scores of the different occupants rise to .14 and .46, suggesting that the same job involves similar interaction structures, even with different occupants. However, the relationship is not as high as when the same job is occupied by the same occupant.

A somewhat different pattern of relationships is found for responsibility and authority as perceived by the members themselves. The same man in the same job tends to see his responsibility as significantly similar on two different occasions. The same man in different jobs tends to perceive his responsibility and authority as similar but not to a significant degree. When one man follows another into the same job, the two do not perceive themselves as having a similar degree of responsibility and authority in the job. These findings suggest that the amount of authority and responsibility that a member perceives himself as having is determined to some extent by the nature of the job but to a larger extent by the member's characteristic manner of approaching a job and evaluating his role in a group.

An additional factor is worthy of mention. An officer's military rank serves as a measure of his status in the military establishment as a whole. Military rank and level of position occupied in an organization are found to be rather highly correlated, but not perfectly so. Many officers are supervised by others of the same rank. In some organizations where highly specialized technical skills and knowledge are involved, high ranking officers may be supervised by officers of lower rank. Stogdill and Jaynes [677] found that, whereas the status level of a job tends to remain constant regardless of its occupant, an officer's rank tends to remain constant regardless of the status of the different jobs he may occupy. Officers of different rank going into the same job hold the same status in the organization. An officer going into a different job, may find that the status of his job has changed, although his military rank remains the same.

These various findings suggest that function and status as formally defined by the organization, responsibility and authority as differentially perceived by self and others, and interaction as determined by self and others, each constitutes a separate system which exerts effects on the other systems in the organized group. Each member is involved in these systems, and it is not surprising that many members find it difficult to comprehend the complex structure of a large group.

# 6

## Group Achievement

MEMBERS may invest a variety of values in different kinds of groups, but in all groups some or all of the members must invest performances, interactions, and expectations. These are the basic dimensions of behavior by means of which groups develop structure, carry out their operations, and accomplish their goals.

The *achievement* of a group may be defined as the totality of the outcomes it experiences as a result of the interrelated performances, interactions, and expectations of its members. Achievement might also be defined as the group outputs resulting from the member inputs, mediated through group structure and operations. Performances, expectations, and interactions may be regarded as the input variables in the theoretical system being developed. These variables in combination describe the structure and operations of the group as an organization and generate the outcomes experienced by the group.

The structure of a group is not an end in itself but facilitates the accomplishment of the group purpose. It is generally assumed that the achievement of a group can be described in terms of its productivity, or effectiveness, in accomplishing the group purpose. But two questions now arise. Why do groups develop structures of extreme complexity if their achievements are simple and unidimensional in nature? Is it possible that the assumption of productive effectiveness is inadequate to account for the totality of group achievement?

With the above questions in mind, let us examine briefly the present state of theory relative to group achievement. Productivity tends to be regarded as the principal measure of achievement. In studies of industrial morale, member satisfaction is regarded as a conditioner of productivity. Group integration, or cohesiveness, tends to be treated in a similar manner in the study of small groups. Performance is treated as an independent variable in some studies, as an intervening variable in others, and as a dependent variable in others. Often, performance is regarded as an input, morale as a conditioning variable, and productivity as an output. Interaction is frequently regarded as an input, cohesiveness as a conditioning variable, and performance as an output. Such variables as performance, interaction, group structure, cohesiveness, morale, and productivity have been studied in a great variety of combinations.

Variance in the productivity of groups has been attributed to differences in member satisfaction, pay, group morale, group integration, and other less well-defined factors. The hypothesis of a stable positive relationship between productivity and such factors as member satisfaction and reward has been challenged by Arensberg and associates [12], Brayfield and Crockett [83], and others. The hypothesis is not found to be supported by research findings. Viteles [741] has found prevailing theories unable to account for a number of apparent discrepancies in experimental findings.

This book was undertaken with the aim of developing an adequate theory of group achievement. The author has not found it possible to construct a logically consistent theory based on the hypothesis that productivity is the only achievement of organization. A great deal of work with a variety of charts, tables, diagrams, equations, and symbolic models was performed in order to arrive at a satisfactory solution. The first models were constructed in terms of the prevailing theories, with performance and interaction as inputs; with expectations, role structure, group integration, and morale as intervening variables; and with productivity as the output. These models failed not only to exhibit any internal consistency but also to account for the experimental findings. Some improvement in these respects was noted when expectation was made an input variable. Increasing improvement was observed as morale and integration were moved farther away from the input segment in the direction of the output segment of the models. Because of the strong set provided by the theoretical and experimental literature, it was very difficult to take the final step of placing morale and integration in the output segment. However, when this had been accomplished, the model exhibited balance and accounted well for the experimental findings.

It is therefore proposed that the essential dimensions of organization achievement are *productivity, morale,* and *integration.* The input variables and the group structures and operational mechanics necessary to generate these outcomes have been described in the preceding chapters. Group *productivity* is defined as the degree of change in expectancy values created by the group operations. Group *integration* is defined as the extent to which structure and operations are capable of being maintained under stress. Group *morale* is defined as degree of freedom from restraint in action toward a goal. It is important to keep in mind that these definitions describe elements of group achievement which may vary from little to much. Morale, for example, is not defined as "good morale," but as a characteristic which can vary over a wide range of values.

The definitions of the three aspects of group achievement are strictly determined by what has been put into the theoretical system. Member performances and interactions create changes in expectation which are positively or negatively valued by the group. The value of the change in goal expectations constitutes the essential measure of group productivity. Group intregation may be regarded as a measure of potentiality for maintaining structure and functional operativeness under conditions of internal and external stress. It has been shown that the structuring of interaction and the reinforcement of expectation provide for freedom of action. Group morale may be regarded as the degree of freedom from restraint exhibited by a group in operating upon a goal objective.

It seems appropriate at this point to reconsider some of the research evidence discussed in Chapter 3. Results of several factor analytic studies were found to be in agreement in identifying five factors which described dimensions of group structure, interaction, and performance. Two factors were descriptive of structure: role structure and interaction structure. The three remaining factors were identified as goal direction, group integration, and within-group interaction facilitation. These findings appear to support the point of view that the outcomes of group operations may be described in terms of goal direction (productivity), integration, and interaction facilitation (morale).

A group may be regarded as a system which tends to maintain itself in balance. However, this balance is precarious. A group is an open system which interacts with its environment. Members come and go. The environment imposes restrictions and demands which require change and adaptation in order to maintain internal balance. In addition, the inputs of a group at the time of its origin do not strictly determine its content and boundaries. New inputs are constantly being added. Also, the possibility exists of some slippage between inputs and outputs. For example, if a member absconds with the funds accumulated by a group, it suffers a slippage in the output it has created.

Despite the fact that a group is an open system, a distinct theoretical advantage is gained from regarding it as a system in precarious balance. The inputs of a group may vary from minute to minute and from day to day depending upon changes in the behaviors and values put into the system. The members differ among themselves, and from time to time, in the intensity and duration of the performances, interactions, and expectations they invest in a group. Productivity, integration, and morale may all increase or decrease simultaneously. However, *when inputs remain constant*, any increase in one factor is achieved at a cost to one or both of the other factors. In other words, with inputs constant, an increase in group integration necessarily involves a decrease in group productivity or morale, or both. However, an increase or decrease in selected inputs may permit one aspect of achievement to rise or fall without affecting the others. The system maintains itself in balance as a totality, although the elements may become unbalanced in relation to each other.

In hypothesizing input-output balance, it is not assumed that the inputs emerge unchanged as outputs. In social and recreational groups, for example, the members invest expectations, performances, and interactions. The productivity values might be regarded as the satisfactions derived from participation in the activities of the group. In addition, the group achieves certain degrees of integration and morale which are valued as indicators of the group's capacity for successful action. The purpose of economic organization has long been regarded as that of operating upon inputs in such a manner as to transform them into outputs which have greater utility than the inputs. The purpose of the organization's accounting system, as a control measure, is to enable it to determine the balance between the cost or value of its inputs (labor, materials, and the like) and the value of its outputs (products or services produced).

The output of a group may produce feedback effects which increase or decrease inputs. For example, experiences of group success may stimulate an increase in performance, interaction, and expectation which has the further effect of increasing morale and perhaps also productivity and integration. Failure may depress the input investments made by the members.

One might expect that morale — vigorous action toward a goal — would be more closely related to productivity than to integration. However, this is not always the case. On a very refractory task, a group may exhibit a high state of morale and integration, but its productivity may be low because of the difficulty of overcoming obstacles in its way.

It has been noted in preceding chapters that performances, interactions, and expectations, acting on each other, account for role structure and enactment. In doing so, they describe the structure and operations of the group. The end effect of these various processes describes the achievements of the group. Since the behaviors of the members are inputs in any group, an organization cannot be regarded as operating upon material values or creating material outputs alone. If no material or monetary values are invested, then the achievement of the group must be evaluated in terms of the changes in input performances, interactions, and expectations redefined as the following outputs: group freedom of action, integrity of group structure, and goal expectancy values of the group.

Organization achievement is usually discussed in terms of the concepts of efficiency or effectiveness. Barnard [34] presents a particularly lucid analysis of the aims of a business firm. He criticizes those theorists who claim that organization should seek to maximize efficiency. The organization may have to pay such a high price for efficiency that it exhausts its resources. Barnard suggests that the achievement of an organization should be evaluated in terms of its effectiveness (maximized productivity or efficiency at minimized cost). Simon [646], contrasting the theory of the firm with the theory of the organization, sees the former as seeking to maximize profit (effectiveness) and the latter as maximizing survival (the continued participation of the members). Both effectiveness and survival would appear to be important outcomes for any group that has an enduring task or service to perform.

## Productivity

Groups organize for the purpose of developing capabilities for creating changes that individuals could not bring about by their sole efforts. Productivity represents the value of the change created in those inputs upon which a group performs operations. Productivity is a direct outcome of task performance.

It is the task of a group to create changes in values. The task may be regarded as an immediate manifestation of its long-time purpose. The end purpose of a group may remain constant. However, in order to accomplish its purpose, it may be required to exhibit sequences of operations which differ from time to time. A group must devote some of its energies to the development of structure and to the maintenance of the group, as well as to task

performance. Although these group functions are carried on simultaneously, they are not emphasized equally at all stages in the
group operations. However, values of some sort are created at
all stages in the operations. Once the objectives of an organization have been specified, positions created to serve that purpose,
and the functions of the positions defined, then the performances
of the members may be evaluated in terms of these definitions and
specifications. But the evaluation of performance as well as the
definition of function and the setting of goals involve value judgments. In the end, one value is validated against another.

The values created by a group may or may not be physical in
nature. A group may have as its purpose the manufacture and
distribution of a material product at a profit to its various members. The group operations are then designed to utilize the performances of the members in such a manner as to accomplish this
purpose. But the group operations are not totally described by
those performances bearing upon the physical products. The performances of many of the members may be concerned with co-
ordination, supervision, accounting, recruitment, pay, maintenance, and the like. Many of the members may neither desire
nor utilize the product made by the group. Nevertheless, they
may like being members of the group. These considerations suggest that the values created by a group for its members are not
to be defined in terms of material product alone.

Value for an individual member has been defined by Rotter
[589] as a set of expectations which the individual prefers or
seeks to reinforce. The group purpose may be regarded as defining the primary set of expectations which the group seeks to reinforce. Therefore, the values created by a group may be regarded
as any outcomes of performance which are capable of exerting
reinforcing effects upon the goal expectations of the group. The
outcomes may or may not involve material products. The outcomes of performance may exhibit high or low potential for reinforcing goal expectation.

Productivity refers to those outcomes designed to satisfy the
expectations of the group as a whole. That is, productivity measures the values created by the members for the group. However,

a portion of these values may be conceived as undergoing redistribution to the members. In creating values for the group, the members also create values for themselves. But it is convenient for theoretical purposes to regard all the effects of group operations as values created for the group. Then the values created for the members are regarded in turn as contributions by the group to the individual. While productivity is achieved at a cost to the members, the satisfaction of the individual values of the members represents a cost to the group.

The values created by a group are so numerous and diverse that they cannot be specified with any degree of precision or completeness. In measuring the productivity of a group, it is necessary to isolate some observable and quantifiable unit of product and to compare this with some observable and quantifiable unit of input. When this has been accomplished, it cannot be assumed that the productive effectiveness of the group has been measured either adequately or completely. However, productivity indices, despite their apparent limitations as measures of group effectiveness, are found to be useful in evaluating the progress of a group.

It has been found very difficult to isolate and measure all the factors that need to be taken into account in evaluating productivity. Troxell [732] has provided a readable analysis of the many complex factors, both internal and external, which affect the productivity of an organization and of an economic system. He points out the fact that an organization creates a great variety of values, both material and non-material. For this reason, the measurement of productivity in terms of units of material product created by the effort of the members can represent at best only a crude approximation of the results of group effort. Ridley and Simon [562] and Gaus [236] have shown that the problem of measuring productivity in governmental, religious, and educational organizations, where no material product is operated upon, is even more precarious.

Siegel's [642] critical analysis of the various conceptions of productivity is particularly helpful. He rejects as impractical any attempt to measure productivity in terms of psychological utilities. The "output per man-hour of work" index is regarded as the soundest and most useful measure thus far devised. However, it is cautioned that this index is to be regarded not as a measure of the efficiency of labor but as a measure of the effectiveness with which labor is utilized in conjunction with other factors. That is, the output per man-hours-available ratio is a measure of the extent to which the productive capability of the group has been utilized. The productivity equations developed by Gold [254] involve measures of physical output, man-hours, fixed investment, and productive capacity.

The productivity index utilized by the U. S. Department of Labor, Bureau of Labor Statistics [735] involves a comparison of outputs with inputs actually utilized and with inputs required for equivalent outputs in a base period of time. It measures the change in man-hours required to produce a given volume of product in one time period compared with the man-hours required to produce the same volume of product in a base period of time. That is, it measures the utilization of productive capacity rather than productivity directly.

Davis [172] defines industrial productivity as "the change in product obtained for the resources expended." Since a group is likely to operate upon a variety of inputs and produce a number of dissimilar outputs, Davis proposes that industrial inputs and outputs be measured in dollar values in order to provide a standard basis of comparison. Then any increase or decrease in output is measured in terms of the output per dollars of input in one period as compared with a base period of time.

The measurement of productivity requires a base of reference that is stable in meaning, objective, and measurable. Psychological values, however, cannot be regarded as either stable or objectively measurable. Men differ not only in what they value but also in the extent to which they value any particular object or referent at different times. It is for this reason that productivity has not been measured satisfactorily in terms of psychological values. However, Craig [160] observes that the substitution of monetary for psychological values does not represent a final solution of the problem. "Money values are merely market reflections of psychological values. Unless market money values are accepted as objective and stable measures of psychological value, there is only precarious hope for measuring productivity over a long range of time in which the product mix of the society changes."

Craig's comments suggest that the economist encounters the same problems in measuring the national product that the psychologist and sociologist face in measuring the productivity of a group. It is difficult to find an objective and stable measure of value. The problem of an adequate criterion is not confined to the study of group productivity. It is inherent in all measurement. The scientist cannot hope for an ultimate and absolute criterion in terms of which all things or any particular thing may be evaluated. The best that he can do is to develop more highly refined, more stable, more reliable, and more useful criteria. Fiske [213] points out the fact that the selection of a criterion of individual or group performance involves a value judgment. The value that is used as a criterion today may be used as a predictive variable tomorrow.

Groups develop criteria for evaluating their performance. Individuals form judgments regarding the productivity of groups and the worthwhileness of groups as productive agencies. Members tend to regard these judgments as having validity. Industrial groups set production quotas and develop accounting systems for making continuous or periodic checks of their productivity. These facts suggest that productivity can be evaluated within degrees of accuracy that are useful for operating purposes.

## Factors Related to Productivity

It was observed in the discussion of role development that the members of groups readily become task involved. They tend to accept the goals of the group and to strive for productivity. This is true even in experimental groups with tasks which have little relevance to the personal interests and goals of the members. The interest of members in the productive achievement of groups is evidenced in the satisfaction they express when a group has made a particularly satisfactory accomplishment and in the regrets they express over having wasted their time attending meetings that appeared to accomplish nothing worthwhile.

Groups, as organized entities, tend to exhibit a high degree of concern relative to the task performances of the members and the goal achievements of the group. Outstanding achievement elevates a group's prestige and status in the community. A positive rather than a negative degree of productivity is nĕcessary in order for the group to survive over a long period of time. If a business group operates at a loss, it soon finds itself unable to purchase the materials and labor necessary for the continuance of its operations. If a group is unable to produce positive reinforcing values for its members, they are likely to become discontented and leave. It is apparent that at least a minimum degree of integration is necessary for productive effort and that the productive success of a group may affect its integration.

Everyday observation convinces us that the motivation of a group can make the difference between its success or failure in an enterprise. A few well-chosen words by a coach can be transformed by a ball team into winning scores. Expressions of recognition and appreciation by a supervisor can be changed into the meeting of emergency quotas by workers. The perception of danger and challenge can be converted by soldiers into heroic action. It has long been recognized that the arousal of drive and its direction toward a goal can facilitate group achievement. Group success acts to reinforce the expectation that further success may be attained by group action. It is apparent that morale is directly related to productivity.

It is generally assumed that the larger a reward, the greater its motivating value. However, Meyer [488] and others have shown that it is not the absolute magnitude of a reward but its value in a perceived range of available values which determines its motivating potential. It is also generally assumed that, once the demands of an individual for a larger reward have been met, he should remain satisfied thereafter. However, it has been shown in an earlier chapter that outcomes which confirm expectation tend to increase rather than decrease expectation. Motivation involves the expectation of further outcomes. This is true not only for individuals but also for groups.

Social systems appear to differ in the extent to which their culturally defined norms tend to legitimize the insatiable demands made by groups upon the individual, while at the same time denying the legitimacy of the continuing demands made by individuals upon groups. Whereas the growth of expectation in response to confirming outcomes is regarded as evidence of gross ingratitude in the individual, the maintenance of continued goal expectation by the group is regarded as a necessity for survival. Groups begin to decline in power when they lose the capacity for continued dissatisfaction and goal striving.

The morale of a group is a function of the motivation and freedom for initiative of its members in interaction. Since productivity in industrial groups is measured in dollar values and since the members are rewarded in dollar values, it is not surprising that various wage incentive plans have been devised in the hopes of increasing productivity. Such plans do tend to increase productivity when they are new. They also tend to prevent the decline of productivity below a more or less constant base level. However, various factors operate to limit the response of productive effort to incentive pay. One factor resides in the incentive wage formula, which yields decreasing increments of gain as worker output exceeds a base level. In other words, a highly skilled worker cannot double his pay by doubling the base rate of output defined for his job.

Workers, whether remunerated under fixed or incentive plans of remuneration, tend over the long run to pace their work at a rate that is endurable from day to day and that leaves some possibility of work for the future. This rate tends to become accepted as a subgroup norm, and workers who deviate too far from the norm are held in low regard by their fellows. When wages are computed on a base rate of worker output determined by time and motion study, conformity to the subgroup norm assumes increased importance. If a number of members greatly exceeds the standard, management is likely to re-evaluate the job so that the members have to work harder to earn the same amount of pay.

Another factor besides the subgroup norm operates to regulate productivity in industrial groups. This is the necessity for operational balance. If one subgroup produces more than can be processed or utilized by other subgroups, the unused portion represents expensive waste. If one subgroup produces so little that it slows down or stops the work of other subgroups depending on it for materials, an expensive waste of man-hours results. The group tends to control operations in such a manner as to keep the output of different subgroups in balance.

A group has access to the acquired potentialities of all its members. These are available as inputs. However, neither a group nor a social order tends to utilize the maximum capabilities of all its members, except in times of crisis. The very necessity of maintaining operational and structural balance tends to regulate performance in such a manner as to depress productivity. However, since it is the purpose of any group to transform inputs into outputs of increased utility, productivity is a constant concern. This concern, although in one sense necessary, is in another sense ineffectual. Group operations must be controlled in order to maintain balance, prevent waste, and create a profit for the group as a whole. However, in order to earn the interest and participation of the members, it is necessary for the group to turn back to them some of the value produced. This fact results in the additional necessity of maintaining a just balance between the values created for the group and those created for the members, while at the same time retaining a sufficient reserve value in the group to support continuing operations. It is one of the primary functions of leadership to maintain an optimum balance among these various factors.

A group is necessarily a conservative system. The necessities of operational balance and of a survival reserve of excess values in the group act to inhibit the group from dissipating its energies and resources. Operational controls tend to regulate and equalize the performances of the members and subgroups in such a manner as to balance the various stages and aspects of productivity. Although the members are usually willing to grant high status members a greater degree of freedom to experience satisfying outcomes, the group tends to equalize the rewards distributed to members who occupy positions that are similar in status and function. This equalizing effect, if not applied by the larger group, is likely to be enforced by the subgroups. Operational controls and group norms are factors of great power for inducing conformity. These factors have been found to operate in a great variety of groups, even those created experimentally.

Thus far in this analysis it has been observed that financial incentives tend to have only short-term effects in raising the output of the members. Subgroups tend to develop norms which regulate productive output at a rate that is comfortable for their average members. The group, in order to maintain operational balance, must establish a standard of productivity that can be fulfilled by all its subgroups. The group and its subgroups impose powerful forces which tend to regulate member task performance. These conclusions seem to imply that there are no methods by means of which productivity can be increased except in emergency situations or by short-term incentives. However there are other solutions to be considered. It has been suggested that each member occupies a position which defines his function and status in the group. The performance of his role in interaction with other members results in a redefinition of his role in terms of the responsibility and authority that he is actually able to exercise in the group. The members who exert the greatest influence upon this redefining process are those who occupy high status positions. They can enlarge or restrict the role boundaries of the members in positions of lower status, thus elevating or depressing their performance. Unless prevented from doing so, the members tend to perform near the outer bounds of their roles as defined by the functions and status of their positions. Pride and satisfaction are derived from demonstrating one's competence to meet the expectations of others. When this possibility exists in a group or subgroup, the norms tend to be elevated to accommodate an enlarged area of responsibility and authority for the group or subgroup and for the individual members.

The considerations outlined above suggest that both the formal group structure and the role structure are instrumental to productivity. Productivity is facilitated when function and status are clearly defined and when those members in high status positions maintain group structure and goal direction. A type of leadership in high status positions which enlarges the responsibility and authority of subordinates to a degree that is permitted by the necessity for controlling operations also tends to facilitate productivity.

The factors that regulate productivity appear to reside in the group structure and operations. These factors can be utilized by a group to increase or decrease productivity. Only short-term benefits can be expected to accrue from the use of external incentives designed to overcome the effects of inherent group factors which depress productivity.

## Morale

Group morale is defined as freedom from restraint in action toward a goal. Freedom to act, freedom to interact, and freedom to reinforce expectations are factors that have been shown to play an important part in the development of group structure, function, and operations. If morale is an aspect of group achievement which has any meaning at all, then it would appear to be defined in terms of these areas of freedom. These areas in combination describe the freedom from restraint which the group members exhibit in attacking their task.

This definition does not imply that all morale is good morale. Morale can be either too high or too low for the welfare of the group. The group may suffer when the members fail to attack their task with sufficient vigor and enthusiasm. A military group may exhibit superb morale but be destroyed by charging wildly into withering enemy fire. There are times when high morale needs to be tempered by a just regard for group integrity and by a careful consideration of the effective means of goal attainment.

It might be argued that two groups of men advancing aggressively side by side under enemy fire do not exhibit equal morale if one is excitedly anticipating hand-to-hand combat while the other is shaking with fear. In terms of the theory being developed, the two groups exhibit equal morale. Subjective feelings are not the critical variables which define morale. The goal direction of activity and its freedom from restraint are the essential factors.

It was noted in discussing interaction that the area of freedom is at a minimum in a group of minimum structure. As the structure of positions in a group becomes more highly differentiated and as roles become more clearly defined, the members experience a greater area of freedom because they know the bounds within which they can act without unfavorable consequences for themselves or for the group as a whole.

But there appear to be upper limits beyond which an increase in rigidity of structure produces no further increase in freedom of action. Studies of bureaucratic organizations indicate that structures may become so rigid as to restrict the area of freedom of the members and the adaptive initiative of the organization as a whole. Therefore, it may be hypothesized that increasing the structure of a group increases its freedom of action to a limit beyond which further increases in structure result in decreases in freedom of action. Morale, then, is a curvilinear function of the degree of structure of a group. Too little or too much structure impose restraints upon a group's freedom of action. The optimum degree of structure for high morale will probably need to be determined empirically for each group.

The reinforcement of goal expectation also appears to enlarge the area of freedom of a group. Successful outcomes reinforce the expectation of further successes. Success brings prestige and high status to a group so that it is expected to exhibit a heightened degree of initiative, freedom, and privilege in keeping with its status. Controlled freedom from restraint tends to facilitate successful action. Successful groups tend to exhibit high morale.

Successful action requires a co-ordinated attack upon the group task or goal. The chances of group success are reduced when each member or subgroup performs according to individual whim without reference to the inherent demands for co-ordinated action. The exercise of operations control is necessary not only for balancing group achievement but also for preventing the fragmentation and dissipation of the group effort in unrestrained individual and subgroup activity which has no relation to the group goal. Operations control may, but need not, reduce freedom of action. It is only when operations control is carried to the extent of reducing too sharply the role boundaries of the individual members that it lowers the morale of the group. Undercontrol permits the group effort to be dissipated in the pursuit of trivial and irrelevant individual or subgroup goals. Overcontrol reduces the effective authority and area of freedom of members and subgroups. Since morale appears to be highest under intermediate degrees of operations control, it may be regarded as a curvilinear function of control.

Co-ordination control is a function of the high status positions in a group. It has been observed that the members who achieve positions of high status tend to be those whose spontaneity stimulates spontaneity in others. It may be inferred that one of the functions of a high status position is the initiation of freedom of action in other group roles. This function is expressly recognized in the theory of formal organization in the principle of delegation. In emergent groups, recognition of the freedom-enlarging function provides the very basis of role differentiation, granting high status and the function of exercising control to a specific member rather than to others who are available. Since group structure and operations control are determined to a very high degree by the leadership of a group and since morale is a function of structure and control, it must be concluded that morale is closely related to group leadership.

The morale of a group is a direct outcome of the freedom of action granted its individual members in the performance of their group-defined roles. However, in order for this freedom to be utilized as group morale, it is necessary for the activities of individual members and of subgroups to be co-ordinated and directed toward the goal of the group. This fact suggests that morale should be related to group integration. A poorly integrated group would be expected to exhibit lower morale than one that is more highly integrated. Also, since morale is increased by reinforcements of the expectation of success, we might expect the productivity of a group to be related to its morale.

It is necessary to distinguish between motivation and morale. Motivation is regarded in the present theory as a function of drive and confirmed desirability estimates. Morale is defined as freedom from restraint in action toward a goal. An individual or a group may be highly motivated but unable to act. Given freedom to act, the degree of morale may be highly related to the strength of motivation. There is a sense in which morale may be regarded as motivation exhibited in overt action toward a goal objective. Motivation provides potential for morale.

The definition of morale as freedom from restraint in action toward a goal carries important implications relative to the nature of group motivation. Applications of pressure and persuasion tend to pervert a group rather than motivate it. The proper motivation of a group consists of setting attainable goal expectations, reinforcing those expectations by experiences of success, providing freedom of action, and providing sufficient structure and control for concerted action upon the goal objective.

## Integration

Group integration is defined as the ability to maintain structure and function under stress. The value of integration is illustrated most dramatically in military operations, where each commander attempts to keep his own lines and communications intact while disrupting those of the enemy forces. The great military commanders in the past have been masters of the art of diagnosing enemy weaknesses and of dividing or flanking the enemy lines. Their writings testify to the doctrine that victory usually goes to the commander who is able to apply a united force against a confused or divided enemy.

The importance of group integration is realized most keenly in times of crisis and emergency. But integration is also valued in routine operations. Groups seek to maintain structural stability, co-ordination, and functional operativeness, and they also show a concern for group unity and loyalty. This fact suggests that one evidence of, or means toward effecting, integration is common agreement among all the members on the goals and values of the group.

That group integration is a complex matter is suggested by the variety of definitions available. Festinger [199] defines group cohesiveness in terms of forces acting upon the members to remain in the group. A group is low in cohesiveness when the induction of forces upon the members to remain in the group are not strong enough to counteract the forces bearing upon the members to leave the group. Moreno and Jennings [503], Criswell [164], and Bronfenbrenner [86] define group integration in terms of the reciprocation of sociometric choices in a group. Group integration is high when a great number of the members of a group are bound together by a network of mutual choices. Hemphill [314] defines group viscidity as the extent to which the members of a group function as a unit and are free from dissension, conflicting interests, and disrupting forces. Cattell [116] views integration as an aspect of group syntality, dependent upon the ability of the group to satisfy the goals of the individual members and to gain their loyalty. Gross and Martin [269], examining various conceptions of group cohesiveness, arrive at the conclusion that cohesiveness should be defined in terms of the resistance of a group to disruptive forces, both internal and external.

The larger a group, and the more routine its operations, the greater the difficulty of assessing its integration. The comparative integration of athletic teams on the playing field is often readily apparent. If two teams are about evenly matched in skill and power, the team which exhibits a breakdown in structure and function under stress is likely to lose the game. The integration of industrial firms may not be so highly visible. The management of a company may go along for years believing that it has a closely knit organization and the firm loyalty of its employees, then suddenly find that it has a serious strike on its hands. Students of industrial relations have observed this situation in firms where management believes that a paternalistic determination of policies relative to employee welfare and wages is sufficient to insure employee loyalty. An associated factor is the lack of provision for upward communication by means of which management may keep itself informed of employee interests and aspirations relative to advancement, job security, recognition for achievement, opportunity for job responsibility, opportunity for making useful suggestions, and the like. Such a beneficent-minded management usually attempts to explain its predicament by concluding that its employees are ungrateful in striking or joining a union.

The proportion of its potential power that a group can bring to bear on an objective is determined by its morale and by its degree of integration. Co-ordinated effort and loyal, enthusiastic support are important not only in military and industrial organizations but also in political parties, religious denominations, labor unions, and organizations of all sorts. In planning any program of action, it is useful to know in advance the state of the organization and the amount of member support that can be depended on when operations are initiated. This widely recognized reality of program planning is seldom associated with the concept of group integration.

Another observable reality that may or may not be associated with integration in the minds of the group members is the concern they show when a member attempts to leave the group. They may appeal to his sense of loyalty or attempt to show that the group really needs him. Both the group as a whole and its subgroups, as well as the individual members, exert pressures toward maintaining the integrity of the group. However, differences in individual goals, relating particularly to the power to control the group and to the differential distribution of the group values, may result in internal conflict. This problem is particularly difficult to solve when the primary issue is the satisfaction of the ego values and power strivings of competing individuals. Such struggles are disturbing to the group members, who are not likely to lend their support to any divisive force so long as their expectations are being met by the group. In other words, the group members and the subgroups are likely to reject the active deviate when they have a clear understanding of the group purpose, are working together to achieve it, and are able to satisfy their individual expectations in doing so.

High status members, even though they experience a comparatively high degree of freedom, are nevertheless bound by the norms of the group and of the subgroup. Conflict within a group tends to be generated when high status members in different subgroups perceive themselves to be competitors for status and power in the larger group. In view of the power of the subgroups to induce conformity, it would appear that high status members can engage in effective contention only when this state of affairs is sanctioned by one or more of the subgroups. The members bring great pressures to bear in the direction of conformity and group integration. Conflict between two different subgroups is perceived as disturbing and disrupting. It can be concluded that the members will voluntarily tolerate disruptive conflict only when the group is failing to satisfy the expectations of one or more of its subgroups.

The desirability of reinforcing formal structure and goal mutuality is more often recognized than is the importance of reinforcing the subgroup norms and individual expectations. The latter two factors, because of their individualistic reference, may be perceived as working in opposition to the group interest. They may or they may not. When individual expectations and subgroup norms are accurately appraised and appropriately reinforced by the group, they tend to reinforce formal structure and goal mutuality.

A group is observed to exhibit both integrative and divisive potentialities. It is one of the paradoxes of organization that, in order to strengthen its integrity, a group must turn some of its attention away from its primary sources of integration in order to reinforce those factors which exhibit the greatest potentiality for division. The most highly rationalized elements of organization

— group purpose, role structure, and operations — exhibit the greatest stability. They are primary referents of attention because of their obvious instrumental utility. The utility of the subgroup norms and individual expectations, because they are changeable, individualistically oriented, and less subject to rational control, is not so obvious. Their continued neglect, however, can result in the increasing fragmentation of the group purpose because of the fact that reference groups not controlled by the membership group are permitted to reinforce the expectations of the members. On the other hand, too much effort devoted to the satisfaction of individual expectations and to the development of integration can deplete the group resources and inhibit productivity. Thus, it is apparent that integrity is to be optimized rather than maximized if the long range survival of the group is being considered.

Considering the individual members, integration is high when the members are loyal to the group, are willing to make strong efforts to support it, and are closely agreed on the goals of the group and the methods of attaining the goals. Considering the subgroups, integration is high when the subgroups are well integrated, when their norms support the structure and objectives of the larger group, and when the activities of the subgroups are well co-ordinated in relation to the group objectives. Considering the group as a whole, integration is high when its structure and operations are strongly supported by its individual members and subgroups. Integration is a function of the degree of intermember unity and co-ordination in the support of the group structure, operations, and goals.

Integration is closely related to the purpose of the group and to its formal and operative structures. The differentiation of roles according to function and status does not reduce group integration. On the contrary, integration is dependent upon a clearly defined role structure. Role confusion and role conflict reduce a member's ability to act decisively and reduce his satisfaction with the organization. Indecision, conflict, and lowered satisfaction all tend to reduce a member's contribution to the cohesiveness of the group.

There are numerous internal and external factors that tend to reduce the inclination of members to support a group. Continued failure of the group to satisfy the expectations of the members relative to reward, status, recognition, and contribution may lower their interest in supporting the group. Members may lose their inclination to support a group that is continuously weak, ineffective, and non-productive. Strong identification with individuals or reference groups that are antagonistic to the group, its purpose, or its status structure may also weaken a member's support of the group.

The less firmly the members support the group, its purpose, and its leadership structure, the easier it is for competing individuals or subgroups to destroy the cohesiveness of the group in disruptive struggles for power and the easier it is for invading individuals to capture the power structure of the group. In view of these facts, and since the potential power of a group is a function of its degree of cohesiveness, the integration of a group must be regarded as an important aspect of its achievement.

In general, it may be concluded that the identity of individual and group goals, member satisfaction with the group and with his role in it, a feeling of acceptance, mutual liking among the members, satisfaction of member expectations, member support of the group leadership, and subgroup support of the group goals are all measures of various aspects of group integration. These factors, built into a stable and clearly differentiated role structure which enables the members to know what they are expected to do and with whom they are expected to co-ordinate their efforts in times of crisis or emergency, contribute to the integration and survival of the group under stress.

## Effects of Reinforcement

According to prevailing theories, member satisfaction should increase group morale and productivity. It is assumed in these theories that satisfied members will be more highly motivated than dissatisfied members and that higher motivation will result in higher production. In accordance with these assumptions, researchers attempt to measure the morale of military, industrial, and other organizations in terms of member satisfaction.

The theory being developed requires us to question the above assumptions. We have observed that both the norms of subgroups and the group requirement for operations control tend to depress the effects of incentives on productivity. Control may also restrict member freedom of action and group morale despite the reinforcement provided by group success. However, neither the subgroup norms nor group controls appear to depress the effects of reinforcement on group integration. It seems necessary to conclude that member satisfaction is more highly related to group integration than to productivity or morale. The integration of a group is a function of the degree of intermember unity in supporting the group structure, operations, and goals. The effect of reinforcement is to increase a member's satisfaction with the group and with his role in the group. Reinforcement confirms the individual's estimate of the value of membership in the group, as well as his estimate of the probability of experiencing further satisfying outcomes as a result of continued membership in the group. The effect of satisfying a member's expectations is to increase his support of the group. Thus, Stagner [667] observes that member satisfaction is at a maximum when individual goals are identical with group goals and can be satisfied in achieving the goals of the group.

Member satisfaction cannot be equated with group integration. The members may exhibit a high degree of satisfaction while in the process of idling, playing, wasting materials, dissipating group resources, undermining the status structure of the group, and otherwise contributing toward its dissolution. Satisfaction contributes toward group integration only when the reinforcement of the members' expectations leads them to support the group structure, operations, and goals. Member satisfaction contributes toward group integration but is not the same as integration. Nor can satisfaction be equated with morale. The members may work strenuously for a group in emergencies, even though they are extremely dissatisfied with it.

If the satisfaction of expectation increases group integration rather than productivity, then it may be asked whether it is worthwhile attempting to keep the members satisfied. The answer to this question depends on whether or not the group values its power and survival. The power that a group can exert upon an objective is dependent upon the maintenance of structure and the co-ordination of effort. The maintenance of structure and co-ordination of operations depends upon sufficient member loyalty to prevent the splitting of the group into independent or competing subgroups and upon sufficient power to oppose individuals intent upon capturing the power structure of the group.

Experimental groups in which the members have very little at stake exhibit a concern for the development and maintenance of structure and for conformity to the group norms. Large, structured organizations can be observed to seek the loyalty of their members and to exhibit concern when members leave in a state of disgruntlement. Although they may not know exactly why they do so, groups as organized systems do appear to value a state of sound integration.

The members, as individuals, also value the integration of the group. When the rank and file members of industrial organizations are asked what they value most in the work situation, they rank first in importance the security of their positions. The significant elements of member satisfaction that are found most frequently among the members of military and industrial organizations are leadership and supervision, job satisfaction, personal rewards, friendly and co-operative co-workers, effective management, adequate working conditions, recognition and opportunity for advancement, and group integration. These factors are concerned with the structure, operations, and integration of the group; with individual role and the conditions of role enactment; and with rewards for role performance. Even in industrial organizations, where financial rewards are set up as the primary incentives to membership and performance, pay is not found to be the reward that is most highly valued by any major segment of the membership. Job security, good leadership, and job challenge and opportunity tend to be more highly valued than monetary reward.

Experimental studies indicate that member satisfaction is positively related to group integration. However, member satisfaction is not found to be highly related to group productivity. On the contrary, satisfaction measures and productivity measures are found more often than not to be negatively related. Therefore, if member satisfaction is accepted as a basis of integration, it must be concluded that group productivity and integration are not highly related, or else are negatively related. That this is a reasonable conclusion will be shown in the following section.

## Achievement Balance

A group may be conceived as a physical system, a biological system, or a social system. It is some of each. If it is a biological system, it needs some sort of chemical input from its environment in order to live, grow, and reproduce. If it is a social system, it needs a minimum set of inputs in the form of performances, interactions, and expectations in order to develop structure, maintain operations, and achieve its purpose. What it achieves as outputs will be dependent upon what is put into the group as it initiates and continues its operations. For theoretical purposes, it is convenient to hypothesize a high degree of input-output equivalence in the group as an instrument of social achievement.

If group outputs bear an approximately one to one relationship to inputs, then, when inputs are held constant, an increase in any one element of group achievement can be accomplished only at the expense of some other element. In order for all elements of achievement to be increased, it is necessary to increase the input investment. Thus, an increase in productivity can be made at the expense of integration or by an additional input in the form of greater effort, improved technology, or some other value.

If total output remains constant under constant total input, then the different elements of group achievement must remain in a state of delicate balance. The probable nature of this balance is stated in the following hypotheses. Productivity and morale are positively related. Morale may be related either positively or negatively to integration. Integration and productivity are negatively related. Morale, productivity, and integration may be positively related when the group is strongly motivated in striving toward goal achievement or when motivation is very low.

The four hypotheses stated above describe the most general condition of balance among the three different elements of group achievement. They appear to be logically consistent, and they account fully for the experimental evidence. Careful research is needed in order to account for the exceptions to these hypotheses.

The hypothesized relationship between productivity and morale seems reasonable. As a group exhibits greater freedom from restraint in attacking a goal objective, it should produce more than when it is listless and restrained. Similarly, in regard to the relationship between productivity and integration, if the group is required to devote its time and effort to the maintenance of integration it cannot devote the same time and effort to productivity. Integration is not an effortless by-product of group action but is accomplished at a cost. The variable relationship between morale and integration is observable in groups under different conditions of frustration and motivation. Under continued threat and frustration, the group tends to heighten its integration but to reduce its freedom from restraint in goal activity. Here, morale and integration are inversely related. In highly motivated goal striving, both integration and freedom from restraint tend to be heightened at the same time. In the latter condition, productivity may also be high if the task obstacles are not too difficult to overcome.

Member satisfaction is found to exert its primary effect upon group integration rather than upon productivity or morale. However, insofar as the reinforcement by the group of a member's expectations tends to confirm his perception of the outer bounds of his role, it may contribute toward his freedom of action on behalf of the group. Continued reinforcements which narrow role boundaries tend to reduce freedom of action. Now it can be shown that the research findings on job satisfaction are reasonable and explainable. Member satisfaction increases group integration, not group productivity. A high degree of satisfaction is not conducive to a high rate of productive effort. However, the reinforcement of expectation is inducive of loyalty, support, and desire to remain in the group.

Leaders of all sorts of groups have been required to operate in terms of a theory of organization which maintains that the executive should act to maximize productive effectiveness. This theory is shown to be in error in that it constitutes only a partial theory of organization. It ignores two important elements of organization achievement: morale and integration. Arrow [17], using symbolic logic to examine the theory of the firm, finds that the concept of maximization in executive decision making is fallible because it ignores an array of social values which are basic to survival. The present theory suggests what those values are.

Although the executive is continuously confronted by the hard facts of organization reality, he has been provided with neither theory nor facts which would enable him to cope rationally with problems of group integration and morale. The present theory suggests that the leader is as fully responsible for the morale and integration of his organization as he is for its productivity. Responsible leadership seldom shows itself slow to accept a clearly defined organizational obligation. There is reason, then, to believe that although a theory does not change the objective facts confronting an executive it may change his approach to them. Since leadership tends to develop the means necessary for the fulfillment of its obligations, the rational acceptance by executives of responsibility for group integration and morale should result in marked advances both in practice and in applied research.

The maximization hypothesis is not tenable in a logically complete theory of organization. Such a theory requires, rather, that the objective of executive decision be to maintain an optimum balance between group productivity, integration, and morale. This requirement applies as well to the industrial firm and the military unit as to any other form of organization.

The criterion of an optimum balance is a matter which must be determined by empirical practice and research. An optimum balance under routine operating conditions is not likely to be the same as that required in emergency situations. Thus, the new theory immediately raises a critical question which cannot be answered in terms of any information now available. However, there is no reason to believe that we are worse off than before the question was raised. It can be counted a gain if the question stimulates thought, effort, and research on the problem of achievement balance.

Nor is executive leadership worse off than before. In the past, the executive has had to deal with morale and integration as unexplainable intrusions of human perverseness into an otherwise rational system. In the present theory, integration and morale are represented as integral and logical outgrowths of organization structure and operations. Granted the validity of the theory, it is necessary to conclude that the initiation, maintenance, and balancing of group productivity, integration, and morale are responsibilities of the executive role. If, as the experimental literature suggests, clarity of role definition facilitates performance, the occupant of a position of high status should be helped rather than hindered by the acknowledgment of his responsibility for group integration and morale.

## RESEARCH ON GROUP ACHIEVEMENT

Research on group achievement has been concerned almost exclusively with problems of productivity. This limitation was dictated by the theories in terms of which the research was designed. Morale and integration are usually regarded as conditioners of productivity rather than aspects of group achievement.

Research on morale bears little relationship to morale as defined for purposes of the present theory. Morale is usually equated with member satisfaction and regarded as a conditioner of productivity. However, freedom of action emerges as an important by-product in several well-conducted studies of group structure and status differentiation.

Highly sophisticated research designs have been devised for the study of group integration, cohesiveness, or viscidity. Integration is usually regarded as instrumental to productivity rather than as an element of group achievement. However, the hypothesis of a positive relationship between integration and productivity is not supported by the research findings.

The theory being developed requires that productivity, morale, and integration be treated as separate elements of group achievement. Member satisfaction is shown to be an aspect of group integration rather than of morale. This formulation readily clarifies and reconciles the discrepancies between hypothesis and experimental results that have plagued both theorist and researcher for a decade or more.

## Productivity

The accounting system of a firm may be regarded as a small scale input-output model. Leontief [409] and others [504] have developed mathematical models for analyzing the national economy as an input-output system. The models require that the national income and the gross national product be measured in dollar values. Allen [6] has produced the most comprehensive and readable formulation of these theories. Both the economist and the accountant are aware of the fact that it is impossible to evaluate all the inputs and outputs of a group in terms of dollar values. Good will of public and of employees is valued by a firm, but it is difficult to place a dollar value on it.

Despite the fact that output per man-hour ratios have been found quite useful for measuring the productivity of business organizations, they have been little utilized in the research conducted by psychologists and sociologists. Productivity is defined in a great variety of ways for research purposes. In small group research, productivity is often defined as the rate or amount of activity exhibited by the members of a group. This is contrary to industrial usage, in which productivity is defined as an effect of member activity. The business firm tends to regard productivity as a measure of output per man-hour. The number of tasks completed per unit of time is also used as a measure of productivity in small group research. Zobel [794] discusses various difficulties involved in devising measures of productivity.

Because of the rapid increase in world population, improved productivity is becoming a matter of international as well as national concern. Troxell's [732] literate and well-balanced analysis indicates it to be a concern of labor, management, scientists, and government. However, the problem is not viewed alike by all parties concerned, as is evidenced by the participants of several discussion panels and conferences on productivity edited by Ross [588], Tripp [729], Peterson [538], and the American Management Association [8].

A group creates a great variety of values and, since it is practically impossible to isolate and measure all these values simultaneously, it appears futile to quarrel with every investigator's definition of productivity. Further, it is difficult to measure social value as a general concept. A more practical definition is required for research purposes. In discussing the research on productivity, each investigator's definition will be accepted at face value. While it is not assumed that the various definitions are equally useful, there is little solid ground for rejecting specific formulations as untenable.

It is necessary to distinguish between activity and productivity. A group may be very active without producing much. Darley, Gross, and Martin [168] found volume of participation to be correlated .02 with group productivity in competing dormitory groups. Norfleet [521] reports that, as group problem solving progresses, the number of contributions judged to further group productivity becomes narrowed to a smaller number of persons, suggesting that activity associated with the differentiation of structure may exert an effect. Horsfall and Arensberg [335] report that the amount of interaction within a group is not related to productivity. Hemphill [314] found that a high participation rate is related to measures of productivity. However, some of the items that describe participation are concerned with task performance rather than with activity in general. These results suggest that it is not the gross amount of activity but the use made of performance that affects productivity.

Contradictory evidence is available on the relation of group size to productivity. Lorge and Brenner [435] reviewed the experimental literature from 1920 to 1957. The productivity of large groups was found to exceed that of small groups on "abstract" problems. Small groups were found to do better than large groups on "concrete" problems. Osborn [523] has analyzed the literature on the efficiency and profitability of manufacturing plants of various sizes. He finds that none of the studies satisfy the criteria necessary for valid measurement and concludes that we know very little about the relationship between group size and efficiency.

Blum [73], Roseborough [581], and Kelley and Thibaut [381], in their reviews of small group experiments, find small groups to be more productive than large ones but point out the fact that as group size changes other variables also change. Marriott [468] found that the productivity of industrial work groups declines as the groups increase in size. South [659] observed that the efficiency of groups of different sizes depends on the type of problem being solved, larger groups being more effective when it is important that incorrect solutions be rejected. Results of experiments conducted by Gibb [246] indicate that the production of ideas increases at a decelerated rate as groups increase in size. James [359], studying subcommittees of the U. S. Senate, found that the mean size of action-taking committees was 6.5 members, while that of committees which do not take action was 14.0. The results of these two studies emphasize the importance of considering the nature of the task in evaluating the effects of group size. Wegner and Zeaman [751] report group learning on a motor task to be greater in groups of four than in groups of two, and there is one-to-one correspondence in groups of four between the rank order of group performance scores and the scores of the most competent members of the respective groups. The superior performance of the larger groups is attributed to the effects of leadership. Bales, Strodtbeck, Mills, and Roseborough [31] find that the difference in total participation between the most active and least active members of a group increases as the size of the group increases in size from 3 to 10. Bass and Norton [45] also report that stratification (variability) increases as groups increase in size from 2, 4, 6, and 8 to 12 in number, but with a maximum at 6 members. These various studies suggest that groups tend to become differentially structured as they increase in size, with the effects that more activity is exhibited, and more influence is exerted, by a few high status members. This fact, along with Moreno's [502] finding that interaction and choice tend to be centered around high status members, may account for any differential effects on productivity. That is, productivity may be more highly related to leadership and group structure than to the numerical size of groups. In this event, no consistent relationship between group size and productivity would be expected.

French [225] found organized groups to be more effective than unorganized ones. Heinicke and Bales [308] and Borgatta and Bales [75] have shown that one of the first tasks undertaken by a newly formed group is that of developing a role structure. After status and function have been defined with some degree of stability, the group then is free to devote its attention to task performance. However, so long as the group is prevented from developing structure, it exhibits a restriction of tension release, a reduced freedom of action, and persistent concern with the development of structure. Structured groups are found to be more efficient than unstructured ones. Smith [652], Hall [290], and Greer, Galanter, and Nordlie [265] present experimental results which indicate that group productivity is higher under conditions of role clarity than under conditions of role confusion.

Bavelas [50] devised an ingenious research design for testing the effects of different group structures upon performance. Leavitt [407], Shaw [626], and Macy, Christie, and Luce [461] using the Bavelas design, report that effectiveness is better when the group structure permits the members to channel communications through a member who occupies a central position than when the structure requires communications to be filtered back and forth through each member. That is, a differentiated structure which provides a co-ordinative function is more effective than an undifferentiated structure. However, the time required for problem solving is increased. Shaw [626, 627], using the Bavelas design, varied the information available to the members in various positions. He found that the member who had access to the information essential for problem solving tended to become the central member. He agrees with Leavitt [407] that a differentiated structure lowers the satisfaction of the group members but increases group efficiency. Heise and Miller [309] found that productivity was depressed in a centrally organized structure.

Guetzkow and Simon [281] repeated the Bavelas experiment under carefully controlled conditions. Using a time and motion analysis of the task, they were able to separate the structural from the operational elements of the communications net. It was found that differences in communication nets introduce important differences in the organizing difficulties encountered. The more difficult the organizational job, the less rapid was the transition to efficient task performance. However, the nets did not produce differences in the time required for handling the operating task when the optimum available organization was used. It was found, further, that the more restrictions imposed on the communication channels the more stable the groups. Complete freedom of communication was found to exert a more limiting effect upon task performance than communication restricted to specified channels. This study emphasizes the importance of differentiating between the structural and operational aspects of group action.

Lanzetta and Roby [404], using a miniature information-command center, varied the functions of the group members. Under one experimental condition, one member was responsible for observation, a second for calculation, and a third for decision. Under the second condition, each of the three members performed all of the functions. Specialization of function was found to result in more efficient performance when the task load was heavy but not under low task loads. These authors report that more useful information can usually be obtained from a single source. When information is dispersed, no single member of the group knows what facts are available or where relevant information is located. These factors become critical under heavy task loads and are perhaps more important to efficient performance than the total load of information to be handled.

Considerable controversy exists regarding the relative merits of vertical as opposed to horizontal differentiation of structure. Out of the great mass of opinion and unsupported conviction, two facts emerge. The first, pointed out by Durkheim [186], Taylor [701], and many others, is that functional (horizontal) differentiation permits the effective application of different skills and professional techniques to the solution of task problems. The second, as noted by Barnard [36], Simon [645], Worthy [783], and others, is that, as function becomes more highly specialized and the organization more finely subdivided, coordination must be pushed higher and higher up the vertical scale in order to maintain operational balance and control. Whether this process is regarded as hindering or facilitating productivity appears to be related to value commitments rather than to objective facts.

A similar conclusion can be drawn relative to the arguments for and against the decentralization of industry. Dale [167] reviewed the studies on centralization and decentralization. He points out the fact that no reliable data are available on the extent of decentralization, nor on the effects of the process. The arguments in its favor are based on the assumption that any dilution of authority is necessarily "progressive" and "good." The primary argument against it is a loss of operational control. Decentralization, once accomplished, is seldom evaluated, because evaluation requires study, checking, record keeping, the preparation of reports, and the analysis of data, all of which are contrary to the principle of diluted control. Baker and France [24] find that chief executives tend to favor the decentralization of industrial relations, so that problems can be handled locally as they arise. In practice, however, this function tends to be centralized because of the necessity of maintaining uniform policies relative to manpower utilization, wage structures, government legislation, union action, and the like. Union leaders, because of their interest in industry-wide bargaining, prefer to deal at high levels on industrial relations problems. Little relation was found between the level of decision making and satisfactory experience in the different plants, except in relation to supervisory and executive development. In regard to those problems, increased centralization improved satisfaction. It can be concluded that not enough is known about the problems involved in decentralization to speak with any high degree of conviction.

Certain aspects of group integration appear to be related to productivity. Maller [464] and Deutsch [177] show that productivity is better when the members work co-operatively on the group task than when they compete or work independently for their own ends. Deutsch also observed greater division of labor and a higher degree of intersubstitutability among the members on the same task under co-operative than under competitive conditions. Grace [262], however, found that the performance (wins) of basketball teams is inversely related to high co-operativeness. Blau [69] found in a government agency that productivity was lower in those departments in which the members were most competitive. However, the more competitive members of competitive departments were more productive than noncompetitive members. No such differences were found in the less competitive departments. Pressure for productivity, while it raised the productivity of the most competitive members of the competitive department, lowered the productivity of the department as a whole.

Competition has also been found to elevate performance. Murphy, Murphy, and Newcomb [510] analyzed fifteen different studies of the effects of competition. The results indicate that the subjects worked harder for self than for a loosely organized group such as a school class. They also worked harder as members of a competing team than for a classroom. Competition between groups, as well as competition between different members within the group, tends to increase speed of performance, but the effect on accuracy is variable. The members of a group do not respond alike to competition. Some members, rather than being challenged, appear threatened and withdraw. Others become tense and overstimulated. Members tend to select as competitors other members of about equal skill or ability.

Rosenthal and Cofer [587], in a study of experimental groups, found that an attitude of indifference and neglect on the part of a single member was sufficient to depress the level of goal expectation among other members both for the attainment of individual goals and group goals. Berkowitz and Levy [63] found that experimental groups which evaluate their performance favorably exhibit greater pride in performance and greater concern with the assigned task than do groups that evaluate their performance unfavorably. When members were made to believe that they could be rewarded for performance independently of other members, they tended to keep to themselves during rest periods and to exhibit poor task motivation. McCurdy and Lambert [453] found, however, that experimental groups do not work more successfully than individuals working alone.

Kelley and Thibaut [381], reviewing the studies of group effects upon individual performance, find that working with others is generally more productive than working alone. This is particularly true of motor tasks. The quantity or quality of intellectual work may be depressed by group stimulation. Originality tends to give way to the popular or commonplace. Reasoning and problem solving tasks are usually performed more efficiently by groups than by individuals because of the greater number of correct solutions offered and the more prompt rejection of erroneous proposals.

Pepinsky, Pepinsky, and Pavlik [530] have developed a theory of motivation for productivity based on the proposition that any task performance exhibits a value dimension and a feasibility dimension. Value refers to the preferential ordering of outcomes, and feasibility to the estimate on the part of the worker that a given response will lead to a preferred outcome. Haire [286] also explains motivation and productivity in terms of the law of effect. That is, performance improves at a rapid rate in response to initial rewards but improves at a decreasing rate of gain in response to later rewards. Pepinsky, Pepinsky, Robin, and Minor [534] used experimental groups to test the hypothesis that productivity will be higher when a group is working on a task that is in accord with its value systems. The hypothesis was only partially supported. Task oriented groups did better than process oriented groups both on rational tasks which they valued and on human relations tasks, which were more highly valued by process oriented groups. In a second study, Pepinsky, Pepinsky, Minor, and Robin [531] obtained results which support the feasibility hypothesis. Under one experimental condition, groups working on a construction task were given advance notice of changes in task specifications confirming their perception of the feasibility of task completion. Under the second condition, the groups were denied access to needed materials, thus contradicting their expectations of task completion. The results indicated that productivity as measured by net profit and net profit per unit of working time was higher under the confirmed than under the contradicted condition.

The two Pepinsky studies, when considered in combination, suggest that the nature of the expectation that has been instated may be less important than the reinforcement of an instated expectation in motivating productive effort. There is evidence, however, that goals differ in their effects on productivity. Georgopoulos, Mahoney, and Jones [239] asked 621 factory workers to rank their goals in order of importance and to make estimates of their daily productivity levels, freedom to set own work pace, and productivity as an aid or hindrance to goal attainment. Support was found for the hypothesis that if a worker sees high productivity as a path to goal attainment he tends to be a high producer. The relation is enhanced when the particular goal is rated high in importance and the worker is free from constraint.

Traditionally, goal incentive has been regarded as a prime conditioner of productivity. It has been assumed that group members produce more when presented with the opportunity to increase their earnings as a result of increased effort. Early experiences in the application of incentive wage systems gave considerable support to this point of view. It was found that some workers, when paid by the number of units produced, could double or triple their daily wages. This state of affairs was usually "corrected" by raising the standard of performance and revising the incentive rate in such a manner as to prevent a worker from increasing his daily earnings above a specified level. Mathewson [472] found that many workers are suspicious of incentive systems. They fear that, if they increase their output enough to make a substantial increase in wages, their jobs may be re-evaluated so as to reduce their earnings. They also fear that too high a rate of productivity may result in unemployment. Therefore, they tend to restrict their output as a protective measure.

Viteles's [741] analysis of the literature suggests more satisfaction than dissatisfaction on the part of management with incentive systems. A recent survey of 198 companies by the National Industrial Conference Board [516] indicates that 58 per cent of the companies report some benefit accruing from profit sharing plans. About 30 per cent of the companies attributed increased productivity to the operation of the plans. Wolf [777] interviewed company executives and union officials in order to compile case histories for twenty-six companies. The general results support the following conclusions. Incentive wages can and often do increase worker output. They reduce production costs. They force management to manage better and to schedule production more efficiently. However, the effects of incentive pay in increasing productivity tends to be limited by factors such as the following: grievances over standards of output, slowdowns, ceilings on output, resistance to change, and frictions between and within work groups.

Balderson [27], Dickinson [178], Lytle [445], and Louden [436] have described the methods for installing and administering incentive wage systems. Belcher [53] presents a brief, but lucid, analysis of the productivity criterion in determining wage levels. Belcher is in agreement with Mills [494], Melman [481], and Kerr [387] that the continued increase in national productivity during the past century must be attributed to the introduction of constantly improved machines and capital equipment rather than to increased worker effort.

Payne, in a series of papers edited by Ross [588], reports the results of a survey of 316 companies. During the fifteen-year period surveyed, 78 per cent of the wage incentive systems surveyed were found to have failed or to have exhibited serious difficulties. Markham [466] argues that incentive wages provide the best means of returning to the worker an equitable share of earnings accruing from his contribution to productivity. Barkin [33] and Roy [593] find that incentive systems tend to lower productivity in the long run because they inhibit the introduction of improved technologies. Haire [286], Lynton [444], Miles [489], Roethlisberger and Dickson [571], Whyte [763], Lincoln [424], Scanlon [602], Viteles [741], and others maintain that monetary reward constitutes only a part, and perhaps not the most important part, of worker motivation.

Murphy, Murphy, and Newcomb [510] have analyzed a variety of experimental studies which indicate that criticism, reproof, public ridicule, and sarcasm tend to depress performance, while judicious praise and encouragement improve it. Burtt [99] finds that workers are more successful when they are selected for jobs that interest them and are suited to their skills and capabilities. Ghiselli and Brown [244], Harrell [300], Ryan and Smith [598], and Tiffin [714] report that rest pauses, shortening the working day, shortening the working week, reducing noise, improving lighting conditions, adapting machines to men, and a variety of other factors have been found to improve productive efficiency. Roethlisberger and Dickson [571] found that almost any change in the work-place will stimulate productivity for a short period of time.

Gibb [245] has reviewed the literature which seeks to define the nature of leader behavior. Evidence is being accumulated which indicates that leadership is related to group productivity in a complicated fashion. Halpin [291] and Shartle [623] report that a pattern of leader behavior which is high both in "consideration" and "the initiation of structure" tends to increase group effectiveness. Katz and associates [376, 377] found that productivity among railroad workers and in an office situation was higher under general supervision than under close supervision. There was also found a direct relationship between group productivity and (1) the "employee orientation" of the supervisor, (2) the assumption of the leadership role by the supervisor, (3) the delegation of authority to the supervisor by his superiors, and (4) the freedom of the supervisor from high level pressure for productivity. Morse [505] has produced experimental evidence which confirms the positive relationship between productivity and general (rather than close) supervision. She found, however, that this generalization needs to be qualified. General supervision tends to raise member expectations. If the supervisor does not have enough influence with his superiors to obtain advancements, pay raises, and other satisfactions of the heightened expectations of his employees, he tends to increase their frustrations and to depress their productivity. These various findings suggest that group productivity is facilitated by a type of leadership that provides role structure and freedom of action and, at the same time, considers and reinforces the expectations of the group members.

In view of the great variety of factors that influence productivity, it would appear to be an easy matter to maintain productivity at a satisfactorily high level of efficiency. However, there are social factors at work within an organized group which tend to regulate productive output. Individuals and subunits or organization differ in ability. If each were permitted to operate at maximum rate, some units of product would be overproduced in relation to others, thus creating expensive wastage. Workers cannot work at maximum output for long periods of time without suffering fatigue, tension, work decrement, illness, and accident. These limiting factors must be taken into account in connection with the organizational reality which demands operational balance as a means toward organization effectiveness. Furthermore, there are social factors which also affect the situation. Mathewson [472], Roethlisberger and Dickson [571], Whyte [763], Horsfall and Arensberg [335], Roy [592], and others have found that subgroups of workers set normative standards designed to equalize performance among the members, thus preventing discrepancies which create interpersonal tensions. These standards also appear to regulate performance in terms of a normative conception of a fair day's work for the pay received. It can be seen that both the incentive system employed by the larger group and the normative system of the subgroup are designed to depress the performance of the most capable members and to elevate the performance of the least capable members. Thus, both systems act toward maintaining operational balance.

A study which clearly illustrates the operation of balancing factors in a group is reported by Whyte [763] and associates. This is a case study of substandard productivity in the paint room of a toy factory. The rate of performance, determined by time and motion study, was governed by a moving chain on which eight girls were to hang painted toys. In spite of a learning bonus for this new method of operation, the girls complained that they could not keep up with the rapid pace set by the moving chain. After a series of discussion sessions, the girls suggested that they be permitted to regulate the speed of the chain. The department foreman was able to gain permission for making this change. After a period of experimentation, the girls operated at "medium" speed at the beginning and end of each half day but operated most of the time at "high" speed, much faster than that set by the engineers. Within three weeks their production increased from 30 to 50 per cent above the standard set by the previous arrangement. Their earnings increased proportionately, so that the girls were then earning more than many highly skilled workers in other parts of the plant. As a result of pressure from other workers, the bonus plan was abolished. All but two of the girls quit their jobs, and the department foreman resigned sometime later. The authors point out the fact that workers like to control their work rather than be controlled by it. They also observe that the increased production in the paint room resulted in an overload at the next stage of operation and in a heavier demand than could be met at the preceding stage of operations. The prestige of the workers in these units was jeopardized. In addition, the wage and status structure of the entire plant was shaken. Changes at one stage of operations usually involve changes at other stages also. The cost of such readjustments to the organization as a whole may outweigh the advantages gained at any one stage of operations.

In summary, results from a variety of studies indicate that a group may be active without producing much. Productivity bears a variable relationship to group size and degree of centralization. However, structured groups are found to be more productive than unstructured ones, even though a part of the group effort must be devoted to the development and maintenance of structure. As structure increases, the members become more sharply differentiated relative to the nature of the contributions they make to the group output. Groups whose structures provide roles for the co-ordination of information and activities are more effective than those without such roles.

Little empirical evidence can be found to support the contention that decentralization and the reduction of vertical structure increase the effectiveness of an organization. The effects of competition and co-operation upon individual and group output are not simple and direct but are conditioned by a complex array of factors. The effects of working alone and working in groups vary with the nature of the task.

Almost any sort of change can act as an incentive to a greater productivity for a time. However, as the novelty of a change wears off, productivity tends to return to its former level. Wage incentive systems, unless accompanied by the consideration of psychological factors, also tend to exert short range effects upon productivity. The granting of responsibility and adequate freedom of action for task performance, accompanied by the satisfaction of member expectations, appears to increase productivity in a wide variety of situations but not in all situations.

Group operations and subgroup norms tend to regulate productivity; thus, the output of subgroups and of their individual members are held in balance throughout the organization. These group-imposed forces are very strong and difficult to overcome.

## Morale

Morale is defined as freedom from restraint in action toward a group goal. This definition resembles more closely the concepts employed by theorists who were writing several decades ago than those of contemporary writers. G. Stanley Hall [288], in 1920, defined morale as a maximum of vital, creative energy, "minimizing, destroying or avoiding all checks, arrests and inhibitions to it." Kurtz [400] presents a similar point of view in defining morale as the "physical, mental, and spiritual fitness that demands release in action against the recognized objective." French [228] and Woods [779] also define morale in terms of action toward a goal. Hocking [327] regarded morale as "fighting power and staying power."

Child [137] and Viteles [741], reviewing recent studies, find that morale tends to be defined in terms of enthusiastic effort, the sharing of goals, striving for a common purpose, a feeling of togetherness, and strong group integration. It is apparent that these definitions regard group integration and morale as identical, or, at least, as common elements of morale. Allport [7] and Watson [749] have emphasized the factors of group unity and common goals in defining morale. Katz [375] and Stogdill [674] have expressed the opinion, based on research results, that morale is a multi-dimensional variable, and they also included elements of group integration among the dimensions of morale.

The identification of integration with morale has been the result of confusion in the theories available. Brayfield and Crockett [83] and Viteles [741], reviewing the literature on morale, find that research results often fail to support the commonly hypothesized relationship between group effectiveness and morale. They, along with Haire and Gottsdanker [287], conclude that attempts to measure morale have been hindered by a lack of systematic theory which will isolate and identify the essential dimensions of morale. It is the author's belief that a useful step in the direction of such clarification is made in differentiating carefully between group integration and morale. The latter is regarded as the degree of freedom from restraint exhibited by a group in action toward a goal. Integration is regarded as the ability of a group to maintain structure and function under stress. The two concepts are quite dissimilar.

Research under the heading of "morale" has been concerned primarily with measures of job satisfaction. Except for the study of Cattell and Stice [118], most of the research that is related to morale as here defined, has been concerned with group structure and integration. Member spontaneity and freedom of action, as well as group initiative and vigor, appear as significant factors in a number of small group experiments but have not been regarded as measures of morale.

Five of twelve factors identified by Cattell and Stice [118] in the study of experimental groups describe different aspects of morale. These are (1) plodding, fortitudinous morale, (2) esprit de corps, (3) integrative morale, (4) morale of effort, and (5) high reward morale. Morale, as defined by four of these factors, is measured by optimism of aspiration, adventurousness, strong group effort, persistence under discomfort, low deliberate will control, and high member freedom of action. The third factor appears to describe group integration, member satisfaction, optimism, and singleness of purpose. Another factor, identified as immediate high synergy, also appears to be related to morale. Items with high loadings on this factor are high group motivation, high degree of leadership, high degree of group orderliness and organization, high we-feeling, and high persistence of effort.

Casual considerations might lead us to suppose that freedom of action would be greatest in those groups which exhibit a minimum of structure and control. Close attention to theoretical considerations forces us to conclude that freedom of action is dependent upon role structure and definition. Experimental results support the latter interpretation.

French [225] found that organized groups exhibit greater task initiative and provide greater freedom of action for their members than do unorganized groups. Heinicke and Bales [308] and others have observed that experimental groups exhibit restraint in task performance until they have solved the problem of developing a stable role structure. Pepitone and Reichling [536] found that highly cohesive groups are less restrained in their actions than are weakly integrated groups. Lanzetta [401] reports that extreme stress deflates the initiative and aggressiveness of a group, while at the same time increasing its cohesiveness.

The experiments of Lippitt and White [431] indicate that morale is related to the leadership of a group. Groups under an authoritarian type of leadership which dictates in detail what shall be done, how it shall be done, and when it shall be done, provide a minimum of individual and group freedom of action. The members respond by a reduction of initiative and by a heightened dependence upon the leader for the initiation of activity. The situation is not improved by another extreme: a *laissez-faire* type of leadership which provides no goal or task structure. Under this condition the members exhibit a high degree of frustration, inactivity, expressions of need for structure, and restricted space of free movement. Freedom of action is maximized by a democratic form of leadership which provides some structure and helpful task facilitation but which places a high degree of responsibility upon the group members for task decision and action. Freedom of action appears to be maximized by intermediate degrees of group structure and task control.

Campbell [101] and Stogdill and Scott [678] report that the freedom of the group members to interact with each other is related to the extent to which superiors delegate authority to their subordinates. Kelley [379], Mills [495], and Thibaut [705] observed that the high status members of a group exhibit greater freedom of action than do the low status members. Jennings [364], and Polansky, Lippitt, and Redl [541] obtained results which indicate that the high status members of a group are valued because their greater spontaneity initiates spontaneity and enlarges the freedom of action of other members.

The morale of a group is shown to be a function of the degree of role structure maintained by the group, the degree of control exercised by the leadership of the group, and the degree of goal motivation exhibited by the members of the group. Morale is high when the members are strongly motivated to attain a goal and when they are operating under optimum rather than minimum or maximum degrees of role structure and leadership control. Little is gained from increasing the motivation of members if their roles are so closely structured as to deny them the right to initiate action. Granting freedom of action cannot be effective if roles are so poorly defined that the members do not know what they are expected to do. Intermediate degrees of structure and control permit member motivation to be released in the form of group morale.

## Integration

It has been suggested that the individual tends in a group situation to react in such a manner as to maintain the integrity of his perceptual and evaluational systems. Groups also appear to make adaptive changes in the direction of maintaining structural integrity and functional operativeness. The fact has been recognized for a long time. However, it is only within the past decade that systematic experiments have been conducted which throw light on the factors at work in this process.

Festinger and Thibaut [205] studied groups which differed in the amount of induced pressure toward conformity of opinion and in the extent to which the members perceived the group as being homogeneously composed. It was found that, as the pressures toward uniformity and perceived homogeneity increase, the greater is the tendency to communicate to members who express deviant opinions, and the greater is the change in the deviating members toward the group norm. In a study of groups which differed in cohesiveness and in the relevance of the issue being considered, Thibaut [705] found that when cohesiveness is held constant a member who expresses deviant opinions is more frequently rejected on relevant than on irrelevant issues. With relevance held constant, the deviate is more frequently rejected in high cohesive than in low cohesive groups. Schachter [603] observed that, the more cohesive the group and the greater the relevance of the issue being considered, the greater is the tendency to reject deviates who will not conform to the group norm. These three studies suggest that, when cohesiveness is highly valued by a group, the members tend to exert pressures upon a deviant member in an effort to integrate him into the group. If this effort fails the members tend to reject him.

Back [22], studying two-man groups which differed in cohesiveness, observed that more influence was exerted in high cohesive than in low cohesive groups, and members of the former felt that more influence was exerted upon them. The members made more effort to agree, and made more changes toward agreement in high cohesive groups. However, the members of high cohesive groups were better able to disagree and reconcile their differences without disrupting the group than were the members of low cohesive groups.

In a study of groups that differed in cohesiveness, task pressure, the presence of experts, and the availability of a correct answer, Festinger and associates [202] found that conformers tend to communicate most with those members who express deviant opinions. Deviates are more ready than conformers to change their opinions. But deviates who do not change tend to communicate most to those members deviating between their extreme position and the position of the conformers, but tend not to communicate with those holding divergent positions. Deviates appear to "redefine the boundaries of the group" so as to exclude those with divergent opinions. Both conformers and deviates in high cohesive groups tend to communicate less when experts are present in the group and when a correct answer is available. In a closely related study, Gerard [240] found that minority members changed more often than majority members, especially in homogeneous, high pressure groups. Majority members communicated more than minority members in high pressure groups, both under homogeneous conditions and heterogeneous conditions. Minority members initiated more influence attempts, especially in homogeneous, high pressure groups. Little change toward uniformity was observed in the heterogeneous groups. A tendency toward group schism was noted in the heterogeneous groups. The author concludes that a minority group will seek stronger support within itself and will be less able to tolerate internal differences than will a majority group.

The latter two studies provide critical insights into the factors at work in group cohesion and division. An isolated deviate, according to Festinger and associates [202], tends to reject other extreme deviates and to seek identification with other deviates somewhat closer to the group norm. In doing so, he tends to identify himself with the group insofar as his values will allow. As the authors observe, the pressures induced by the group upon a member toward remaining in the group are very strong. Gerard's [240] findings indicate that the pressures exerted upon minority groups are also strong. When deviant members constitute a minority group, they tend to reject the member who does not conform to the norms of their subgroup. This rejection would appear to represent a means of maintaining the cohesiveness of the subgroup, but the increased unity of the subgroup may serve to sharpen its separation from the larger group. Festinger and associates [202] found that individual deviates and minority subgroups in a larger group are less able to tolerate differences than is the larger group. The larger group and the members who conform to its norms appear to experience a sense of security or solidarity which enables them to tolerate a greater degree of deviation than the individual deviate or the minority group is able to endure.

Small groups were found by Hare [296] to be more cohesive than large groups. In small groups, each member is better able to interact with every other member. As the size of the group increases, less opportunity is afforded each member to express himself, particularly in discussions and similar interactive tasks. Those members who feel that they will be unable to make a contribution to the group tend to withdraw from interaction and productive effort. Groups of twelve show a greater tendency than groups of five members to split into competing factions. Cleland [143] found small industrial plants to exhibit a higher degree of integration and freedom from union-management conflict than large plants in the same geographical areas.

Simmel [644] observed that groups tend to exhibit divisive as

well as integrative tendencies. He suggested that groups of three
members tend to divide into a pair and an isolate. Mills [496],
Caplow [106], and others have demonstrated this effect experimentally. Bion [66] found that members of groups working under
conditions of extreme tension and frustration tend to evade the
task by pairing or by exhibiting individual dependency, fight, or
flight. Thelen and associates [704] studied adult discussion groups
in order to test the Bion hypothesis. They found five clusters of
patterns of group behavior. Cluster A members rejected fight and
pairing and developed leadership roles as a means of preventing schism and domination and in order to provide structure and
control. Cluster B members showed a preference for dependent
relationships and for direct aggressive outlets. Cluster C members
accepted flight and avoided power struggles, dissension, and responsibility. Cluster A C members supported their leader and
looked to him for support of their status needs. They opposed any
member who attempted to dominate the group, create conflict, or
threaten their status. Cluster B C members accepted flight and
accepted their leader in order to avoid disharmony, mediate conflict, and maintain group cohesiveness. These groups appear to
have exhibited stronger tendencies toward maintaining integration than toward cleavage. Martin, Darley, and Gross [470] suggest that a high degree of mutuality in sociometric choice may be
indicative of division into highly integrated subgroups rather
than of integration in the group as a whole.

Lippitt and White [431] found group cohesiveness to be higher
under a democratic form of leadership that provided moderate
structure than under forms of leadership that imposed a high degree of authoritarian control or refused to provide any structure
at all. French [224] also found that there are disruptive as well
as cohesive forces at work in groups. He subjected previously
organized and unorganized groups to frustration by requiring
them to solve insoluble problems. Minor disruptions in the form
of interpersonal aggressions, temporary escape from the field, and
general disorganization of activity occurred more frequently in
the organized groups. Splitting into antagonistic factions and the
permanent withdrawal of individuals occurred only in the unor-

ganized groups. French observed that previous organization of the group tends to produce a greater sense of identity among the members with each other and with the group, more equal participation, greater interdependence, and greater social freedom. Greater social freedom reduces the barriers against intermember aggressions. As interdependence among the members and identification with others and the group increases, task involvement also increases. As task involvement increases, interference with activity increases frustration; thus, the stronger the motivation the stronger the frustration, which, under conditions of increased social freedom, leads to aggression. However, the increased sense of identification with other members and with the group permits the members to absorb their interpersonal aggressions without splitting into subgroups. French points out the fact that the more completely a member's goals are involved in, and identified with, the group goals, the greater is the likelihood of conflict, since individuals often disagree on the goals to be attained and on the methods for attaining them. Thus, every group contains within itself the potentiality for conflict and division.

Pepitone and Reichling [536] found that high cohesive groups are able to express more hostility and to express it more directly against an aggressive member than are low cohesive groups. The behavior of high cohesive groups is less restrained. Having once exhibited aggressive behavior against a member, high cohesive groups are better able than low cohesive groups to accept him afterward. Thibaut and Coules [706] observed that group members permitted to communicate back to an aggressor later showed relatively more friendly responses toward the aggressor than members not permitted to communicate. Paterson [527] demonstrated that it was possible to reduce air accidents in fighter squadrons by using the informal communication channel to build up the concept of "weather" as the enemy. Harvey [305] found that members tend to rate each other's performance higher when in the presence of a hostile outgroup than when in the presence of a friendly outgroup. The members tended to close ranks in the presence of hostility. Pepitone and Kleiner [535] found that a reduction in the expectation of loss of status tended to increase group cohesiveness, but an increase in the expectation of gain did not increase cohesiveness. However, a low expectation of gain resulted in a withdrawal symptom evidenced in reduced competition with other groups and in increased co-operation among the group members. Lanzetta [401, 402] conducted a series of experiments on unorganized groups which indicates that external as well as internal threat has the effect upon a group of reducing its forcefulness, activity, effectiveness in attacking a problem, and interactional tensions, while increasing the efforts of the members to establish satisfying interpersonal relationships. These various findings suggest that groups respond to threat by increasing their cohesiveness. Threat may lower the forcefulness and activity, or morale, of groups, while at the same time increasing their integration. However, Mills [495] found that the power structure is more stable in cohesive groups, and Thibaut [705] and Sherif and Sherif [633] have shown that integrated groups are better able than poorly integrated groups to repel external aggression. According to Torrance [725], permanently structured groups are not only more cohesive but more willing than temporarily assembled groups to jeopardize their survival in order to care for a disabled group member.

Sociometric studies have shown that persons tend to prefer the association of other group members whom they perceive to be similar to themselves, particularly in social values. French and Chadwick [223] have shown that the need for affiliation is something more than a mere fear of isolation. Fiedler [207] shows that group members tend to prefer other members whom they perceive to be similar to themselves, but they do not necessarily choose their preferred associates as task partners. Jackson [354] finds that the most highly valued members of a group tend to be those who contribute to goal achievement and conform to group standards.

Not only is the individual important to the group, as is indicated in the tendency of the group to induce pressures toward conformity, but the group is also important to the individual. McKeachie [459] reports that, as members perceive the norms of the group to change, their attitudes tend to change in conformity with those of the group. Festinger, Torrey, and Willerman [206] observe that, the stronger the attraction of a member to his group, the stronger his feeling of inadequacy when he does less well than other members of the group. Festinger and Hutte [203] also report that when the members of a group feel that those members whom they like best dislike each other they exhibit uncertainty and instability in their interpersonal relations in the group. Rasmussen and Zander [553] found that the more attractive a group is to a member and the more he deviates from the standard he attributes to the group, the more he perceives his own performance as falling below his ideal performance. Kelley and Shapiro [380] found that when members are made to feel that they are not highly valued they place a lower value on membership in the group and tend to conform less to the group norms. These various studies suggest that the individuals place a high value on group integration. They tend to evaluate themselves as group members in terms of their contributions to the group and the contribution of the group to their own values.

Membership in a group serves purposes other than the satisfaction of desires for affiliation and companionship. It provides a means for the realizations of personal goals. It also serves to accomplish group purposes which the individual may value. It seems reasonable to believe that the integrity of the group will depend to a considerable degree upon the conformity of personal goals with the goals of the group. May and Doob [476], in formulating a theory of co-operation, advance, among others, the hypothesis that individuals will co-operate rather than compete when co-operation is perceived as a means toward achieving shared goals. Deutsch [177] finds that member co-operation, as opposed to within-group competition, facilitates group integration and productivity. Co-operation also results in greater subdivision of activity, diversity in the contributions of the members, achievement pressure, mutual attractiveness, and favorable attitude toward the group. Blau [69] and Grossack [273] also report that an attitude of co-operativeness increases group cohesiveness. Mutual co-operation might well be regarded as one of the major factors in group integration.

If a correspondence between personal and group goals, buttressed by mutual striving toward the accomplishment of group goals is a factor in group integrity, then any marked discrepancy between personal and group goals would be expected to jeopardize the integrity of the group. Fouriezos, Hutt, and Guetzkow [220] observed that the expression of self-oriented needs in conference groups tends to produce conflict. Gross [268] found that cohesive groups are characterized by a high degree of consensus on general values, while groups with little cohesion are merely aggregates of isolates who are dominated by their own immediate needs. These results suggest that the failure to co-operate need not always be regarded as evidence of malicious or deliberate intent. Some group members may be so closely bound by their personal goals that they cannot become effectively involved in work for the group.

Lewis [417] has presented evidence which indicates that not all group members are dominated by a drive for ego satisfaction and the accomplishment of personal goals. Members are frequently motivated directly by the demands of the objective situation, including the requirements of other members. The whole history of heroism and of self-sacrifice indicates a similar story. The fact that groups are able to organize and operate provides evidence of the subordination of individual interests to the group purpose. But this is not equivalent to saying that members will be satisfied with, or will strongly support, a group in which they are unable to realize their personal goals.

The experimental results and theories presented by Stouffer [687], Walter [746], and Wispé [774], although not bearing directly on the subject of group integration, suggest that role conflict may be expected to affect integration adversely. When a group member is subjected to conflicts in demands, loyalties, judgments, and commands, his behavior is either inhibited or tends to exhibit a comparatively high degree of variability and indecision. In either event, it is poorly designed to satisfy the expectations of other members. The integrity of a group is dependent to a high degree upon a role structure that is sufficiently stable to let each member know what is expected of him. When this structure of expectations is placed under tension or conflict, the integration of the organization is correspondingly weakened. Thus, it is not surprising that French, Deutsch, and others find that an organized group with a defined role structure is more cohesive than an unorganized aggregate of isolated or competing individuals. Nor is it surprising that Haythorn [306] and Guetzkow and Gyr [280] find that the expression of self-oriented need and striving for individual status are disruptive of group integration.

If a correspondence between individual and group values is important to group integrity, a correspondence between subgroup and group goals would appear to be more so. Firey [212], in an insightful analysis of group schism, points out the fact that the forces acting upon the subgroups of a system are not necessarily the same as those acting on the total system. However, it is necessary for the subgroups and the total system to share the same utilities. Schism is evidenced when different subgroups strive to achieve contradictory goals or compete for the group utilities. Evidence to support this point of view is presented in the numerous studies of industrial conflict. Hartmann and Newcomb and some twenty collaborators [303] report that the causes of industrial conflict are extremely complex. The struggle for power between management and union officials appears to be a dominant feature. Differences in this area are not easily reconciled. Agreement is reached more readily when managers and labor leaders work toward a common goal. Kornhauser, Dubin, and Ross [397], summarizing a more recent series of studies, conclude that conflicts of interest are more readily resolved when they are recognized and dealt with openly than when they are suppressed. As organizations become stronger and more inclusive the destructive potentialities of conflict are increased. Conflicts over local industrial issues appear to be on the wane, while conflict in the political sphere appears to be increasing.

Stagner [666] has developed a systematic treatment of industrial conflict. Beginning with the basic factors of perception and motivation, he analyzes factors within the industrial organization, within the union organization, between the two organizations, and relationships of the worker to union and management. A mass of empirical data is brought to bear on the problem. Although none of these data can be regarded as irrelevant to the present discussion, it will serve the purpose to abstract only such findings as apply to groups in general. It was found that conflict tends to be focused upon distribution of the group values. The group (or group management) applies pressures aimed at increasing the differential between profit and wages. When the members feel that they are not sharing equitably in the values they create for the group, they institute measures designed to reduce the discrepancy. Among these measures are the "slow-down" of productive performance and a direct demand for a greater share in the group profits. Stagner finds that the members often perceive a wider discrepancy than actually exists. This misunderstanding is less apparent in organizations which communicate clearly and fully with the members relative to the operations of the group and the distribution of the values created. Stagner finds that the members have no desire to demand such a large share of the group values that the survival of the organization will be jeopardized. The emphasis on material values often covers a state of dissatisfaction with non-material values. Job, security, opportunities for advancement, status, recognition, feeling valued and involved are values which often take precedence over material reward. There is noted an increasing trend for conflicts in the industrial situation to be concerned with human relations problems involving the control of the job. For the solution of group conflict, Stagner proposes a threefold approach: perceptual, motivational, and institutional. These involve an increase in understanding among managers, union leaders and workers; the development of common norms and loyalties; and maintenance of a balance of power aimed at the co-operative solution of mutual problems.

Stagner [665], Purcell [549], Rosen [583], and Kerr and Gottlieb [390] find that co-operation between management and union tends to structure the attitudes of workers along integrative rather than divisive lines. However, when workers are dissatisfied with either union or management, they tend to be dissatisfied with both. These findings suggest that the group members in general tend to be disturbed by power struggles within the group. Kerr [387], Levinson [411], and Reynolds and Taft [560] find that workers have benefited less than commonly supposed from the conflict between management and labor. Moore [499], Bakke [25], Troxell [732], Dale [166], Selekman and Selekman [617], Golden and Ruttenberg [256], and others stress, among other variables, the importance of mutual goals, mutual understanding, mutual involvement, and mutual sharing, as factors which produce group integration and harmony. Arensberg and McGregor [13], Warner and Low [747], and Gouldner [261], among others, have shown that industrial organizations may go for long periods of time with a mistaken estimate of the condition of their integration.

Cartwright and Zander [114] have analyzed the theory and definition of group cohesiveness for small group research. They also discuss the advantages and disadvantages of different measures of cohesiveness. Bakke [25] has skillfully combined theory and research in a study of the internal conditions of, and the relationships between, a telephone company and a union. The "bonds of organization" were analyzed in relation to functional specifications, status system, communication system, reward-penalty system, and organization charter.

The critical studies edited by Chamberlain, Pierson, and Wolfson [127] and Arensberg and associates [12] suggest the need, in the study of group conflict, for improved theory, the discard of unsupported hypothesis, and the design of research with adequate controls. Merton's [484] proposals for research on *anomie,* if executed, should improve our understanding of the basic processes underlying the disorganization and decline of groups. Durkheim's [187] definition of anomie as a state of normlessness has been elaborated and refined by American sociologists. Merton [484] observes that forces toward anomie are induced in a group which strongly reinforces the goal orientation of its members but fails to provide any legitimized means to goal attainment that are equally available to all its members. The conflict between the normatively defined goal and the availability of legitimized structural means to goal attainment produces a strain toward anomie: the deterioration and disintegration of value systems.

Shartle [623] points out the fact that organizations, if they survive for any length of time, exhibit cyclical periods of growth and decline. They often experience difficulties and hardships in the early stages of development, then exhibit a period of revitalization, reorganization, and growing achievement. After reaching a period of peak achievement, they begin to weaken and experience increasingly serious difficulties. Under extreme deterioration, they either dissolve, are absorbed, or become rejuvenated and start a new cycle.

The period of group decline is often accompanied by extreme discontent and confusion among the group members, by conflicts in values and goals among different subgroups, and by increasing rigidity in group structures. Weber [750] and others have observed that such a condition of organization provides a fertile ground for the activities of individuals whose primary qualification for leadership is the ability to structure and mobilize member discontent in the support of change. A group can best maintain control over its own destiny by instituting procedures for coping with change on a rational and foresightful basis.

Ginzberg and Reilley [253] have outlined the general principles, policies, and factors that need to be considered in effecting change in large organizations. Lippitt, Watson, and Westley [430] have analyzed the basic, clinical factors to be considered in planning for organization change. Problems involved in overcoming resistance to change in organizations have been studied by means of the planned experiment and by the case history method. The detailed case studies presented by Jaques [360], Ronken and Lawrence [580], and Spicer [662] indicate that the introduction of change involves numerous complex factors, and that many unanticipated effects of change in one segment of organization may be observed in other parts of the system. An excellent, step-by-step description of the procedures followed in the installation of a new program has been published by Low [437].

In controlled experimental studies of change, Baumgartel [49],

Jenkins [363], and Zander and Gyr [790] found that the feedback of information relative to the effects of change facilitates the acceptance of a new program. French [226] and Coch and French [144] obtained results which indicate that the acceptance of change by the members of a group is in direct proportion to the extent to which they are involved in the process of planning and initiating change. Bennett [57] finds that discussion is most effective when accompanied by decision and consensus. Cartwright [113] has outlined the group processes which retard, and those which facilitate, the acceptance of change. Cartwright observes that any proposal for change which is contrary to the group norms will encounter resistance. The more attractive a group is to its members, and the more relevant an issue to the basis of attraction, the greater the influence that the group can exert on its members. The greater the shared perception of the need for change among the members, the greater will be the internal group pressure for change. The greater the extent to which the members who are affected by change participate in the planning, discussion, and installation of change, the greater the likelihood that they will share in the perceived need for change. Cartwright's paper indicates that a program for the initiation of change should be based on a consideration of the basic processes of group formation and structure.

In summary, evidence has been presented which indicates that various kinds of groups adopt different methods for reducing their tensions and maintaining their integrity. Groups that are highly structured and integrated tend to exert pressures on the deviate in an effort to bring him into the group. If this effort does not succeed, the deviate is isolated or rejected, thus preserving the integrity of the system. Minority groups, because of the pressure exerted upon them to conform to the group norms, appear to be less able than the larger group to absorb the deviate. Groups that are not highly integrated appear to make comparatively less effort to keep deviant members in the system.

In general, it may be concluded that the identity of individual and group goals, member conformity to group norms, a feeling of mutual acceptance, mutual liking among the members, satisfaction of member expectations, member support of the group leadership, and subgroup support of the group goals are all measures of various aspects of group integration. These factors, built into a stable and clearly differentiated role structure which enables the members to know what they are expected to do and with whom they are expected to co-ordinate their efforts, contribute to the integration and survival of the group under stress. At the same time, the group must maintain sufficient freedom of action throughout the role system to permit the handling of emergencies and the coping responses needed for adaptations to stress and change.

Group integration is found to involve formal and operative structures, communication structures, role structures, group purpose and norms, subgroup purpose and norms, and individual goals and expectations. Group integration is high when structure, functional operativeness, and communications are maintained and when all members and subgroups are working in co-ordination to support the group and its purpose.

## Effects of Reinforcement

Studies of member satisfaction are often referred to as "morale surveys." A high degree of satisfaction among the group members is assumed to be an evidence of high morale. Since there are theoretical reasons for questioning this assumption, we shall use the term "satisfaction" rather than "morale" in discussing the research in this area.

Robinson [566], summarizing the reviews published by Hoppock and Robinson over a period of 21 years, found 343 percentages ranging from 1 to 92 per cent of dissatisfaction among employees. The median of these studies was 13 per cent dissatisfied. In another analysis, Robinson [565] summarized the reviews of Hoppock and Robinson during the years 1946 to 1953. The average per cent of dissatisfaction reported in various surveys declined from 21 per cent in 1946 to 13 per cent in 1953. These results suggest that worker satisfaction varies from company to company and from time to time. Dissatisfaction appears to be less prevalent than often supposed.

Various factor analytic studies have been made in an effort to define the important dimensions of job satisfaction. The author tabulated and compared the factors identified in the following studies: Baehr [23], Burns [97], Conklin [154], Kahn [371], Katz [375], Gordon [258], Schreiber, Smith, and Harrell [607], Smith and Westen [654], Van Zelst [737], and Wherry [760]. Satisfaction with supervision, job satisfaction, and satisfaction with personal rewards emerged as factors in at least five of the studies listed above. Company management and operations, friendly co-workers, and working conditions were found in four of the studies. Group integration, personal recognition and advancement, the company as an organization, and freedom and responsibility in role enactment were identified as factors in two or three of the studies. The differences in the factors found by different investigators are dependent to a considerable degree upon the kinds of items investigated and also upon differences in the groups studied. Wherry [762] combined the results of four factorial studies. This procedure resulted in the identification of eight factors, identified as general satisfaction, fellow workers, supervisors, working conditions, confidence in management, financial reward, personal development, and personnel actions.

The different factors of job satisfaction may be regarded as defining independent areas of member expectation. The satisfaction of one area of expectation does not necessarily satisfy other expectations. Pattern of supervisory behavior, behavior of fellow workers, characteristics of the job, working conditions, rewards for performance, recognition and advancement, freedom for responsible role enactment, group integration, confidence in management, and reason for pride in organization represent areas of member expectation which require differential consideration and action on the part of a group in order to provide adequate confirmation. In view of the number and complexity of the expectations that a group must satisfy, the problem of maintaining member satisfaction cannot be regarded as an easy one.

Kahn and Morse [373], influenced by factorial studies, developed a theory of morale based on the following dimensions: job satisfaction, involvement in the immediate work group, identification with the larger organization, satisfaction with supervisor, and satisfaction with rewards. These are, for the most part, measures of group integration rather than of morale.

Viteles [741], in his admirable survey of the research on industrial morale, finds that job satisfaction is related to type of job, status in the group, size of work groups, perceived adequacy of pay, method of wage payments, job security, opportunity for advancement, recognition of contribution, type of supervision, working conditions, hours of work, adequacy of equipment, identification with company, identification with union, participation in decision making, task involvement, adequacy of information about company policies and practices, relations with fellow workers, and a great variety of other factors. In addition to the above factors, Child [137] mentions the opportunity to remedy frustration and annoyances. But these factors do not affect all employees alike. Various combinations of situational influences operate to determine the impact of any one factor upon the individual and upon the group at any given time. In addition, the variables may not act in isolation to affect satisfaction in a direct, uncomplicated fashion; but several interrelated variables are usually found in the better designed studies to act in combination to determine job satisfaction.

When people are asked what they value most in a job, their answers resemble those given when they are asked to describe their satisfactions and dissatisfactions. Chant [128], Blum and Russ [72], Jurgensen [368], and others have found that what workers in general value most highly are job security and opportunity for advancement. Next in order of preference are type of work, opportunity to learn and use ideas, a good boss, congenial work companions, and good pay. Of lesser value are good working conditions, good hours, easy work, and supplemental benefits. These items appear to be more closely related to group integration than to morale. Opportunity to learn, to use ideas, and to advance in the company might be interpreted as evidences of an interest in freedom of action. All of these items were among those most highly valued. But the workers were not questioned relative to their desires for responsibility, authority, and freedom of action because these items were not regarded as essential elements in morale.

Herzberg, Mausner, Peterson, and Capwell [321] analyzed sixteen studies in which 16,000 employees ranked various aspects of job satisfaction in order of importance. The following average ranking was obtained, in decreasing order of importance: job security, job interest, opportunity for advancement, appreciation by supervisors, company and management, intrinsic aspects of the job, wages, supervision, social aspects of the job, working conditions, communication, and benefits. Both management personnel and union officials were found to overestimate the importance of wages and financial benefits to employees.

Viteles [741], Hoppock [332], Lynton [444], Louden [436], and others have observed that pay tends to be emphasized as an incentive method. Furthermore, these authors, along with Mace [455] and many others, find that as wages rise above the subsistence level, other factors become important to the worker. Among these are status, self-respect, participation, recognition of contributions, fair treatment, and other social factors. The need for improved supervision which recognizes the importance of these social factors is particularly noted.

It was hypothesized in a preceding chapter that a new member enters a group entertaining certain personal goals and values. The interest in job security, advancement, pay, and the like might be regarded as expressions of the more easily verbalized of these values. Social custom makes its more difficult to express an overt interest in high status, increased responsibility and authority, fair treatment, and the like. To do so might be interpreted by other members as an expression of intention to infringe upon their own rights and interests.

It has also been observed that the members of a group do not all value the same things. Troxell [731] reports that the high status members of industrial groups place a high value on work that is interesting and challenging. Lower status members are more interested in pay, job security, and good supervision, and knowing definitely what is expected of them. Baehr [23], Centers [120], Raube [554], and others report similar results. Jurgensen [369] finds that as education increases, type of work becomes more important. Among less highly educated workers, type of supervision, job security, company, and co-workers become highly important. Wyatt [786] found that doing the type of work one liked was directly related to the effectiveness of an incentive wage plan. Productivity did not increase under incentive pay for work that was disliked, but it did increase in proportion to the degree of liking for the type of work being done. The importance attached to type of work suggests that the functional aspects of role differentiation enter into the expectations and satisfactions of the members. High status members value a role that presents a challenge and a degree of uncertainty, while low status members desire a comparatively high degree of security and certainty. It may be that high status members are valued because of their capacity to make decisions which involve a high degree of uncertainty.

Renck [559], Uhrbrock [734], Centers [121], Campbell [102], Kolstad [394], Lenski [408], Yoder, Heneman, and Cheit [787], and others have shown that satisfaction is positively related to status in the organization. The morale of managers is higher than that of foremen, and the morale of foremen is higher than that of the worker. These findings are in accord with the theoretical prediction that a higher degree of freedom to initiate action and to reinforce personal expectations would result in a greater degree of satisfaction among high status members.

Scott [610] found that satisfaction is related to a clearly defined status structure. Satisfaction is higher when the members of the group know who their superiors and subordinates are. Stouffer and associates [688] report that the higher a member's status, the more strongly he supports the formal structure of the organization. Bernberg [64] used questionnaires to test two hypotheses relative to the nature of "morale." One hypothesis, as proposed by Roethlisberger [570] and Krech and Crutchfield [398], holds that "morale" is a subgroup phenomenon. The other holds that "morale" is expressed in terms of acceptance of the formal organization. Bernberg found that individual behaviors, such as absences and tardiness, are not related to satisfaction scores but do differentiate significantly between departments. Both the morale hypotheses predict group differences but do not predict individual differences in behavior.

Stouffer and associates [688], Goode and Fowler [257], and Whyte [763] observe that informal subgroups may operate to support the requirements of the formal organization, even when satisfaction is low. Goode and Fowler observed this to be particularly true when group goals, function, and status are clearly defined. Sayles [601] found that, in spite of efforts made by management to set an equitable wage structure, individuals and subgroups are always comparing their earnings, working conditions, hours, and other factors with those of other individuals and subgroups. When the comparisons are judged to be unfavorable, some form of discontent is usually expressed. Union officers, because of their perceived political interests, are no more able than management personnel to argue about the reasonableness or unreasonableness of these considerations. It is not the absolute, but the comparative, amount of reward that determines member satisfaction. Management can cope with this factor better at the subgroup than at the individual level.

Benge and Copell [55], Hull [343], and Stouffer and associates [688] report that the satisfaction of new members of a group is usually much higher than that of rank and file members who have been in the organization for longer periods of time. An analysis of 23 studies by Herzberg and associates [321] indicates that workers start on a new job with considerable satisfaction, but this satisfaction wanes after a time, then begins to rise. Very young workers show a high rate of satisfaction. The lowest degree of satisfaction is found among workers who are 20 to 30 years of age. Beyond this age range, job satisfaction increases with increasing age. The factors that operate to produce these effects have not been adequately investigated. It may be, as Merton and Kitt [486] and Shils [639] suggest, that identification with different reference groups begins to operate after a period of time, so that the member feels relatively deprived in comparing his own experiences with the outcomes experienced by the groups with which he identifies himself. The usual attitude or morale survey is unable to answer questions of this sort. Studies conducted by Bullock [96] and by Friend and Haggard [232] are exceptions. The latter found that both personal adjustment and work adjustment were related to family background. The better adjusted men were found to come from secure homes that were described as closely knit and unified. The poorly adjusted men come from disorganized homes in which the parents had set the pattern for poor job adjustment and interpersonal maladaptation. Bullock [96] found social background factors to be highly related to job satisfaction. Among the most critical background factors, were the attitudes of the worker's friends and family members toward his job. The worker tended to be dissatisfied with the job if his family and friends held it in low regard. These findings suggest that the group members carry with them attitudes and expectations which, independently of the nature of the group, may determine their adjustment to the group.

Stockford and Kunze [672] interviewed aircraft factory workers in their homes. Those who started in the factory at a salary lower than that earned in their previous jobs expressed a less favorable attitude toward the company and were rated lower in performance by their supervisors. The unfavorable effect of a low starting wage was found to last in many cases beyond the point at which the worker had been advanced to a pay level higher than he had ever earned before. Centers and Cantril [122] interviewed 1,239 workers representative of a national sample. It was found that 86 per cent wanted higher pay. The lower the pay received, the larger the percentage of increase needed, except in the high income groups. The higher a worker's income, the better satisfied he is with it and the smaller the proportionate increase he wants. However, for the person who is dissatisfied, the more money he makes the more he wants.

Scientists have begun only recently to conduct experiments that are specifically designed to take into account the factor of expectations in group performances and morale. Stogdill, Scott, and Jaynes [679], Morse [505], Harnquist [298], Rosen and Rosen

[584], Spector [660], and Weitz [755] have published in this area. Rosen and Rosen [584] asked their subjects (a) what should be done? (b) what is being done?, and (c) how satisfied are you with what is being done? Satisfaction was found to be higher when expectations were perceived to have been met. To do or receive more than expected was not always satisfying. The dissatisfied subjects usually thought that more should be done in the direction of their own expectations.

Harnquist [298] studied the expectations of Naval conscripts in Sweden. He found that identification with different civilian reference groups significantly affected expectations relative to military life. Those identified with higher income groups expected to suffer the most deprivation and to be less satisfied with military leadership. Within the organization, behavioral adjustment was more highly determined by the military norm system than by the norms of the conscript subgroups. These findings are in conformity with those reported by Stouffer and associates [688] and Merton and Lazarsfeld [487] in their studies of the American soldier.

Spector [660] used experimentally created groups in which it was possible to manipulate the expectation of promotion and the degree of success in achieving promotion. The members of groups in which the probability of promotion was high did not differ as widely from those of low probability groups in desire for promotion as in the expectation of being promoted. Satisfaction was higher in the low probability groups than in the high probability groups and was higher in the promoted than in the non-promoted groups. Promotion was a significant determiner of satisfaction with the group and with the task. It was concluded that a person's satisfaction is partly a function of how certain he feels that a given outcome will be effected. Satisfaction did not appear to be adversely affected by failure to achieve an attractive goal if a person's expectations of achieving the goal were low. These results suggest that satisfaction is related not only to the referents of expectation but also to the perceived probability of reinforcing expectations.

Weitz [755], in an investigation of factors related to the high job mortality rate among insurance agents, designed a letter and a booklet describing the duties of the agent's job. The letter and booklet were sent by a high ranking company official to 226 applicants for the position of agent. A control group of 248 applicants received no letter or booklet. Resignations occurred among 27 per cent of the control group but only among 19 per cent of the experimental group, suggesting that a clear structuring of expectations relative to the nature of the agent's job reduced resignations.

In a comparative study of a bankrupt company and a similar company of sound financial status, Grove and Kerr [275] found that the prospect of being discharged lowered satisfaction significantly in the bankrupt company. Satisfaction was low, not only in relation to job security but also in relation to pay, associates, supervision, and a number of other factors not logically related to job insecurity. Satisfaction with these various factors was not highly intercorrelated, requiring that the classical halo hypothesis be rejected. One factor, the financial insecurity of the company, affected other factors which were not highly interrelated.

The findings of the several studies cited above indicate that expectations do not operate in an uncomplicated and direct manner to affect satisfaction. Nor can morale be properly understood when it is regarded as a simple feeling of well-being and satisfaction. The morale of the individual members is rather to be interpreted in terms of the area of freedom available to them in the group for realizing their personal goals and expectations. Their satisfaction with the group will be determined not only by the level of their aspirations but also by the perceived probability of experiencing satisfying outcomes. A great complex of factors operates to determine aspirations and satisfaction with experienced outcomes. Among these are expectations structured by the groups as well as by internal and external reference groups.

Studies of workers who quit their jobs indicate that a high percentage of separations are due to factors that are remediable by the organization and its management. Koran [395] found that the reasons most frequently given by employees for leaving a company are poor initial job orientation, unkept promises, unsatisfactory wages and benefits, unsatisfactory hours, lack of communication, unfair treatment by supervisors, and the like. Several of these items suggest the failure of the company to meet the expectations of the worker. Loken [434] found the reasons given by 415 workers for quitting their jobs could be classified under poor supervision, dislike for jobs, poor working conditions, and unbalanced work load. Weitz and Nuckols [756] found among insurance agents who liked the companies for which they had worked, that the majority quit because of dissatisfactions in the areas of supervision and training. Dissatisfaction with supervision received ranked high in each of these studies. These findings suggest that the satisfactions experienced by the members of a group tend to be determined by the ability of the group leaders to satisfy the expectations of the members.

Hemphill, Seigel, and Westie [318] have produced convincing evidence of the effects of reinforcement upon group integration. They asked members of 100 groups to describe the behavior of the group leaders on eight "dimensions" of leader behavior. The same eight dimension scales were used to describe what the leader was expected to do. In addition, 14 scales were used to describe different characteristics of the 100 groups. The scores for reported leader behavior were subtracted from the scores for expected leader behavior to yield eight discrepancy scores for each leader. The discrepancy scores were then correlated with each of the 14 group-dimension scores. The eight discrepancy scores were found to be highly and significantly related to viscidity (integration). The correlation coefficients ranged from —.40 to —.60. The greater the discrepancy between the behavior expected of a leader and the behavior exhibited by him, the less integration perceived in the group. These results suggest that the failure of a leader to confirm the expectations of the members exerts a strong negative effect upon the integration of the group. The leader's failure to confirm member expectations also reduces the perceived polarity, or unity of goal direction, of the group.

The satisfaction of member expectation is found to exert its strongest effects on group integration. A state of member satisfaction is not necessarily equivalent to a state of group integration. Member satisfaction contributes to group integration by reinforcing the expectations of the members relative to the value of group membership. It reinforces group loyalty and support and reduces member separation from the group. The leadership of the group is found to play an important part in satisfying the expectations of the members.

Katz and associates [376, 377] found in two studies, one with office workers and the other with railroad section workers, that intrinsic job satisfaction was negatively related to productivity, but not to a significant degree in the clerical situation. Neither satisfaction with company nor with rewards was related to productivity. A direct relation was found between section productivity and the employees' evaluations of the productivity of their work groups, but the relationship was not statistically significant in the railroad study. In both studies, productivity is directly related to the assumption of leadership by the supervisor. Productivity is higher under general rather than under close supervision, and under employee oriented supervision rather than a type of supervision which pushes for productivity. However, productivity is lowered when the supervisor permits or requires his subordinates to assume leadership functions in the group. Comrey, Pfiffner, and Beem [152], in a study of the administration of U. S. forests, also found that job satisfaction and personal competence are not related to organization effectiveness. However, effectiveness is directly related to a type of high level supervision which is described as democratic, sympathetic and which keeps subordinates informed. Medalia and Miller [480] report that unit efficiency and unit satisfaction are mutually reinforcing only when some differential reward is given to those units which operate at high efficiency.

The most competently designed study of satisfaction thus far available has been conducted by Morse [505]. In a study of job satisfaction, financial and status satisfaction, and company involvement among 742 clerical workers, she found that education increases the need for pay and job status. Satisfaction was higher among those doing skilled, varied work than among those doing repetitive work. There was no high relationship between pay level and satisfaction with the company. Dissatisfaction was related to the feeling that the worker was not experiencing the return to be expected in terms of his education, experience, length of service, and contribution. The need for pay and job status increases with increasing length of service. A prolonged discrepancy between the pay and status desired and that attained leads to dissatisfaction. Satisfaction was significantly related to good interpersonal relations among employees and the desire to stay in the company. Satisfaction with the immediate work group was higher under general than under close supervision. However, this favorable attitude may not be extended to the company if the supervisor, by virtue of the greater freedom allowed and the higher expectations induced, is not able to influence higher management to fulfill the workers' expectations. The supervisor who supervises closely allows little opportunity for developing improved skills and higher aspirations. As a result, his subordinates are better satisfied with their pay and with the company in general but not with the immediate work group. Productivity was found to be higher under a supervisor who delegates, gives considerable freedom of action, exerts little pressure for productivity, and treats his subordinates in a warm and understanding manner. However, general supervision was not related to higher productivity in a section doing routine and monotonous work. Satisfaction was positively related to general supervision and freedom of action only when the members were able to fulfill the higher levels of expectation arising from a greater degree of freedom.

In general, member satisfaction is found to be related to a great array of variables which measure group integration. Satisfaction is not highly related to measures of group productivity. In some studies the two measures are negatively related. Morale, or freedom of action, is positively related to productivity. Morale is positively related to satisfaction when freedom of action leads to the reinforcement of expectation.

## Achievement Balance

Research on achievement balance is particularly weak in the area of morale, defined as enthusiastic effort and freedom of action. Further research will be required in order to determine the relationship between morale and productivity, and between morale and integration. A convincing body of evidence is available concerning the relationship between integration and productivity.

The preceding discussion has shown that productivity, integration, and morale are related to group structure. Member freedom of action is higher under moderate than under extreme degrees of role definition. When structure is lacking, the members contend with each other in an effort to define status and function, thus reducing productivity and increasing the efforts toward inducing member conformity and group integration. If the group is too highly structured, the role boundaries of the members are restricted, their initiative is reduced, and subgroup integration is increased at the expense of the integration of the larger group. Group productivity, integration, and morale appear to be maximized under intermediate degrees of structure.

*Morale and productivity* are positively related. Lippitt and White [431] found that members exhibit greater freedom of action and spend more time in productive work in the absence of the leader under conditions of moderate structure and democratic control than under conditions of extremely high or low structure and control. Darley, Gross, and Martin [169] found that task enthusiasm is significantly related to measures of group productivity. Katz, Maccoby, and Morse [376] and Likert and Katz [423] have observed that group productivity is increased by a type of supervision that gives a worker responsibility for his job and freedom of action necessary to carry out his responsibilities. Bass [38] reports that raising the satisfaction of group members by increasing their participation, responsibility, and freedom of action has the effect of increasing productive effectiveness in pleasant groups but not in unpleasant groups. Lanzetta, Haefner, Langham, and Axelrod [402] found that groups under threat were less forceful and active in attacking the task problem and were less effective but more variable in performance than groups not subjected to threat. Cervin and Ketchum [125] have also reported a decline in group effort and productivity under continued frustration. Sorokin's [656] studies of war, famine, and catastrophe suggest that groups tend to exhibit physical and spiritual debilitation and apathy under conditions of extreme deprivation. The above results from a few, but highly competent, studies suggest that conditions which increase the initiative, enthusiastic effort, and freedom of action of the members also increase the productivity of the group. Conditions which lower group morale also tend to depress productivity.

*Morale and integration* may be positively or negatively related. Examination of the factor loadings reported by Cattell and Stice [118] indicate that items which measure integration and morale are loaded in the same direction in some factors, but are loaded in opposite directions in other factors. Guetzkow and Gyr [280] observed that consensus in affective conflict involving interpersonal struggles by group members is achieved when the participants withdrawn from problem solving and show little interest in the task. Lanzetta [401] and Lanzetta, Haefner, Langham, and Axelrod [402] report that groups under conditions of threat exhibit increased cohesiveness but are less forceful and active in attacking the task problem. Haythorn [306] found a factor identified as group goal facilitating behavior to be positively related to satisfaction, co-operativeness, and interest in task completion. A second factor, independent of the first and identified as striving for individual prominence, was negatively related to mutual friendliness. The results of these studies suggest that group integration or cohesiveness may be independent of morale defined as freedom of action toward a goal.

French [225] observed that organized groups exceeded unorganized groups in social freedom, integration, interdependence, and interpersonal aggression. Cattell, Saunders, and Stice [117] also report that democratic freedom in a group is associated with group structure and orderly procedures. Lippitt's [428, 431] studies indicate that both group cohesiveness and member freedom of action are higher under moderate than under extreme, high or low, degrees of structure. French [224], Lippitt [428], Thibaut [705], and Lanzetta [401] found that the cohesiveness of groups tends to increase under threat and frustration. According to Torrance [725], permanently structured groups are not only more cohesive but more willing than temporarily assembled groups to jeopardize their survival in order to care for a disabled group member. It would appear, then, that cohesiveness can be so strong as to threaten the welfare of the group as a whole. The results of studies conducted by Deutsch [177] indicate that member co-operativeness increases co-ordination of effort, achievement pressure, and group integration. Wickert [766] found that members who stayed with a group, when compared with those who had separated, were those who reported that they were permitted to make decisions and felt that they were making a contribution to the success of the group. Morse and Reimer [506] made experimental changes in four departments of a large organization. When the authority structure was changed to enlarge the opportunity of workers to make decisions, their satisfaction increased. However, satisfaction decreased when the change in authority structure reduced the area of decision making of the workers. Productivity increased under both conditions of change, with a somewhat greater increase being observed under centralized control.

Two different sets of studies indicate that morale may be related either positively or negatively with integration. Vigorous, active goal striving appears to be associated with a heightened degree of group integration. However, threat and frustration appear to result in a reduction in overt goal striving and in an increase in integrative efforts.

*Integration and productivity* are negatively related. Although group integration provides conditions under which productive operations may be maintained, the effort that is devoted to the development of integration might be conceived as a substraction from the efforts that are devoted to productivity. Evidence in this direction is presented by Fiedler [207] and Torrance [726], who report that unsuccessful groups tend to value those members who build group cohesiveness and interpersonal rapport, while successful groups tend to value those members who further group productivity. Additional evidence is provided by Lanzetta [401] and Borgatta and Bales [76], who observed that groups are not able to concern themselves with productive effort until a stable role structure has been achieved.

French [228] found that group cohesion is negatively related to performance in drill competitions between military groups. Norfleet [521] finds that personal liking is little related to productive contributions in discussion groups. Schachter, Ellertson, McBride, and Gregory [604] and Berkowitz [60] report that productivity increased under conditions of both high and low cohesiveness in problem solving groups. Berkowitz observed that high cohesiveness and high production standards interact to improve productivity. Hemphill [314] found effective synergy to be positively related to productivity in experimental groups, but that group viscidity is not related to administrative effectiveness in a large, structured organization. Schachter, Ellertson, McBride, and Gregory [604] observed that productivity increased in both high and low cohesive groups under persuasion to increase productivity. However, communications calling for a decrease in productivity resulted in a greater decrease in the high than in the low cohesive groups. Seashore [613] found that high cohesiveness is associated with either high or low productivity standards, depending on the degree to which workers feel secure with the company. A high degree of security is associated with lower productivity and greater conformity with subgroup norms. Darley, Gross, and Martin [169] found productivity to be related positively with cohesiveness. However, in a later study, Gross, Martin, and Darley [270] observed that the variance between groups in productivity and cohesiveness is to be accounted for in terms of differences in leadership rather than cohesiveness. Lanzetta [401] found that group integration increased under stress, but productivity declined under both high and low stress. Productivity was higher under moderate degrees of stress.

Studies of job satisfaction provide further evidence of the low or inverse relationship between group integration and productivity. Brayfield and Crockett [83] have surveyed the most competent studies of job satisfaction conducted during the period 1927 to 1955. Measures of individual job satisfaction are not significantly related to productivity in 13 of the 15 studies analyzed. Averaging the scores of individuals to produce an index of group satisfaction also fails to show any consistent relationship between satisfaction and productivity. Herzberg and associates [321] have analyzed 26 studies in which job attitude scores were correlated with objective measures of productivity. The results indicate that 14 of the studies yield positive correlations, some of which are close to zero, while 12 of the studies yield zero or negative relations. In a separate analysis of 24 studies concerned with employee separations and turnover, 21 showed a positive relation between job satisfaction and low turnover. Satisfaction acts to keep the group intact, thereby contributing toward its integration. However, member satisfaction does not show any consistently high relationship to group productivity.

The results of group experiments and of job satisfaction surveys suggest that group integration and productivity are not highly related. In many groups, integration and productivity are negatively related. Berkowitz [60, 61] has conducted experiments which indicate that integration and productivity are positively related when the group is highly motivated and operating under strong task urgency.

*Productivity, morale, and integration* may rise or fall simultaneously. The studies by Berkowitz [60, 61] cited above indicate that productivity and integration may be high when morale is high. Deutsch [176] suggests that intermember co-operation increases group productivity, integration, and activity. However, a great array of internal and external factors may operate to change the balance among these three elements of group achievement. Observations made by Horsfall and Arensberg [335] suggest that closely integrated groups which exhibit a high degree of enthusiastic mutual friendliness, sociability, and horseplay are likely to be low producers. Thus, it is apparent that both integration and freedom of action may be high in a group at the same time, but productivity may suffer if the freedom is not utilized in the accomplishment of the group goals. This is particularly likely to be the case, as suggested by Horsfall and Arensberg, when the subgroups organize to oppose the demands of management and work counter to the purposes of the larger group.

*In summary,* high group morale appears to be associated with high productivity. The greater the freedom from restraint, within limits, that a group exhibits in attacking its task, the more it is able to produce. Morale may be related either positively or negatively with integration. High cohesiveness is related to high morale when the group is actively engaged in operations upon a goal objective. However, high cohesiveness is related to low morale under conditions of continued threat and frustration. Integration and productivity tend to be related inversely. The time and effort spent on the maintenance of integration cannot be devoted at the same time to productivity. However, both productivity and integration may be high under conditions of high morale, task motivation, and effort. These findings appear to lend some support to the hypothesis that a group is a system which tends to maintain a continuous balance among its various achievement outputs. With inputs held constant, an increase in one achievement factor is accomplished at the cost of some other achievement element. A simultaneous increase in productivity, integration, and morale can only be accomplished at the expense of an increase in some form of input value or effort.

7

## Summary and Discussion

A RATHER exacting and laborious procedure has been followed in developing a theory of group achievement and
examining it in reference to the pertinent experimental data. In
order to construct a satisfactory system, it has been necessary to
start with concepts that are firmly anchored in the scientific
literature, to define them strictly, to examine the interrelationships among them, and to trace in systematic detail the effects
generated by their interactions upon each other.

A group is regarded as an input-output system. The inputs
are the performances, expectations, and interactions of the group
members. These variables in combination account for the development of group structure and for the initiation and maintenance of group operations. The input behaviors, transformed
into group structure and operations, result in outcomes which
describe the achievement of the group. The logical development
of the system has required that group achievement be analyzed
in terms of productivity, integration, and morale. A group may
be examined at any stage in its operations to evaluate its status
in respect to these three aspects of achievement.

Various concepts used in the system are reviewed in the following sections.

### Characteristics of Individuals and of Groups

Performance and expectation are characteristics of individuals. Interaction is an interpersonal form of behavior. A group by

definition involves interactions and performances (actions and reactions). A group also involves expectations. The structuring of positions in a group tends to confirm differential expectations relative to the predictable initiative of certain members and the predictable reactions of other members. In addition, the members tend to confirm for each other a normative set of values relative to the group purpose and member behavior affecting the group purpose. Not only do the members in interaction develop norms which define expected behavior, but they exert strong pressures upon each other to conform with the norms of the group. Purpose and norms represent mutually confirmed sets of expectations which must be regarded as characteristics of groups. Structure and operations are also characteristics of groups.

## The Input Behaviors

The concepts *performance, interaction,* and *expectation* must be regarded as abstractions which refer to observed or inferred aspects of behavior that are recognized in general conversation as well as in the scientific literature. The concepts have been defined in the scientific literature by a variety of research operations. For this reason, we know more about the concepts and the behaviors to which they refer than we do about various other concepts that might have been used for the theory. The fact that several concepts have been redefined according to the demands of the theory and in order to bring them into closer conformity with research findings requires us to keep in mind the scientific rather than the cultural meanings of the terms.

Interaction is defined as an action-reaction sequence in which the reactions of each participant in the sequence are responses to actions initiated by other participants. A *group* is defined as an interaction system. It must be regarded as an open system because it gains and loses members, and exchanges values with its environment. The structure of a group is determined by the actions and reactions of its members. A position in a group is defined as a predictable sequence of actions by a member which elicits predictable reactions from other members of the system. Successive interactions and the gain or loss of members do not change the identity of the system. Although interaction is not self-perpetuating, the continuance of interaction, at least intermittently, is necessary to maintain the identity of the system. The degree of structure of a system determines the freedom of action permitted its members. The concept of interaction, as here developed, enables us to account for group structure, identity, and freedom of action, which are important concepts in a theory of groups.

Performance is defined as any action exhibited by an individual which identifies him as a member of a group. A performance may be an action initiated by a member or a reaction to the action of another member. Each action and each reaction is a performance. The nature or content of an interaction sequence is described in terms of the performances (actions and reactions) involved. The performances of the members, singly or in interaction, accomplish the work of the group and describe the operations of the group. The concept of performance increases our ability to explain group identity. It enables us to describe the nature of interaction. It provides a means of explaining group operations, or group task performance.

Expectation is defined as readiness for reinforcement. It is regarded in this theory as a function of drive, the estimated level of desirability of a possible outcome, and the estimated probability of the outcome. A reinforcing outcome confirms or disconfirms desirability estimates and probability estimates. A reinforcing outcome usually, but not always, reduces drive temporarily. Successive reinforcements increase expectation, but add progressively smaller increments of strength. Inconsistent schedules of reinforcement reduce freedom of action in that they mobilize drive and maintain the organism in a state of constant readiness for the reinforcement of a dominant expectation.

Motivation is regarded as a function of drive and confirmed desirability estimates. The confirmation of desirability estimates determines the value of an outcome in relation to a scale of value or previously confirmed desirability estimate. Secondary reinforcement and generalization account for the development of value systems, which may be regarded as sets of desirability estimates whose confirmation is not dependent upon the confirmation of probability estimates. Value systems provide the individual with stable reference scales for the evaluation and direction of behavior in an environment that exhibits a high degree of uncertainty and unpredictability. The concept of expectation enables us to account for the goal direction and continuity of behavior, as well as for prediction and value.

## Group Structure and Operations

Variance among the members in the initiation of behavior and in response to the initiative of others results in the differentiation of a structure of positions in a group. The mutual confirmation of expectation among the members that comes about in the process of establishing the structure of positions tends to define the contribution of each position to the accomplishment of the group purpose. These expectations, when mutually acknowledged and confirmed, define the function and status of each position in the system. Since function and status are defined in relation to the group purpose, they tend to remain unchanged even though a succession of different persons may occupy a given position.

In order to accomplish the group purpose, it is necessary for the members to act and interact in carrying out the tasks assigned to each position. These performances and interactions describe the operations of the group. Because of the impact of environmental pressures and changing operational requirements, and because of differences between individuals, function and status cannot define in detail the manner in which a member is expected to behave in a group. Successive occupants of the same position are not expected to act alike. The members in interaction develop mutually confirmed expectations relative to the role that each is expected to play as a participant in the changing group operations. A member's role defines the responsibility and authority he is expected to exercise by virtue of the functions and status of his position, the demands made upon him by changing group operations, and the kind of person he is perceived to be. The mutual acknowledgement and confirmation of positions and roles tends to legitimize these systems and to insure their stability. Both role definition and group norms tend to specify a set of sanctions which reward conformity and penalize non-conformity. The continued legitimation of a role depends on the correspondence between the behavior of a member and the specifications and norms pertaining to his role. A member may act in such a manner as to undermine the legitimacy of his role without affecting the legitimacy of the function and status defined for his position. Role conflict occurs when contradictory expectations are made upon the occupant of a position.

Groups are found to develop structures of positions and roles as means of subdividing the group task, controlling group operations, and insuring unity of goal direction. The provision for operations control gives some members greater access to power than is available to others. Conflict within groups tends to center around the legitimation of the uses of power. Power is defined as the differential right to control the reinforcement of expectation.

It is found that the concepts of performance, interaction, and expectation, when used in combination, are able to account for group structure and operations. They are also able to account for group achievement.

## Group Achievement

Achievement is defined as the group outcome resulting from the member inputs, mediated through group structure and operations. The achievement of a group at any stage of its operations may be analyzed in terms of its productivity, morale, and integration. Productivity is defined as the degree of change in expectancy values resulting from group operations. Integration is a measure of capacity to maintain structure and function under stress. Morale is defined as freedom from restraint in action toward a group goal.

The three aspects of achievement are necessarily defined in terms of group capacity. The standards of reference for measuring group achievement involve time and capacity. Productivity measures the extent to which operational capability has been utilized with past performance as a standard of reference. Morale is a measure of the degree to which a group actually utilizes its potentiality for freedom of action at the time of observation. Integration has a future reference, in that it is a measure of capacity to maintain structure and function under conditions of stress.

Because of the fact that the achievement of a group is valued differently by different members as well as by observers who are not members, it is difficult to establish any absolute standards for evaluating different aspects of achievement. Nevertheless, both members and outside observers make evaluative judgments of group achievement and tend to accept such appraisals as valid.

An increase or decrease in inputs permits an increase or decrease in productivity, morale, and integration simultaneously. However, with inputs constant, an increase in productivity is accomplished at some expense to integration. An increase in integration involves some decrease in productivity. Morale is usually, but not always, related positively to productivity. Morale tends to be higher under medium degrees of integration than under extremely high or low degrees of integration.

## Balance and Counterbalance

Membership provides a means for the accomplishment of individual goals while aiding in the achievement of group goals. An organization is usually interested in the creation of specific productivity values which are defined in its declaration of purpose. The end values created by the performances of the members and the operations of the group are accomplished at a cost to the members and to the group. The cost to the members is reckoned in terms of the time and effort they devote to the group, the dues they pay, the illnesses and accidents they suffer in the performance of their duties, the frustrations and disappointments they experience, the freedom of self-determination they surrender, and the subordination of personal loyalties and goals to the welfare of the group. Such factors as these are costs to the members, even though they cannot all be measured in dollars and cents.

The group also must pay a cost of one sort or another for the participation of the members. It must create for the members such values as are necessary to reinforce their expectations. Groups, as collectivities of individuals, generally expect the contributions of the members to be related to the productive purpose of the group. In turn, they expect the members to be content with rewards that may be derived from the accomplishment of the group purpose. If it is the purpose of the group to produce material values, the members are expected to be satisfied with material rewards. In athletic groups the return to the members may be the fun of playing the game or of watching others play it. In religious groups it may be the reinforcement of personal value systems and perhaps the rendering of humanitarian services. In business groups it may be the financial reward for the effort and responsibility invested in task performance. In a social group it may be the pleasure of interaction, mutual stimulation, and emotional support. However, these primary values are not the only ones that the members expect to derive from a group. Some members value the pride that comes with membership in a high prestige organization. Others value the opportunity provided by a group to exercise responsibility and authority and to experience a sense of achievement. Some members value the sense of security provided by a group, while others derive satisfaction from the opportunity for innovation, advancement in status, and the exercise of power. The members of a group may differ widely among themselves depending upon differences in social background, training, and reference group identifications. The meeting of these various expectations takes time and effort which the group might otherwise devote to task performance, and thus represents a cost to the group.

All that is a cost to a member represents an input for the group. Some of the input may not be highly valued, but it will exert an effect someplace in the group. Although inputs that have a high positive or negative value are often recognized, groups as organized entities appear to exhibit little awareness of the total costs paid by their members. Thus, there is usually more invested in a group than is recognized as constituting individual and collective input. Correspondingly, the group creates outputs, such as integration and morale, which are seldom recognized as aspects of achievement.

Performance is regulated to a high degree by operational demands and subgroup norms which may bear no close relationship to the amount, nature, or relevance of the rewards for performance. Group structures, on the other hand, exhibit numerous mechanisms for their mutual reinforcement. Value systems are highly reinforcible. Although work decrement in response to dissatisfaction is to be observed, productive effectiveness may be maintained at high levels despite a state of extreme dissatisfaction among the members. Griping, hostility, absenteeism, accidents, separations, malco-ordination, and other evidences of low group integration are observed instead. It is the structural-functional integrity of the group that is most vulnerable to inadequate or inappropriate reinforcement.

A member tends to judge the outcomes he experiences as satisfying or unsatisfying in reference to his own expectations and in comparison with the outcomes he perceives other members to be experiencing in the group. If he perceives some members to be receiving excessive rewards, he sees the group as potentially able to increase his own rewards as well.

When the members permit the group to accumulate a surplus of values, they realize that this surplus gives the group a degree of power that the members could not exert individually if the surplus were divided equally among them. Therefore, all the members, except perhaps a few who are antagonistic to certain of its goals, are interested in seeing that the group has a sufficient reserve to insure its power to operate and to fulfill its purpose. The greater the extent to which their own welfare is perceived to be dependent upon, and served by, the activities of the group, the greater the interest of the members in the adequate reserve power of the group.

The decision by a group to play a game or perform a task involves much more than the accomplishment of the stated objective. It involves also the differentiation of function and status, a process which places different values on the contributions of the various members. Thus, the basic process of organizing creates a situation which is likely to reward certain members but to disappoint the expectations of certain others. Although this outcome may not be avoidable, the integration of the group may depend upon the extent to which the group sensitizes itself to the expectations of its members and succeeds in satisfying or else restructuring them.

Organization seeks to establish stable structures of expectations relative to interaction, performance, and outcomes. However, the model structure can never anticipate nor represent all the demands that the organization will be required to fulfill. Therefore, it is confronted by two extreme alternatives with a wide range of values in between. It can spend all its energy on the reinforcement of structural integrity, or it can devote all its energies to task achievement. The former solution represents little advantage over the primal group, for it merely formalizes the original struggle for structure in the form of a non-productive ritualism. The latter solution may be expected eventually to jeopardize integration and morale. Therefore, a realistic concern for the survival of the group demands a solution that lies between these two extremes.

In times of crisis, the members may sacrifice most, if not all, of their personal goals for the benefit of the organization. The internal problems of the group are likely to be simplified under these circumstances because it can devote most of its attention to maximizing productive effectiveness. Nevertheless, many groups that do not live under continued crisis, persist in operating under routine conditions as if crisis were ever present. Under continued pressure for productivity when no crisis exists, the members are likely to become wearied and disillusioned. When this occurs, the time has passed for the group to have sensitized itself to the expectations of its members and to its structural integrity and morale.

The real test of the integrity of a group is whether its members will support it in time of crisis. A member's loyalty to a group appears to be determined by some ratio between the personal cost he has to pay to support the group and the magnitude of the discrepancy between his expectations and the outcomes he experiences in the group. When this ratio becomes so unbalanced that the member feels cheaply valued or that his interests are betrayed, he may also feel inclined to let the organization suffer whatever reverses may be in store for it.

The formal organization does, or should, structure the expectations of the members. Correspondingly, it is the responsibility of the formal structure to fulfill the relevant expectations of the members. The integration of a group is founded on its formal structure and on the correspondence between individual goals and group goals. This mutual support is brought about by the clear definition of roles, by the careful structuring of expectations, and by the reinforcement of those expectations.

Not only the group as a system, but the members as individuals, are interested in the primary purpose of the group, its productive achievement. However, the necessity of maintaining operational balance, and the setting of limits upon the personal reward that can be achieved for increased effort tend to counteract the attempts made by the group to increase productivity through the use of various motivating measures. In addition, the subgroups tend to demand uniformity of performance and rewards, and the solution of problems by formula. For example, they may expect promotions to be based on seniority, technical ability, or some other standard formula. A group can hardly hope to devise a formula which will satisfy all the members. It is difficult for the group, even when it realizes the desirability of doing so, to sensitize itself to the expectations of the individual members with the aim of satisfying each in a maximum degree. In fact, the primary concern of the group is for the welfare and accomplishment of the group as a whole rather than for the satisfaction of the individual members, and it tends to reject those members who cannot conform to this concern.

High status members are found to experience a greater degree of personal freedom in the group, to enlarge the area of freedom of other members, and to be more tolerant and supportive of the deviate. Thus, there are some functions which neither the group as a whole nor the various subgroups can perform, but which the members will permit high status members to perform. It now becomes clear why group productivity is related to supervisory leadership rather than to satisfaction with the job or the group as a whole. The group is conservative by nature and necessity. It must maintain balance and control if it is to survive. Productivity among the various subgroups must be equalized in order to prevent a wastage of group resources, and the rewards to peers in the same subgroup must be equalized in order to prevent dissension. The members tend to produce more when they are given freedom to perform and interact in conformity with the demands of their tasks and roles. Excessive degrees of freedom are observed to result in indecision, confusion, and malco-ordination. The desirability of balancing responsibility and authority is more than a trite saying. It is a requirement for effective performance. The high status member provides freedom of action, definition of structure, and co-ordination control.

There are many balancing and counterbalancing factors at work in an organized group. An excess in any one factor may be accomplished at the cost of a deficiency in others. The exercise of a high degree of control over performance and interaction reduces satisfaction and productivity. Granting an optimum degree of freedom of action increases productivity and satisfaction but weakens co-ordination control. Under a maximum degree of freedom, co-ordination breaks down, production is reduced, and satisfaction is lowered. If disproportionate amounts of time and effort are devoted to the structuring and reinforcement of expectations, satisfaction tends to increase, but productivity suffers. On the other hand, if the member expectations relative to status and function, responsibility and authority, recognition and reward are disregarded, satisfaction and loyalty to the organization are depressed.

The subgroups develop norms which tend to regulate performance. On the other hand, the subgroups may exert pressures which induce conformity to the group standards. The subgroups may also provide support which enables members to resist the attempts of internal and external agents to alienate them from the group. It is equally true that an alienated subgroup may make life very difficult for a member who is loyal to the group. In the interests of survival, it is important for the group to structure and satisfy the legitimate expectations of its members. The development of structural integrity under normal operating conditions, even at the expense of productive effectiveness, strengthens the group for times of crisis.

If responsibility and authority are too rigidly structured and controlled, the members suffer a reduction in their freedom of action. Thus, a too rigid role structure may incapacitate the organization for coping with changing environmental demands. However, if roles are not clearly defined, the members may not know what they are expected to do in the way of task performance or interaction with other members. As a result, initiative is lowered, operations become disorganized, and dissatisfaction increases.

In order for an organization to cope with changing conditions, it is necessary that initiative and freedom of decision be permitted at the operative levels where technical problems are encountered first hand. This is true, not only for combat troops in the field, but for civilian organizations as well. Even when the technical details of task performance are strictly prescribed and controlled, there are always situations arising which demand technical knowledge and action on the spot. Lacking freedom to decide and act within his defined area of responsibility, the individual feels frustrated and distrusted in the performance of his task. Given too much freedom, the member may feel confused and inhibited lest he overstep his authority or make decisions which conflict with those made by other members.

Group productivity, as well as morale and integration, are dependent upon structure and control. All aspects of achievement are frustrated when structure is not firmly controlled. All are inhibited when structure is too rigid and operations control is too firm. The maintenance of an optimum balance among the different elements of group achievement requires insightful attention to the problems involved in group structure and operations.

An organized group may be regarded as a complex system of overlapping and interacting input values, structures, operations, and output values. The various elements and subsystems of elements are in constant balance, change, and counterbalance. The theory that we have developed outlines the structure and functioning of a group as a generally conceptualized operating system. Although the theory cannot describe in detail the many specific variations to be found in different groups, it should be of value in specifying the important variables to be considered in analyzing the problems of groups in general.

## Change and Survival

The survival of a group may depend upon the manner in which it responds to the demand for change. The problems created by the demand for change and those resulting from the requirement for stability are not identical. Neither are they entirely contradictory.

We have observed that function and status define the stable relationship of a position to the group purpose. The formal acknowledgment of function and status provides the formal structure of positions with a high degree of legitimation in the expectations of the members. This legitimation is attached to the position and is independent of the behaviors of different occupants of the position. The formal system tends to exhibit a profound degree of stability as long as group purpose remains unchanged.

Whereas function and status are defined in general terms, responsibility and authority are given flexible, detailed definitions which provide for a high degree of adaptation to changing operational demands. The role that a member can play in a group is determined not only by the extent to which his responsibility and authority are acknowledged by himself and others but also by the extent to which others knowingly or unknowingly exercise responsibilities and authority defined for his role or permit him to invade the boundaries of their roles. It is more difficult for a member to establish the legitimacy of his role behavior in a group than it is to establish the legitimacy of his position. A member in a high status position may be granted an enlarged or a restricted role in initiating and controlling group operations, depending on the contribution he is perceived to make to group productivity, morale, and integration. Role performance is expected to change as operations change and as the environment imposes forces which demand adaptation or resistance in order to cope with the problem of change.

An organized group contains structures which are well designed to preserve its stability and other structures which enable it to cope with change. The continued power of a group depends upon its ability to maintain the legitimation of these structures, to utilize them continuously, and to keep them in balance.

Continued change in a group is dependent upon a structure that exhibits stability. A structure that disintegrates under the influence of change cannot continue to change because it no longer exists. At the opposite extreme, a completely rigid structure may collapse under the impact of internal or external stresses. There appears to be a median range within which flexibility and stability optimize the capacity for survival.

Numerous factors operate to complicate the problem of change. The overlapping structures of a group are not easy to perceive. The more clearly defined the structures of a group, the greater the utility of the structures for rational decision and action on the part of all the group members. However, individuals differ in the extent to which they will acknowledge the legitimacy of structure not controlled by themselves or by reference groups with which they identify themselves. Group members also differ in the extent to which they value stability and change. Many persons feel threatened by change. Others appear highly motivated to promote group improvement and growth. Still others seem to thrive on turmoil and confusion. When active proponents of these differing ideologies begin operating in a group, both the group and its individual members have much at stake.

Reactions to proposals for change are likely to differ, depending on the part of the organization affected. Change in the formal structure of a group is likely to be accepted by the members if they perceive the change to be instrumental to more effective group achievement. They are likely to resist change in the formal structure when such change is perceived as a device for reinforcing the power available to individuals who seek to exploit the group. Members are also likely to resist change which results in lowering the status of their positions. A member feels devalued when he loses status in a legitimized status structure.

Changes in the role structure may affect a member's responsibility and authority directly, or indirectly by enlarging or restricting the responsibility and authority of associated roles. A member may welcome a change in role if it gives him a valued responsibility or relieves him of an unwanted burden. He may oppose role change if it takes away a valued responsibility or burdens him with a "dirty job." A member's reactions to marked changes in group operations and operational technologies are likely to be determined by his perception of the impact of the changes on his role.

Members in different status levels tend to react differently to the same proposal for change. Those in low status positions tend to be affected most seriously by change in operational technologies. Those in high status positions are more directly affected by change in formal structure. Changes in the occupancy of high status positions may affect all the members.

The readiness of individuals and subgroups to accept change may depend upon the origin of the proposal. Changes proposed by superiors, peers, subordinates, and outsiders are not viewed alike. Whether or not a proposal is regarded as potentially beneficial to the group or to its members as individuals tends to be determined by the members' perceptions of the motive behind the proposal. Both individuals and subgroups are likely to oppose a change which challenges the legitimacy of their roles, dislodges them from their positions, reduces the value of the outcomes they can experience in the group, imposes unnecessary hardships, or places them at a comparative disadvantage in relation to other individuals or subgroups.

Any effective disparagement of the formal system and the goal values it supports is most damaging to a group. Such action tends to undermine the legitimacy of the organization in the eyes of its members and reduces their capacity to support it as vigorously as they might otherwise do. Actions on the part of a member which cause others to challenge the legitimacy of his role, and power struggles between individuals or factions, are likely to be perceived by most members as threatening to the survival of a group. The direction in which the members throw their support may or may not be related to the objective merits of the issue being contested. Any action they take is likely to be determined by the extent to which the group has served as an effective medium for the reinforcement of their expectations.

We have observed that groups contain within themselves the structures necessary to preserve their stability and to cope with change. Granted a formal structure that is adequate to serve the group purpose, a group can best insure its survival by a continuously sensitive regard for the definition and utilization of its role system in conformity with the norm systems of the group. In concrete terms, this means that each member is permitted to perform near the outer bounds of his role as clearly defined by his responsibility and authority, and in conformity with the norms pertaining to his role. The more responsibly a member is engaged in the solution of operational problems defined for his role, the greater his opportunity to perceive the need for useful change. The more effectively he is involved in the planning and initiation of change, the greater his acceptance of it. The more adequate the authority of a member to carry out the responsibilities in which he is effectively involved, the greater his support of the role system which provides him with these satisfying outcomes. It must be admitted that these observations apply most directly to organizations that start out "right" and keep going that way. They are not necessarily invalid when applied to organizations with a less fortunate history, but they are certainly more difficult to put into effect.

## Applications

A theory need not define an applied technology. However, a useful theory may stimulate the development of a variety of technologies. Although a theory provides a set of concepts and hypotheses that may be used for analytical purposes, neither the theory nor the technologies derived from it can yield a solution to a problem until analytical operations have been performed. This fact is generally understood in regard to the physical sciences. However, a theory in the behavior sciences tends to be regarded as useful only if it provides answers and solutions to practical problems without the necessity of diagnosis and analysis. This misconception of the nature of theory in the social sciences has at times resulted in considerable disillusionment relative to the value of the sciences. In order to avoid the disappointment of expectation, it is necessary to regard a theory, both in the physical and the social sciences, as a systematic method for increasing our understanding rather than as a given solution to all problems that may arise.

The theory presented in this book is based upon, and incorporates, a variety of sub-theories, the validities of which are well documented. The integration accomplished by this system defines related sets of problems for the scientist and for the practitioner. For the scientist, it has shown the need for more clearly defined research on expectation, particularly in regard to the relationships between drive, desirability estimates, and probability estimates. It has suggested a new approach to the design of research on group achievement. It points out the strong need that exists for refinement of methods for measuring morale and integration. The current methods of measuring productivity are far from satisfactory. The set of hypotheses relative to the relationships between productivity, integration, and morale should be subjected to rigorous experimental testing. There is need for research in a wide variety of operating organizations to determine the exact conditions under which various remedial measures may be applied effectively.

Despite its research orientation, the theory here proposed has generated a number of hypotheses which are relevant to the administration of organized groups. These hypotheses challenge the viewpoint that productive effectiveness is the only value with which managerial leadership need concern itself. Group integration and morale are here shown to be achievement values which are equal in importance with productivity. If this theory is confirmed by the results of further systematic research, it will necessitate a new formulation of the basic responsibilities of managerial leadership.

The theory presented does not suggest any ready-made solutions to group problems. However, it defines a set of concepts that may be useful for the diagnosis of problems. Although the theory cannot relieve the members or the leadership of a group from the responsibility for continued analysis of their concrete situations, it can be counted a gain if it sensitizes them to the important factors that need to be considered in their efforts to understand the problems of organization structure, operations, and achievement.

# References

1. Abruzzi, A. *Work, workers and work measurement.* New York: Columbia University Press, 1956.
2. Adams, S. Status congruency as a variable in small group performance. *Soc. Forces,* 1953, *32,* 16–22.
3. Adorno, T. W., Frenkel-Brunswick, Else, Levinson, D. J., and Sanford, R. N. *The authoritarian personality.* New York: Harper, 1950.
4. Allee, W. C., et al. *Principles of animal ecology.* Philadelphia: Saunders, 1949.
5. Allee, W. C. *Cooperation among animals, with human implications.* New York: Henry Schuman, 1951.
6. Allen, R. G. D. *Mathematical economics.* London: Macmillan, 1957.
7. Allport, G. W. The nature of democratic morale. In G. Watson, *Civilian morale.* Boston: Houghton Mifflin, 1942.
8. American Management Association. *The union's role in production management.* New York: American Management Association, 1950.
9. Ammons, R. B. Effects of knowledge of performance: a survey and tentative theoretical formulation. *J. gen. Psychol.,* 1956, *54,* 279–99.
10. Anderson, E. H. and Schwenning, G. T. *The science of production organization.* New York: Wiley, 1938.
11. Anderson, H. H. and Brandt, H. F. A study of motivation, involving self-announced goals of fifth-grade children and the concept of the level of aspiration. *J. soc. Psychol.,* 1939, *10,* 209–32.
12. Arensberg, C. M., et al. *Research in industrial human relations: a critical appraisal.* New York: Harper, 1957.
13. Arensberg, C. M. and McGregor, D. Determination of morale in an industrial company. *Appl. Anthrop.,* 1942, *1* (2), 12–34.
14. Argyle, M. Social pressure in public and private situations. *J. abnorm. soc. Psychol.,* 1957, *54,* 172–5.

15. Argyris, C. The individual and organization: some problems of mutual adjustment. *Admin. Sci. Quar.*, 1957, 2, 1–24.
16. Arrington, Ruth E. Time sampling in studies of social behavior: a critical review of techniques and results with research suggestions. *Psychol. Bull.*, 1943, 40, 81–124.
17. Arrow, K. J. *Social choice and individual values.* New York: Wiley, 1951.
18. Artin, E. *Modern higher algebra: Galois theory.* New York: New York University, Inst. Mathematics and Mechanics, 1947. Mimeo.
19. Asch, S. E. *Social psychology.* New York: Prentice-Hall, 1952.
20. Atkinson, J. W. and Reitman, W. R. Performance as a function of motive strength and expectancy of goal-attainment. *J. abnorm. soc. Psychol.*, 1956, 53, 361–6.
21. Atkinson, J. W. and Walker, E. L. The affiliation motive and perceptual sensitivity to faces. *J. abnorm. soc. Psychol.*, 1956, 53, 38–41.
22. Back, K. W. Influence through social communication. *J. abnorm. soc. Psychol.*, 1951, 46, 9–23.
23. Baehr, Melany E. A factorial study of the SRA Employee Inventory. *Personnel Psychol.*, 1954, 7, 319–36.
24. Baker, Helen and France, R. R. *Centralization and decentralization in industrial relations.* Princeton: Princeton University, Industrial Relat. Section, 1954.
25. Bakke, E. W. *Bonds of organization; an appraisal of corporate human relations.* New York: Harper, 1950.
26. Bakke, E. W. *The fusion process.* New Haven: Yale University, Labor and Management Center, 1953.
27. Balderson, C. C. *Group incentives.* Philadelphia: University of Pennsylvania Press, 1930.
28. Bales, R. F. *Interaction process analysis; a method for the study of small groups.* Cambridge: Addison-Wesley, 1950.
29. Bales, R. F. and Borgatta, E. F. Size of group as a factor in the interaction profile. In P. Hare, E. F. Borgatta, and R. F. Bales, *Small groups.* New York: Knopf, 1955.
30. Bales, R. F. and Strodtbeck, F. L. Phases in group problem-solving. *J. abnorm soc. Psychol.*, 1951, 46, 485–95.
31. Bales, R. F., Strodtbeck, F. L., Mills, T. M., and Roseborough, Mary E. Channels of communication in groups. *Amer. sociol. Rev.*, 1951. 16, 461–8.
32. Barker, R. G. The social interrelations of strangers and acquaintances. *Sociometry*, 1942, 5, 169–79.
33. Barkin, S. Management's attitude toward wage incentive systems. *Indus. lab. relat. Rev.*, 1951, 5, 92–107.

34. Barnard, C. I. *The functions of the executive.* Cambridge: Harvard University Press, 1938.

35. Barnard, C. I. *Organization and management.* Cambridge: Harvard University Press, 1948.

36. Barnard, C. I. Functions and pathology of status systems in formal organizations. In W. F. Whyte, *Industry and society.* New York: McGraw-Hill, 1946.

37. Barnes, R. M. *Work measurement manual.* Dubuque, Iowa: W. C. Brown, 1951.

38. Bass, B. M. Feelings of pleasantness and work group efficiency. *Personnel Psychol.,* 1954, *7,* 81–91.

39. Bass, B. M. *Behavior in groups.* II. *Increased attraction to the group as a function of individual and group goal attainment.* Baton Rouge: Louisiana State University, unpublished report, 1955.

40. Bass, B. M. *Behavior in groups.* III. *Consistent differences in the objectively measured performance of members and groups.* Baton Rouge: Louisiana State University, unpublished report, 1955.

41. Bass, B. M. *Behavior in groups.* IV. *Interrelations among measurements of member and group performance.* Baton Rouge: Louisiana State University, unpublished report, 1955.

42. Bass, B. M. Authoritarianism or acquiescence? *J. abnorm. soc. Psychol.,* 1955, *51,* 616–23.

43. Bass, B. M. Development and evaluation of a scale for measuring social acquiescence. *J. abnorm. soc. Psychol.,* 1956, *53,* 296–9.

44. Bass, B. M., Pryer, Margaret W., Gaier, E. L., and Flint, A. W. Interacting effects of control, motivation, group practice, and problem difficulty on attempted leadership. *J. abnorm. soc. Psychol.,* 1958, *56,* 352–8.

45. Bass, B. M. and Norton, Fay-Tyler M. Group size and leaderless discussions. *J. appl. Psychol.,* 1951, *35,* 397–400.

46. Bates, A. P. and Cloyd, J. S. Toward the development of operations for defining group norms and member roles. *Sociometry,* 1956, *19,* 26–39.

47. Bates, F. L. Position, role, and status: a reformulation of concepts. *Soc. Forces,* 1956, *34,* 313–21.

48. Baumback, C. M. *Incentive wage problems in collective bargaining and in arbitration.* Iowa City: State University of Iowa, Bur. Labor and Mgmt. Res. Series No. 14, 1956.

49. Baumgartel, H. *The survey feedback experiment.* Ann Arbor: University of Michigan, Survey Research Center, 1953. Mimeo.

50. Bavelas, A. A mathematical model for group structures. *Appl. Anthrop.*, 1948, 7, 16–30.

51. Bavelas, A. Some problems of organizational change. *J. soc. Issues*, 1948, 4 (3), 48–52.

52. Bavelas, A. Communication patterns in task oriented groups. *J. accoustical Soc. Amer.*, 1950, 22, 725–30.

53. Belcher, D. W. *Wage and salary administration.* Englewood Cliffs: Prentice-Hall, 1956.

54. Bendix, R. and Lipset, S. M. *Class, status and power: a reader in social stratification.* Glencoe: Free Press, 1953.

55. Benge, E. J. and Copell, D. F. Employee morale survey. *Modern Mgmt.*, 1947, 7, 19–22.

56. Benne, K. D. and Sheats, P. Functional roles of group members. *J. soc. Issues*, 1948, 4 (2), 41–9.

57. Bennett, Edith B. Discussion, decision, committment, and consensus in group decision. *Hum. Relat.*, 1955, 8, 251–73.

58. Bennett, J. W. and Tumin, M. M. *Social life: structure and function.* New York: Knopf, 1948.

59. Berg, J. Cooperation without communication and observation. *J. soc. Psychol.*, 1955, 41, 287–96.

60. Berkowitz, L. Group standards, cohesiveness, and productivity. *Hum. Relat.*, 1954, 7, 509–19.

61. Berkowitz, L. Group norms among bomber crews: patterns of perceived crew attitudes, "actual" crew attitudes, and crew liking related to air crew effectiveness in Far Eastern combat. *Sociometry*, 1956, 19, 141–53.

62. Berkowitz, L. Effects of perceived dependency relationships upon conformity to group expectations. *J. abnorm. soc. Psychol.*, 1957, 55, 350–54.

63. Berkowitz, L. and Levy, B. I. Pride in group performance and group-task motivation. *J. abnorm. soc. Psychol.*, 1956, 53, 300–306.

64. Bernberg, R. E. Socio-psychological factors in industrial morale: I. The prediction of specific indicators. *J. soc. Psychol.*, 1952, 36, 73–82.

65. Bettelheim, B., Janowitz, M., and Shils, E. A. A study of the social, economic, and psychological correlates of intolerance among urban veterans of enlisted rank. *Amer. Psychol.*, 1947, 2, 323.

66. Bion, W. R. Experiences in groups. *Hum. Relat.*, 1948, 1, 314–20, 487–96.

67. Blake, R. R., Mouton, Jane S., and Fruchter, B. The consistency of interpersonal behavior judgments made on the basis of short-

term interactions in three-man groups. *J. abnorm. soc. Psychol.*, 1954, *49*, 573–8.

68. Blake, R. R., Helson, H., and Mouton, Jane S. The generality of conformity behavior as a function of factual anchorage, difficulty of task, and amount of social pressure. *J. Pers.*, 1957, *25*, 294–305.

69. Blau, P. M. Cooperation and competition in a bureaucracy. *Amer. J. Sociol.*, 1954, *59*, 530–35.

70. Blau, P. M. *The dynamics of bureacracy.* Chicago: University of Chicago Press, 1955.

71. Blau, P. M. *Bureaucracy in modern society.* New York: Random House, 1956.

72. Blum, M. L. and Russ, J. J. A study of employee attitude toward various incentives. *Personnel*, 1942, *19*, 438–44.

73. Blum, R. *The study of groups.* Washington, D. C.: George Washington University, Human Resources Research Office, 1953. Mimeo.

74. Borgatta, E. F. Analysis of social interaction: actual, role playing, and projective. *J. abnorm. soc. Psychol.*, 1955, *51*, 394–405.

75. Borgatta, E. F. and Bales, R. F. Task and accumulation of experience as factors in the interaction of small groups. *Sociometry*, 1953, *16*, 239–52.

76. Borgatta, E. F. and Bales, R. F. Interaction of individuals in reconstituted groups. *Sociometry*, 1953, *16*, 302–20.

77. Borgatta, E. F. and Bales, R. F. Sociometric status patterns and characteristics of interaction. *J. soc. Psychol.*, 1956, *43*, 289–97.

78. Borgatta, E. F., Bales, R. F., and Couch, A. S. Some findings on the great man theory of leadership. *Amer. sociol. Rev.*, 1954, *19*, 755–9.

79. Borgatta, E. F. and Cottrell, L. S. On the classification of groups. In J. L. Moreno, *Sociometry and the science of man.* New York: Beacon House, 1956.

80. Borgatta, E. F., Cottrell, L. S., and Meyer, H. J. On the dimensions of group behavior. *Sociometry*, 1956, *19*, 223–40.

81. Bovard, E. W., Jr. Conformity to social norms and attraction to the group. *Science*, 1953, *118*, 598–9.

82. Bowman, Mary Jean. The conference on research on expectations, uncertainty, and business behavior. *Soc. Science Res. Council Items*, 1956, *10*, 32–7.

83. Brayfield, A. H. and Crockett, W. H. Employee attitudes and employee performance. *Psychol. Bull.*, 1955, *52*, 396–424.

84. Brim, O. G., Jr. and Hoff, D. B. Individual and situational differences in desire for certainty. *J. abnorm. soc. Psychol.*, 1957, *54*, 225–9.

85. Brodbeck, May. The role of small groups in mediating the effects of propaganda. *J. abnorm. soc. Psychol.*, 1956, 52, 166–70.

86. Bronfenbrenner, U. The measurement of sociometric status, structure and development. *Sociometry Monogr.*, 1945, No. 6.

87. Brooks, E. What successful executives do. *Personnel*, 1955, 32, 210–25.

88. Brown, E. J. Informal participation of active and inactive formal participants. *Rural Sociol.*, 1954, 19, 365–70.

89. Brown, R. W. A determination of the relationship between rigidity and authoritarianism. *J. abnorm. soc. Psychol.*, 1953, 48, 469–76.

90. Browne, C. G. Study of executive leadership in business. I. The R, A, and D scales. *J. appl. Psychol.*, 1949, 33, 521–6.

91. Browne, C. G. Study of executive leadership in business. II. Social group patterns. *J. appl. Psychol.*, 1950, 34, 12–15.

92. Bruner, J. S. Personality dynamics and the process of perceiving. In R. R. Blake and G. V. Ramsey, *Perception: an approach to personality*. New York: Ronald Press, 1951.

93. Bruner, J. S., Goodnow, J. J., and Austin, G. A. *A study of thinking*. New York: Wiley, 1956.

94. Bruner, J. S. and Postman, L. Symbolic value as an organizing factor in perception. *J. soc. Psychol.*, 1948, 27, 203–8.

95. Bruner, J. S., Postman, L., and Rodrigues, J. Expectation and the perception of color. *Amer. J. Psychol.*, 1951, 64, 216–27.

96. Bullock, R. P. *Social factors related to job satisfaction*. Columbus: Ohio State University, Bur. Business Research Monogr. No. 70, 1952.

97. Burns, R. Employee morale — its meaning and measurement. In L. R. Tripp, *Proceedings Fourth Annual Meeting*. Madison: Industrial Relations Research Association, 1951.

98. Burnside, W. *Theory of groups of finite order*. Cambridge: Cambridge University Press, 1911.

99. Burtt, H. E. *Applied psychology*. New York: Prentice-Hall, 1957.

100. Butler, R. A. and Harlow, H. F. Discrimination learning and learning sets to visual exploration incentives. *J. gen. Psychol.*, 1957, 57, 257–64.

101. Campbell, D. T. *Leadership and its effect upon the group*. Columbus: Ohio State University, Bur. Business Research Monogr. No. 83, 1956.

102. Campbell, J. W. An attitude survey in a typical manufacturing firm. *Personnel Psychol.*, 1948, 1, 31–9.

103. Cannons, H. G. T. *Bibliography of industrial efficiency and management*. London: Routledge, 1920.

104. Cantril, H. The prediction of social events. *J. abnorm. soc. Psychol.*, 1938, 33, 364–89.

105. Caplow, T. *The sociology of work.* Minneapolis: University of Minnesota Press, 1954.
106. Caplow, T. A theory of coalitions in the triad. *Amer. sociol. Rev.*, 1956, *21*, 489–93.
107. Carlson, S. *Executive behavior.* Stockholm: Strombergs, 1951.
108. Carmichael, R. *Introduction to the theory of groups of finite order.* New York: Dover, 1956.
109. Carter, L. F. Evaluating the performance of individuals as members of small groups. *Personnel Psychol.*, 1954, *7*, 477–84.
110. Carter, L. F., Haythorn, W., Meirowitz, B., and Lanzetta, J. The relation of categorizations and ratings in the observation of group behavior. *Hum. Relat.*, 1951, *4*, 239–54.
111. Carter, L. F. and Nixon, Mary. An investigation of the relationship between four criteria of leadership ability for three different tasks. *J. Psychol.*, 1949, *27*, 245–61.
112. Cartwright, D. The effect of interruption, completion and failure upon the attractiveness of activities. *J. exp. Psychol.*, 1942, *31*, 1–16.
113. Cartwright, D. Achieving change in people: some applications of group dynamics theory. *Hum. Relat.*, 1951, *4*, 381–92.
114. Cartwright, D. and Zander, A. *Group dynamics: research and theory.* Evanston: Row, Peterson, 1953.
115. Castaneda, A. *A systematic investigation of the concept of expectancy as conceived within Rotter's "Social Learning Theory of Personality."* Columbus: Ohio State University, Doctor's dissertation, 1952.
116. Cattell, R. B. Concepts and methods in the measurement of group syntality. *Psychol. Rev.*, 1948, *55*, 48–63.
117. Cattell, R. B., Saunders, D. R., and Stice, G. F. The dimensions of syntality in small groups. *Hum. Relat.*, 1953, *6*, 331–56.
118. Cattell, R. B. and Stice, G. F. *The psychodynamics of small groups.* Urbana: University of Illinois, Lab. Personality Assessment and Group Behavior, 1953. Mimeo.
119. Cattell, R. B. and Wispé, L. G. The dimensions of syntality in small groups. *J. soc. Psychol.*, 1948, *28*, 57–78.
120. Centers, R. Motivational aspects of occupational stratification. *J. soc. Psychol.*, 1948, *28*, 187–217.
121. Centers, R. *The psychology of social classes.* Princeton: Princeton University Press, 1949.
122. Centers, R. and Cantril, H. Income satisfaction and income aspiration. *J. abnorm. soc. Psychol.*, 1946, *41*, 64–9.
123. Cervin, V. Experimental investigation of behavior in social situations: I. Behavior under opposition. *Canad. J. Psychol.*, 1955, *9*, 107–16.

124. Cervin, V. Experimental investigation of behavior in social situations: II. Individual behavior effects of change in group attitude from opposition to co-operation. *Canad. J. Psychol.*, 1955, 9, 155–60.

125. Cervin, V. and Ketchum, J. D. Experimental investigation of behavior in social situations: III. Behavior under frustration. *Canad. J. Psychol.*, 1956, 10, 23–30.

126. Chamberlain, N. W. *The union challenge to management control.* New York: Harper, 1948.

127. Chamberlain, N. W., Pierson, F. C., and Wolfson, Theresa. *A decade of industrial relations research: 1946–1956.* New York: Harper, 1958.

128. Chant, S. N. F. Measuring the factors that make a job interesting. *Personnel J.*, 1932, 11, 1–4.

129. Chapin, F. S. A three-dimensional model for visual analysis of group structure. *Soc. Forces*, 1952, 31, 20–25.

130. Chapin, F. S. and Tsouderos, J. E. Formalization observed in ten voluntary associations: concepts, morphology, process. *Soc. Forces*, 1955, 33, 306–309.

131. Chapin, F. S. and Tsouderos, J. E. The formalization process in voluntary associations. *Soc. Forces*, 1956, 34, 342–44.

132. Chapman, D. W. and Volkman, J. A. A social determinant of the level of aspiration. *J. abnorm. soc. Psychol.*, 1939, 34, 225–38.

133. Chapman, L. J. and Campbell, D. T. Response set in the F scale. *J. abnorm. soc. Psychol.*, 1957, 54, 129–32.

134. Chapman, L. J. and Campbell, D. T. An attempt to predict the performance of three-man teams from attitude measures. *J. soc. Psychol.*, 1957, 46, 277–86.

135. Chapple, E. D. The interaction chronograph: its evolution and present application. *Personnel*, 1949, 25, 295–307.

136. Chapple, E. D. and Donald, G., Jr. A method of evaluating supervisory personnel. *Harvard bus. Rev.*, 1946, 24, 197–214.

137. Child, I. L. Morale: a bibliographical review. *Psychol. Bull.*, 1941, 38, 393–420.

138. Christie, R. Authoritarianism re-examined. In R. Christie and M. Jahoda, *Studies in the scope and method of "The Authoritarian Personality."* Glencoe: Free Press, 1954.

139. Church, A. H. *The science and practice of management.* New York: Engineering Magazine Co., 1914.

140. Churchman, C. W., Ackoff, R. L., and Arnoff, E. L. *Introduction to operations research.* New York: Wiley, 1957.

141. Clark, B. R. Organizational adaptation and precarious values: a case study. *Amer. sociol. Rev.*, 1956, 21, 327–36.

142. Clark, R. A. Analyzing the group structure of combat rifle squads. *Amer. Psychol.*, 1953, *8*, 333.

143. Cleland, S. *The influence of plant size on industrial relations.* Princeton: Princeton University, Industrial Relations Section, 1955.

144. Coch, L. and French, J. R. P., Jr. Overcoming resistance to change. *Hum. Relat.*, 1948, *1*, 512–32.

145. Coffin, T. E. Some conditions of suggestion and suggestibility: a study of some attitudinal and situational factors influencing the process of suggestion. *Psychol. Monogr.*, 1941, No. 241.

146. Cohen, A. R. The effects of individual self-esteem and situational structure on threat-oriented reactions to power. *Dissertation Abstr.*, 1954, *14*, 727–8.

147. Cohen, A. R. Experimental effects of ego-defense preference on interpersonal relations. *J. abnorm. soc. Psychol.*, 1956, *52*, 19–27.

148. Cohen, E. Stimulus conditions as factors in social change. *Amer. Psychol.*, 1956, *11*, 407.

149. Cohen, J. and Hansel, M. *Risk and gambling: a study of subjective probability.* New York: Philosophical Library, 1956.

150. Cohn, T. S. The relation of the F scale to a response set to answer positively. *J. soc. Psychol.*, 1956, *44*, 129–33.

151. Comrey, A. L. Group performance in a manual dexterity task. *J. appl. Psychol.*, 1953, *37*, 207–10.

152. Comrey, A. L., Pfiffner, J. M., and Beem, Helen P. Factors influencing organizational effectiveness. I. The U. S. Forest Survey. *Personnel Psychol.*, 1952, *5*, 307–28.

153. Comrey, A. L. and Staats, C. K. Group performance in a cognitive task. *J. appl. Psychol.*, 1955, *39*, 354–6.

154. Conklin, E. H. *A multiple factor analysis of morale data from small ships.* Ohio State University, Master's thesis, 1950.

155. Cooley, C. H. *Social organization.* New York: Scribners, 1909.

156. Copeland, M. T. *The executive at work.* Cambridge: Harvard University Press, 1952.

157. Cornell, W. B. *Organization and management.* New York: Ronald Press, 1936.

158. Coutu, W. Role-playing vs. role-taking: an appeal for clarification. *Amer. sociol. Rev.*, 1951, *16*, 180–87.

159. Cowles, J. T. and Nissen, H. W. Reward expectancy in delayed responses of chimpanzees. *J. compar. Psychol.*, 1937, *24*, 345–58.

160. Craig, P. G. Remarks on the measurement of productivity. Unpublished communication, 1957.

161. Crandall, V. J., Solomon, D., and Kellaway, R. The value of anticipated events as a determinant of expectancy learning and extinction. *Amer. Psychol.*, 1955, *10*, 466.

162. Creamer, D. *Personal income during business cycles.* Princeton: Princeton University Press, 1956.
163. Crespi, L. P. Quantitative variation of incentive and performance in the white rat. *Amer. J. Psychol.*, 1942, 55, 467–517.
164. Criswell, Joan H. The measurement of group integration. *Sociometry*, 1947, 10, 259–67.
165. Crow, W. J. and Hammond, K. R. The generality of accuracy and response sets in interpersonal perception. *J. abnorm. soc. Psychol.*, 1957, 54, 384–90.
166. Dale, E. *Greater productivity through labor-management cooperation; analysis of company and union experience.* New York: American Management Association, 1949.
167. Dale, E. Centralization versus decentralization. *Advanced Management*, 1955, 20, 11–16.
168. Darley, J. G., Gross, N., and Martin, W. E. Studies of group behavior: stability, change and interrelations of psychometric and sociometric variables. *J. abnorm. soc. Psychol.*, 1951, 46, 564–76.
169. Darley, J. G., Gross, N., and Martin, W. E. Studies of group behavior: factors associated with the productivity of groups. *J. appl. Psychol.*, 1952, 36, 396–403.
170. Davids, A. Some personality and intellectual correlates of intolerance of ambiguity. *J. abnorm. soc. Psychol.*, 1955, 51, 415–20.
171. Davis, A. *Social-class influences upon learning.* Cambridge: Harvard University Press, 1948.
172. Davis, H. S. *Productivity accounting.* Philadelphia: University of Pennsylvania Press, 1955.
173. Davis, K. *Human society.* New York: Macmillan, 1949.
174. Davis, R. C. *The influence of the unit of supervision and span of executive control on the economy of line organization structure.* Columbus: Ohio State University, Bur. Business Research Monogr. No. 26, 1941.
175. Davis, R. C. *Industrial organization and management.* New York: Harper, 1957.
176. Deutsch, M. A theory of cooperation and competition. *Hum. Relat.*, 1949, 2, 129–52.
177. Deutsch, M. An experimental study of the effects of cooperation and competition upon group process. *Hum. Relat.*, 1949, 2, 199–232.
178. Dickinson, Z. C. *Compensating industrial effort.* New York: Ronald Press, 1937.
179. Diemer, H. *Factory organization and administration.* New York: McGraw-Hill, 1910.

180. Dittes, J. E. and Kelley, H. H. Effects of different conditions of acceptance upon conformity to group norms. *J. abnorm. soc. Psychol.*, 1956, *53*, 100–107.

181. Dodd, S. C. *Dimensions of society.* New York: Macmillan, 1942.

182. Dodd, S. C. Sociomatrices and levels of interaction for dealing with plurals, groups and organizations. *Sociometry*, 1951, *14*, 237–48.

183. Dreyer, A. S. Aspiration behavior as influenced by expectation and group comparison. *Hum. Relat.*, 1954, *7*, 175–90.

184. Drury, H. B. *Scientific management: a history and criticism.* New York: Longmans, Green, 1918.

185. Dubin, R. Power and union-management relations. *Admin. Sci. Quar.*, 1957, *2*, 60–81.

186. Durkheim, E. *The division of labor in society.* (Trans. by G. Simpson). Glencoe: Free Press, 1947.

187. Durkheim, E. *Suicide: a study in sociology.* (Trans. by G. Simpson). Glencoe: Free Press, 1951.

188. Edwards, A. L. *The social desirability variable in personality assessment and research.* New York: Dryden Press, 1957.

189. Edwards, W. Probability preferences in gambling behavior. *Amer. J. Psychol.*, 1953, *66*, 349–64.

190. Eisenstadt, S. N. Studies in reference group behavior: 1. Reference norms and the social structure. *Hum. Relat.*, 1954, *7*, 191–216.

191. Escalona, Sybille K. The effect of success and failure upon the level of aspiration and behavior in manic-depressive psychoses. *Univ. of Iowa, Stud. Child Welf.*, 1940, *16*, 199–307.

192. Estes, W. K. An experimental study of punishment. *Psychol. Monogr.*, 1944, No. 263.

193. Estes, W. K. Of models and men. *Amer. Psychol.*, 1957, *12*, 609–17.

194. Exline, R. V. Group climate as a factor in the relevance and accuracy of social perception. *J. abnorm. soc. Psychol.*, 1957, *55*, 382–8.

195. Fenchel, G. H., Monderer, J. H., and Hartley, E. L. Subjective status and the equilibration hypothesis. *J. abnorm. soc. Psychol.*, 1951, *46*, 476–9.

196. Fensterheim, H. and Tresselt, M. E. The influence of value systems on the perception of people. *J. abnorm. soc. Psychol.*, 1953, *48*, 93–8.

197. Festinger, L. Wish, expectation and group standards as factors influencing level of aspiration. *J. abnorm. soc. Psychol.*, 1942, *37*, 184–200.

198. Festinger, L. The analysis of sociograms using matrix algebra. *Hum. Relat.*, 1949, 2, 153–8.

199. Festinger, L. Informal social communication. *Psychol. Rev.*, 1950, 57, 271–82.

200. Festinger, L. A theory of social comparison processes. *Hum. Relat.*, 1954, 7, 117–40.

201. Festinger, L. *A theory of cognitive dissonance.* Evanston: Row, Peterson, 1957.

202. Festinger, L., Gerard, H. B., Hymovitch, B., Kelley, H. H., and Raven, B. The influence process in the presence of extreme deviates. *Hum. Relat.*, 1952, 5, 327–46.

203. Festinger, L. and Hutte, H. A. An experimental investigation of the effect of unstable interpersonal relations in a group. *J. abnorm. soc. Psychol.*, 1954, 49, 513–22.

204. Festinger, L., Pepitone, A., and Newcomb, T. Some consequences of de-individuation in a group. *J. abnorm. soc. Psychol.*, 1952, 47, 382–9.

205. Festinger, L. and Thibaut, J. Interpersonal communication in small groups. *J. abnorm. soc. Psychol.*, 1951, 46, 92–9.

206. Festinger, L., Torrey, Jane, and Willerman, B. Self-evaluation as a function of attraction to the group. *Hum. Relat.*, 1954, 7, 161–74.

207. Fiedler, F. E. Assumed similarity measures as predictors of team effectiveness. *J. abnorm. soc. Psychol.*, 1954, 49, 381–8.

208. Fiedler, F. E., Warrington, W. G., and Blaisdell, F. J. Unconscious attitudes as correlates of sociometric choice in a group. *J. abnorm. soc. Psychol.*, 1952, 47, 790–96.

209. Filer, R. J. Frustration, satisfaction, and other factors affecting the attractiveness of goal objects. *J. abnorm. soc. Psychol.*, 1952, 47, 203–12.

210. Filipetti, G. *Industrial management in transition.* Homewood, Ill.: Richard D. Irwin, 1953.

211. Fine, S. A. and Heinz, C. A. The estimates of worker trait requirements for 4,000 jobs. *Person. guid. J.*, 1957, 36, 168–74.

212. Firey, W. Informal organization and the theory of schism. *Amer. sociol. Rev.*, 1948, 13, 15–24.

213. Fiske, D. W. Values, theory, and the criterion problem. *Personnel Psychol.*, 1951, 4, 93–8.

214. Flanagan, J. C. Critical requirements: a new approach to employee evaluation. *Personnel Psychol.*, 1949, 2, 419–25.

215. Fleishman, E. A. Testing for psychomotor abilities by means of apparatus tests. *Psychol. Bull.*, 1953, 50, 241–62.

216. Fleishman, E. A. Differences between military and industrial organizations. In R. M. Stogdill and C. L. Shartle, *Patterns of ad-*

*ministrative performance.* Columbus: Ohio State University, Bur. Business Research Monogr. No. 81, 1956.

217. Fleishman, E. A. and Hempel, W. E. A factor analysis of dexterity tests. *Personnel Psychol.,* 1954, 7, 15–32.

218. Florence, Edwiges de C. *The construction of a forced-choice technique for the evaluation of college students' goals.* Columbus: Ohio State University, Doctoral dissertation, 1956.

219. Forsyth, E. and Katz, L. A matrix approach to the analysis of sociometric data: a preliminary report. *Sociometry,* 1946, 9, 340–47.

220. Fouriezos, N., Hutt, M., and Guetzkow, H. Measurement of self-oriented needs in discussion groups. *J. abnorm. soc. Psychol.,* 1950, 45, 682–90.

221. Frank, J. D. Recent studies of the level of aspiration. *Psychol. Bull.,* 1941, 38, 218–26.

222. French, Elizabeth G. Motivation as a variable in work-partner selection. *J. abnorm. soc. Psychol.,* 1956, 53, 96–9.

223. French, Elizabeth G. and Chadwick, I. Some characteristics of affiliation motivation. *J. abnorm. soc. Psychol.,* 1956, 52, 296–300.

224. French, J. R. P., Jr. The disruption and cohesion of groups. *J. abnorm. soc. Psychol.,* 1941, 36, 361–77.

225. French, J. R. P., Jr. Organized and unorganized groups under fear and frustration. *Univ. of Iowa, Stud. Child Welf.,* 1944, 20, 231–308.

226. French, J. R. P., Jr. Field experiments: changing group productivity. In J. G. Miller, *Experiments in social process.* New York: McGraw-Hill, 1950.

227. French, J. R. P., Jr. A formal theory of social power. *Psychol. Rev.,* 1956, 63, 181–94.

228. French, R. L. Morale and leadership. In *Human factors in undersea warfare.* Washington: National Research Council, 1949.

229. French, J. W. *The description of aptitude and achievement tests in terms of related factors.* Chicago: University of Chicago, Psychometr. Monogr. No. 5, 1951.

230. Frenkel-Brunswick, Else. Further exploration by a contributor to "The Authoritarian Personality." In R. Christie and M. Jahoda, *Studies in the scope and method of "The Authoritarian Personality."* Glencoe: Free Press, 1954.

231. Frenkel-Brunswick, Else. Social research and the problem of values: a reply. *J. abnorm. soc. Psychol.,* 1954, 49, 466–71.

232. Friend, Jeannette G. and Haggard, E. A. Work adjustment in relation to family background. *Appl. Psychol. Monogr.,* 1948, No. 16.

233. Fryer, D. *The measurement of interests in relation to human adjustment.* New York: Holt, 1931.
234. Gardner, B. B. and Whyte, W. F. The man in the middle. *Appl. Anthropol.*, 1945, *4* (2), 1–28.
235. Gardner, E. F. and Thompson, G. G. *Social relations and morale in small groups.* New York: Appleton-Century-Crofts, 1956.
236. Gaus, J. M. *Reflections on public administration.* University, Alabama: University of Alabama Press, 1947.
237. Gebhard, Mildred E. Changes in the attractiveness of activities: the effect of expectation preceding performance. *J. exp. Psychol.*, 1949, *39*, 404–13.
238. Gebhard, Mildred E. The effect of success and failure upon the attractiveness of activities as a function of experience, expectation and need. *J. exp. Psychol.*, 1948, *38*, 371–8.
239. Georgopoulos, B. S., Mahoney, G. M., and Jones, N. W. A path-goal approach to productivity. *J. appl. Psychol.*, 1957, *41*, 345–53.
240. Gerard, H. B. The effect of different dimensions of disagreement on the communication process in small groups. *Hum. Relat.*, 1953, *6*, 249–71.
241. Gerard, H. B. The anchorage of opinions in face-to-face groups. *Hum. Relat.*, 1954, *7*, 313–25.
242. Gerard, H. B. Some factors affecting an individual's estimate of his probable success in a group situation. *J. abnorm. soc. Psychol.*, 1956, *52*, 235–9.
243. Getzels, J. W. and Guba, E. G. Role, role conflict, and effectiveness: an empirical study. *Amer. sociol. Rev.*, 1954, *19*, 164–75.
244. Ghiselli, E. E. and Brown, C. W. *Personnel and industrial psychology.* New York: McGraw-Hill, 1955.
245. Gibb, C. A. Leadership. In G. Lindzey, *Handbook of social psychology.* Cambridge: Addison-Wesley, 1954.
246. Gibb, J. R. The effects of group size and of threat reduction upon creativity in a problem-solving situation. *Amer. Psychol.*, 1951, *6*, 324.
247. Gibb, J. R., Platts, Grace N., and Miller, Lorraine F. *Dynamics of participative groups.* St. Louis: Swift, 1951.
248. Gibson, J. J. *The perception of the visual world.* Boston: Houghton Mifflin, 1950.
249. Gilbert, G. M. *The psychology of dictatorship; based on an examination of the leaders of Nazi Germany.* New York: Ronald Press, 1950.
250. Gilbreth, F. B. and Gilbreth, Lillian M. *Applied motion study.* New York: Macmillan, 1919.

251. Gilchrist, J. C. The formation of social groups under conditions of success and failure. *J. abnorm. soc. Psychol.*, 1952, *47*, 174–87.

252. Gilchrist, J. C., Ludeman, J. F., and Lysak, W. Values as determinants of word-recognition thresholds. *J. abnorm. soc. Psychol.*, 1954, *49*, 423–6.

253. Ginzberg, E. and Reilley, E. W. *Effecting change in large organizations.* New York: Columbia University Press, 1957.

254. Gold, B. *Foundations of productivity analysis.* Pittsburgh: University of Pittsburgh Press, 1955.

255. Goldberg, S. C. Three situational determinants of conformity to social norms. *J. abnorm. soc. Psychol.*, 1954, *49*, 325–9.

256. Golden, C. S. and Ruttenberg, H. J. *The dynamics of industrial democracy.* New York: Harper, 1942.

257. Goode, W. J. and Fowler, I. Incentive factors in a low morale plant. *Amer. sociol. Rev.*, 1949, *14*, 618–24.

258. Gordon, O. J. A factor analysis of human needs and industrial morale. *Personnel Psychol.*, 1955, *8*, 1–18.

259. Gottlieb, B. and Kerr, W. A. An experiment in industrial harmony. *Personnel Psychol.*, 1950, *3*, 445–53.

260. Gould, Rosalind. An experimental analysis of level of aspiration. *Genet. Psychol. Monogr.*, 1939, *21*, 3–115.

261. Gouldner, A. W. *Wildcat strike.* Yellow Springs, Ohio: Antioch Press, 1954.

262. Grace, H. A. Conformance and performance. *J. soc. Psychol.*, 1954, *40*, 333–5.

263. Graicunas, V. A. Relationship in organization. In L. Gulick and L. Urwick, *Papers on the science of administration.* New York: Institute of Public Administration, 1937.

264. Grant, D. A., Hake, H. W., and Hornseth, J. P. Acquisition and extinction of a verbal conditioned response with differing percentages of reinforcement. *J. exp. Psychol.*, 1951, *42*, 1–5.

265. Greer, F. L., Galanter, E. H., and Nordlie, P. G. Interpersonal knowledge and individual and group effectiveness. *J. abnorm. soc. Psychol.*, 1954, *49*, 411–14.

266. Gronlund, N. E. Sociometric status and sociometric perception. *Sociometry*, 1955, *18*, 122–8.

267. Gross, E. Some functional consequences of primary controls in formal work organizations. *Amer. sociol. Rev.*, 1953, *18*, 368–73.

268. Gross, E. Primary functions of the small group. *Amer. J. Sociol.*, 1954, *60*, 24–9.

269. Gross, N. and Martin, W. E. On group cohesiveness. *Amer. J. Sociol.*, 1952, *57*, 546–54.

270. Gross, N., Martin, W. E., and Darley, J. G. Studies of group behavior: leadership structures in small organized groups. *J. abnorm. soc. Psychol.*, 1953, *48*, 429–32.

271. Gross, N., Mason, W. S., and McEachern, A. W. *Explorations in role analysis.* New York: Wiley, 1958.

272. Grossack, M. M. Cues, expectations, and first impressions. *J. Psychol.*, 1953, *35*, 245–52.

273. Grossack, M. M. Some effects of cooperation and competition upon small group behavior. *J. abnorm. soc. Psychol.*, 1954, *49*, 341–8.

274. Grosser, D., Polansky, N., and Lippitt, R. A laboratory study of behavorial contagion. *Hum. Relat.*, 1951, *4*, 115–42.

275. Grove, E. A. and Kerr, W. A. Specific evidence of halo effect in measurement of employee morale. *J. soc. Psychol.*, 1951, *34*, 165–170.

276. Guetzkow, H. *Groups, leadership and men; research in human relations.* Pittsburgh: Carnegie Press, 1951.

277. Guetzkow, H. An exploratory empirical study of the role of conflict in decision making conferences. *Int. Soc. Sci. Bull.*, 1953, *5*, 286–300.

278. Guetzkow, H. Differentiation of roles in task-oriented groups. Unpublished report.

279. Guetzkow, H. and Dill, W. R. Factors in the organizational development of task-oriented groups. *Sociometry*, 1957, *20*, 175–204.

280. Guetzkow, H. and Gyr, J. An analysis of conflict in decision-making groups. *Hum. Relat.*, 1954, *7*, 367–82.

281. Guetzkow, H. and Simon, H. A. The impact of certain communication nets upon organization and performance in task-oriented groups. *Mgmt. Science*, 1955, *1*, 233–50.

282. Gulick, L. and Urwick, L. *Papers on the science of administration.* New York: Institute of Public Administration, 1937.

283. Guthrie, E. R. *The psychology of human conflict.* New York: Harper, 1938.

284. Haber, W. and Levinson, H. M. *Labor relations and productivity in the building trades.* Ann Arbor: University of Michigan, Bureau of Labor Relations, 1956.

285. Haigh, G. V. and Fiske, D. W. Corroboration of personal values as selective factors in perception. *J. abnorm. soc. Psychol.*, 1952, *47*, 394–8.

286. Haire, M. *Psychology in management.* New York: McGraw-Hill, 1956.

287. Haire, M. and Gottsdanker, Josephine S. Factors influencing industrial morale. *Personnel*, 1951, *27*, 445–54.

288. Hall, G. S. *Morale*. New York: Appleton, 1920.
289. Hall, Patricia and Locke, H. W. *Incentives and contentment: a study made in a British factory*. London: Pitman, 1938.
290. Hall, R. L. Group performance under feedback that confounds responses of group members. *Sociometry*, 1957, 20, 297–305.
291. Halpin, A. W. *The leader behavior of school superintendents*. Columbus: Ohio State University, College of Education, 1956.
292. Halpin, A. W. *Administrative theory in education*. Chicago: Midwest Administration Center, 1958.
293. Hamilton, J. A. and Krechevsky, I. Studies in the effect of shock upon behavior plasticity in the rat. *J. comp. Psychol.*, 1933, 16, 237–53.
294. Harary, F. and Norman, R. Z. *Graph theory as a mathematical model in social science*. Ann Arbor: University of Michigan, Institute for Social Research, 1953.
295. Harbison, F. H. and Dubin, R. *Patterns of union-management relations*. Chicago: Science Research Associates, 1947.
296. Hare, A. P. A Study of interaction and consensus in different sized groups. *Amer. sociol. Rev.*, 1952, 17, 261–7.
297. Hare, A. P., Borgatta, E. F., and Bales, R. F. *Small groups: Studies in social interaction*. New York: Knopf, 1955.
298. Harnquist, K. *Adjustment: leadership and group relations in a military training situation*. Stockholm: Almquist and Wiksell, 1956.
299. Harrell, T. W. A factor analysis of mechanical ability tests. *Psychometrika*, 1940, 5, 17–33.
300. Harrell, T. W. *Industrial psychology*. New York: Rinehart, 1949.
301. Harrell, T. W. and Harrell, Margaret S. Army general classification test scores for civilian occupations. *Educ. psychol. Meas.*, 1945, 5, 229–39.
302. Hartley, E. L. and Hartley, Ruth E. *Fundamentals of social psychology*. New York: Knopf, 1952.
303. Hartmann, G. and Newcomb, T. *Industrial conflict*. New York: Cordon, 1939.
304. Harvey, O. J. An experimental approach to the study of status relations in informal groups. *Amer. sociol. Rev.*, 1953, 18, 357–67.
305. Harvey, O. J. An experimental investigation of negative and positive relations between small groups through judgmental indices. *Sociometry*, 1956, 19, 201–209.
306. Haythorn, W. The influence of individual members on the characteristics of small groups. *J. abnorm. soc. Psychol.*, 1953, 48, 276–84.
307. Healey, J. H. *Executive coordination and control*. Columbus: Ohio State University, Bur. Business Research Monogr. No. 78, 1956.

308. Heinicke, C. and Bales, R. F. Developmental trends in the structure of small groups. *Sociometry*, 1953, *16*, 7–38.

309. Heise, G. A. and Miller, G. A. Problem solving by small groups using various communication nets. *J. abnorm. soc. Psychol.*, 1951, *46*, 327–35.

310. Helson, H. Adaptation-level as a basis for a quantitative theory of frames of reference. *Psychol. Rev.*, 1948, *55*, 297–313.

311. Hemphill, J. K. *Situational factors in leadership*. Columbus: Ohio State University, Bur. Educational Research Monogr. No. 32, 1949.

312. Hemphill, J. K. Relations between the size of the group and the behavior of "superior" leaders. *J. soc. Psychol.*, 1950, *32*, 11–22.

313. Hemphill, J. K. A proposed theory of leadership in small groups. In J. K. Hemphill, et al., *Leadership acts: 1. An investigation of the relation between the possession of task relevant information and attempts to lead*. Columbus: Ohio State University, Personnel Research Board, 1954. Mimeo.

314. Hemphill, J. K. *Group dimensions: a manual for their measurement*. Columbus: Ohio State University, Bur. Business Research Monogr. No. 87, 1956.

315. Hemphill, J. K. and Coons, A. E. Development of the leader behavior description questionnaire. In R. M. Stogdill and A. E. Coons, *Leader behavior: its description and measurement*. Columbus: Ohio State University, Bur. Business Research Monogr. No. 88, 1957.

316. Hemphill, J. K., Pepinsky, Pauline N., Shevitz, R. N., Jaynes, W. E., and Christner, C. A. *Leadership acts: 1. An investigation of the relation between possession of task relevant information and attempts to lead*. Columbus: Ohio State University, Personnel Research Board, 1954. Mimeo.

317. Hemphill, J. K. and Sechrest, L. B. A comparison of three criteria of aircrew effectiveness in combat over Korea. *J. appl. Psychol.*, 1952, *36*, 323–7.

318. Hemphill, J. K., Seigel, Ann, and Westie, C. M. *An exploratory study of relations between perceptions of leader behavior, group characteristics, and expectations concerning the behavior of ideal leaders*. Columbus: Ohio State University, Personnel Research Board, 1951. Unpublished.

319. Hemphill, J. K. and Westie, C. M. The measurement of group dimensions. *J. Psychol.*, 1950, *29*, 325–42.

320. Hertz, D. B. and Livingston, R. T. Contemporary organizational theory: a review of current concepts and methods. *Hum. Relat.*, 1950, *3*, 373–94.

321. Herzberg, F., Mausner, B., Peterson, R. O., and Capwell, Dora F.

*Job attitudes: review of research and opinion.* Pittsburgh: Psychological Service of Pittsburgh, 1957.

322. Heyns, R. W. and Lippitt, R. Systematic observational techniques. In G. Lindzey, *Handbook of social psychology.* Cambridge: Addison-Wesley, 1954.

323. Hickman, C. A. and Kuhn, M. H. *Individuals, groups, and economic behavior.* New York: Dryden Press, 1956.

324. Higgin, G. The effect of reference group functions on social ratings. *Brit. J. Psychol.,* 1954, *45,* 88–93.

325. Hilgard, E. R. *Theories of learning.* New York: Appleton-Century-Crofts, 1956.

326. Hochbaum, G. M. The relation between group members' self-confidence and their reactions to group pressures to uniformity. *Amer. sociol. Rev.,* 1954, *19,* 678–87.

327. Hocking, W. E. *Morale and its enemies.* New Haven: Yale University Press, 1918.

328. Hoffman, P. J., Festinger, L., and Lawrence, D. H. Tendencies toward group comparability in competitive bargaining. *Hum. Relat.,* 1954, *7,* 141–59.

329. Hollander, E. P. and Bair, J. T. Attitudes toward authority-figures as correlates of motivation among naval aviation cadets. *J. appl. Psychol.,* 1954, *38,* 21–5.

330. Hollingshead, A. B. *Elmtown's youth.* New York: Wiley, 1949.

331. Homans, G. C. *The human group.* New York: Harcourt, Brace, 1950.

332. Hoppock, R. *Job satisfaction.* New York: Harper, 1935.

333. Hoppock, R. and Robinson, H. A. Job satisfaction researches of 1948. *Occupations,* 1949, *28,* 153–61.

334. Horowitz, M. W., Lyons, J., and Perlmutter, H. V. Induction of forces in discussion groups. *Hum. Relat.,* 1951, *4,* 57–76.

335. Horsfall, A. B. and Arensberg, C. M. Teamwork and productivity in a shoe factory. *Hum. Organization,* 1949, *8* (1), 13–25.

336. Horwitz, M. The conceptual status of group dynamics. *Rev. educ. Res.,* 1953, *23,* 309–28.

337. Horwitz, M. The recall of interrupted group tasks: an experimental study of individual motivation in relation to group goals. *Hum. Relat.,* 1954, *7,* 3–38.

338. Horwitz, M. and Lee, F. J. Effects of decision making by group members on recall of finished and unfinished tasks. *J. abnorm. soc. Psychol.,* 1954, *49,* 201–10.

339. Hovland, C. I., Janis, I. L., and Kelley, H. H. *Communication and persuasion.* New Haven: Yale University Press, 1953.

340. Hughes, E. C. Institutional office and the person. *Amer. J. Sociol.,* 1937, *43,* 404–14.

341. Hull, C. L. *Essentials of behavior*. New Haven: Yale University Press, 1951.

342. Hull, C. L. *A behavior system: an introduction to behavior theory concerning the individual organism*. New Haven: Yale University Press, 1952.

343. Hull, R. L. Measuring employee attitudes — a proving ground for personnel policy and practices. *Conference Bd. Mgmt. Record*, 1939, 165–72.

344. Humphreys, L. G. Acquisition and extinction of verbal expectations in a situation analogous to conditioning. *J. exp. Psychol.*, 1939, 25, 294–301.

345. Humphreys, L. G. The effect of random alternation of reinforcement on the acquisition and extinction of conditioned eyelid reactions. *J. exp. Psychol.*, 1939, 25, 141–58.

346. Hunt, D. E. Changes in goal-object preference as a function of expectancy for social reinforcement. *J. abnorm. soc. Psychol.*, 1955, 50, 372–7.

347. Hurwitz, J. I., Zander, A. F., and Hymovitch, B. Some effects of power on the relations among group members. In D. Cartwright and A. Zander, *Group dynamics*. Evanston: Row, Peterson, 1953.

348. Hyman, H. H. The psychology of status. *Arch. Psychol.*, 1942, No. 269.

349. Hyman, R. and Jenkin, N. S. Involvement and set as determinants of behavior stereotypy. *Amer. Psychol.*, 1955, 10, 466–7.

350. Irwin, F. W. The realism of expectations. *Psychol. Rev.*, 1944, 51, 120–26.

351. Irwin, F. W. Stated expectations as functions of probability and desirability of outcome. *J. Pers.*, 1953, 21, 329–35.

352. Israel, J. *Self-evaluation and rejection in groups*. Stockholm: Almquist and Wiksell, 1956.

353. Jackson, D. N. and Messick, S. J. A note on "ethnocentrism" and acquiescent response sets. *J. abnorm. soc. Psychol.*, 1957, 54, 132–4.

354. Jackson, J. M. *The relation between attraction, being valued, and communication in a formal organization*. Ann Arbor: University of Michigan, Institute for Social Research, 1953. Mimeo.

355. Jackson, J. M. and Saltzstein, H. D. *Group membership and conformity processes*. Ann Arbor: University of Michigan, Institute of Social Research, 1956.

356. Jacobson, E., Charters, W. W., Jr., and Lieberman, S. The use of the role concept in the study of complex organizations. *J. soc. Issues*, 1951, 7, 18–27.

357. Jacobson, E. and Seashore, S. Communication practices in complex organizations. *J. soc. Issues*, 1951, 7, 28–9.

358. Jambor, H. *Discrepancies in role expectations for the supervisory position.* Minneapolis: University of Minnesota, Doctoral dissertation, 1954.

359. James, J. A preliminary study of the size determinant in small group interaction. *Amer. sociol. Rev.,* 1951, *16,* 474–7.

360. Jaques, E. *The changing culture of a factory.* New York: Dryden Press, 1952.

361. Jaques, E. *Measurement of responsibility.* Cambridge: Harvard University Press, 1956.

362. Jaynes, W. E. Differences between jobs and between organizations. In R. M. Stogdill and C. L. Shartle, *Patterns of administrative performance.* Columbus: Ohio State University, Bur. Business Research Monogr. No. 81, 1956.

363. Jenkins, D. H. Feedback and group self-evaluation. *J. soc. Issues,* 1948, *4* (2), 50–60.

364. Jennings, Helen H. *Leadership and isolation.* New York: Longmans, Green, 1950.

365. Jessor, R. *A methodological investigation of the strength and generalization of verbal reinforcement.* Columbus: Ohio State University, Doctoral dissertation, 1951.

366. Jessor, R. and Readio, J. The influence of the value of an event upon the expectancy of its occurrence. *J. genl. Psychol.,* 1957, *56,* 219–28.

367. Jurgensen, C. E. What job applicants look for in a company. *Personnel Psychol.,* 1948, *1,* 433–45.

368. Jurgensen, C. E. What do job applicants want? *Personnel,* 1949, *25,* 352–5.

369. Jurgensen, C. E. Selected factors which influence job preferences. *J. appl. Psychol.,* 1947, *31,* 553–64.

370. Kahl, J. A. *The American class structure.* New York: Rinehart, 1957.

371. Kahn, R. L. An analysis of supervisory practices and components of morale. In H. Guetzkow, *Groups, leadership and men.* Pittsburgh: Carnegie Press, 1951.

372. Kahn, R. L. and Katz, D. Leadership practices in relation to productivity and morale. In D. Cartwright, and A. Zander, *Group dynamics.* Evanston: Row, Peterson, 1953.

373. Kahn, R. L. and Morse, Nancy C. The relationship of productivity to morale. *J. soc. Issues,* 1951, *7,* 8–17.

374. Kanareff, Vera T. and Lanzetta, J. T. The acquisition of imitative and opposition responses under two conditions of instruction induced set. Unpublished report, 1958.

375. Katz, D. The Survey Research Center: an overview of the human relations program. In H. Guetzkow, *Groups, leadership and men.* Pittsburgh: Carnegie Press, 1951.

376. Katz, D., Maccoby, N., Gurin, G., and Floor, L. G. *Productivity, supervision and morale among railroad workers.* Ann Arbor: University of Michigan, Institute for Social Research, 1951.

377. Katz, D., Maccoby, N., and Morse, Nancy C. *Productivity, supervision and morale in an office situation.* Ann Arbor: University of Michigan, Institute for Social Research, 1950.

378. Katz, E. and Lazarsfeld, P. F. *Personal Influence.* Glencoe: Free Press, 1955.

379. Kelley, H. H. Communication in experimentally created hierarchies. *Hum. Relat.*, 1951, 4, 39–56.

380. Kelley, H. H. and Shapiro, M. M. An experiment on conformity to group norms where conformity is detrimental to group achievement. *Amer. sociol. Rev.*, 1954, 19, 667–77.

381. Kelley, H. H. and Thibaut, J. W. Experimental studies of group problem solving and process. In G. Lindzey, *Handbook of social psychology.* Cambridge: Addison-Wesley, 1954.

382. Kelley, H. H. and Volkart, E. H. The resistance to change of group-anchored attitudes. *Amer. sociol. Rev.*, 1952, 17, 453–65.

383. Kelly, G. A. *The psychology of personal constructs.* New York: Norton, 1955.

384. Kemeny, J. G., Snell, J. L., and Thompson, G. L. *Introduction to finite mathematics.* New York: Prentice-Hall, 1957.

385. Kennedy, V. D. *Union policy and incentive wage methods.* New York: Columbia University Press, 1945.

386. Kerr, C. The short-run behavior of physical productivity and average hourly earnings. *Rev. Econ. and Stat.*, 1949, 31, 299–309.

387. Kerr, C. Productivity and labor relations. Princeton: Inter-University Study of Labor Problems in Economic Development, Reprint No. 13, 1957.

388. Kerr, W. A. Labor turnover and its correlates. *J. appl. Psychol.*, 1947, 31, 366–71.

389. Kerr, W. A. Dual allegiance to union and management (a symposium). III. Dual allegiance and emotional acceptance-rejection in industry. *Personnel Psychol.*, 1954, 7, 59–66.

390. Kerr, W. A. and Gottlieb, B. An experiment in industrial harmony. In M. Derber, *Proceedings of third annual meeting, IRRA.* Champaign, Ill.: Industrial Relations Research Association, 1951.

391. Kidd, J. S. and Campbell, D. T. Conformity to groups as a function of group success. *J. abnorm. soc. Psychol.*, 1955, 51, 390–93.

392. Kimball, D. S. *Principles of industrial organization.* New York: McGraw-Hill, 1913.

393. Kogan, N. Authoritarianism and repression. *J. abnorm. soc. Psychol.*, 1956, 53, 34–7.

394. Kolstad, A. Attitudes of employees and their supervisors. *Personnel*, 1944, *20*, 241–50.

395. Koran, S. W. Controlling office turnover. *Mgmt. Rev.*, 1955, *44* (1), 25–35.

396. Kornhauser, A. *Problems of power in American democracy.* Detroit: Wayne State University Press, 1957.

397. Kornhauser, A., Dubin, R., and Ross, A. M. *Industrial conflict.* New York: McGraw-Hill, 1954.

398. Krech, D. and Crutchfield, R. S. *Theory and problems of social psychology.* New York: McGraw-Hill, 1948.

399. Kruisinga, H. J. *The balance between centralization and decentralization in managerial control.* Oxford: Blackwell, 1954.

400. Kurtz, Le R. H. The morale function of the executive. *Personnel*, 1944, *20*, 202–20.

401. Lanzetta, J. T. Group behavior under stress. *Hum. Relat.*, 1955, *8*, 29–52.

402. Lanzetta, J. T., Haefner, D., Langham, P., and Axelrod, H. Some effects of situational threat on group behavior. *J. abnorm. soc. Psychol.*, 1954, *49*, 445–53.

403. Lanzetta, J. T. and Roby, T. B. Effects of work-group structure and certain task variables on group performance. *J. abnorm. soc. Psychol.*, 1956, *53*, 307–14.

404. Lanzetta, J. T. and Roby, T. B. Group performance as a function of work-distribution patterns and task load. *Sociometry*, 1956, *19*, 95–104.

405. Lanzetta, J. T. and Roby, T. B. Group learning and communication as a function of task and structure "demands." *J. abnorm. soc. Psychol.*, 1957, *55*, 121–31.

406. Lauterbach, A. *Men, motives and money: psychological frontiers of economics.* Ithaca: Cornell University Press, 1954.

407. Leavitt, H. J. Some effects of certain communication patterns on group performance. *J. abnorm. soc. Psychol.*, 1951, *46*, 38–50.

408. Lenski, G. E. Social participation and status crystallization. *Amer. sociol. Rev.*, 1956, *21*, 458–64.

409. Leontief, W. W. *Studies on the structure of the American economy: theoretical and empirical explorations in input-output analysis.* New York: Oxford University Press, 1953.

410. Levinger, G., Morrison, H. W., and French, J. R. P., Jr. Coercive power and forces affecting conformity. *Amer. Psychol.*, 1957, *12*, 393.

411. Levinson, H. M. *Unionism, wage trends, and income distribution, 1914–1947.* Ann Arbor: University of Michigan Press, 1951.

412. Levy, L. and McCandless, B. Expectancy of punishment as a func-

tion of type of differentiation in original learning. *J. abnorm. soc. Psychol.*, 1952, *47*, 520–25.

413. Lewin, K. *A dynamic theory of personality.* (Trans. by D. K. Adams and K. E. Zener.) New York: McGraw-Hill, 1935.

414. Lewin, K. *Resolving social conflicts; selected papers on group dynamics.* New York: Harper, 1948.

415. Lewin, K. *Field theory in social science.* New York: Harper, 1951.

416. Lewin, K., Dembo, Tamara, Festinger, L., and Sears, Pauline. Level of aspiration. In J. McV. Hunt, *Personality and the behavior disorders.* New York: Ronald Press, 1944.

417. Lewis, H. B. An experimental study of the role of the ego in work. I. The role of the ego in cooperative work. *J. exp. Psychol.*, 1944, *34*, 113–26.

418. Lewis, J. S. *The commercial organization of factories.* London: Spon Books, 1896.

419. Lichtenberg, P. Time perspective and the initiation of cooperation. *J. soc. Psychol.*, 1956, *43*, 247–60.

420. Liddell, H. The role of vigilance in the development of animal neurosis. In P. Hoch and J. Zubin, *Anxiety.* New York: Grune and Stratton, 1950.

421. Lienau, C. C. Quantitative aspects of organization. *Hum. Biol.*, 1947, *19*, 163–216.

422. Likert, R. Developing patterns of management: II. In *Amer. Mgmt. Ass'n., genl. Mgmt. Series* No. 182, 1956.

423. Likert, R. and Katz, D. Supervisory practices and organizational structures as they affect employee productivity and morale. *Amer. Mgmt. Assn., Personn. Series* No. 120, 1948.

424. Lincoln, J. F. *Lincoln's incentive system.* New York: McGraw-Hill, 1946.

425. Lindzey, G. *Handbook of social psychology.* 2 vols. Cambridge: Addison-Wesley, 1954.

426. Lindzey, G. An experimental examination of the scape-goat theory of prejudice. *J. abnorm. soc. Psychol.*, 1950, *45*, 296–309.

427. Linton, R. *The study of man.* New York: Appleton-Century, 1936.

428. Lippitt, R. An experimental study of the effect of democratic and authoritarian group atmospheres. *Univ. of Iowa, Stud. Child Welf.*, 1940, *16*, 43–195.

429. Lippitt, R., Polansky, N., and Rosen, S. The dynamics of power. *Hum. Relat.*, 1952, *5*, 37–64.

430. Lippitt, R., Watson, Jeanne, and Westley, B. *The dynamics of planned change.* New York: Harcourt, Brace, 1958.

431. Lippitt, R. and White, R. K. The social climate of children's groups. In R. G. Barker, J. S. Kounin, and H. F. Wright, *Child behavior and development.* New York: McGraw-Hill, 1943.

432. Livingstone, Elizabeth. Attitudes of women operatives to promotion. *Occup. Psychol.*, 1953, *27*, 191–9.

433. Logan, F. A., Olmsted, D. L., Rosner, B. S., Schwartz, R. D., and Stevens, C. M. *Behavior theory and social science.* New Haven: Yale University Press, 1955.

434. Loken, R. D. *Why they quit, a survey of Illinois employees who quit their jobs in 1949; retail, clerical, manufacturing.* Urbana: University of Illinois, 1951.

435. Lorge, I. and Brenner, M. *A survey of studies contrasting the quality of group performance and individual performance: 1920–1957.* New York: Columbia University, Bur. Applied Social Research, 1957. Mimeo.

436. Louden, J. K. *Wage incentives.* New York: Wiley, 1944.

437. Low, Lillian. Resolving employee resistance to new personnel policies: a case study. *Personnel Psychol.*, 1948, *1*, 185–96.

438. Lowenthal, L. and Guterman, N. *Prophets of deceit; a study of the techniques of the American agitator.* New York: Harper, 1949.

439. Luce, R. D. Connectivity and generalized cliques in sociometric group structure. *Psychometrika*, 1950, *15*, 169–90.

440. Luce, R. D. and Raiffa, H. *Games and decisions: introduction and critical survey.* New York: Wiley, 1957.

441. Luchins, A. S. Personality and prejudice: a critique. *J. soc. Psychol.*, 1950, *32*, 79–94.

442. Luchins, A. S. and Luchins, E. H. Previous experience with ambiguous and non-ambiguous stimuli under various social influences. *J. soc. Psychol.*, 1955, *42*, 249–70.

443. Lundberg, G. A. Some problems of group classification and measurement. *Amer. sociol. Rev.*, 1940, *5*, 351–60.

444. Lynton, R. P. *Incentives and management in British industry.* London: Routledge and Kegan Paul, 1949.

445. Lytle, C. W. *Wage incentive methods.* New York: Ronald Press, 1942.

446. McClelland, D. C., Atkinson, J. W., Clark, R. A., and Lowell, E. L. *The achievement motive.* New York: Appleton-Century-Crofts, 1953.

447. McCloskey, J. F. and Trefethen, F. N. *Operations research for management.* Baltimore: Johns Hopkins Press, 1954.

448. McClothlin, W. H. Decision-making under uncertainty. *Amer. Psychol.*, 1955, *10*, 493.

449. Maccoby, Eleanor, Newcomb, T. M., and Hartley, E. L. *Readings in social psychology.* New York: Holt, 1958.

450. McCormick, E. J., Finn, R. H., and Scheips, C. D. Patterns of job requirements. *J. appl. Psychol.*, 1957, *41*, 358–64.

451. McCormick, E. J. and North, W. E. The analysis of an experimental job evaluation system as applied to enlisted naval jobs. *J. appl. Psychol.*, 1954, 38, 233–7.

452. MacCorquodale, K. and Meehl, P. E. Preliminary suggestions as to a formalization of expectancy theory. *Psychol. Rev.*, 1953, 60, 55–63.

453. McCurdy, H. G. and Lambert, W. E. The efficiency of small human groups in the solution of problems requiring genuine cooperation. *J. Pers.*, 1952, 20, 478–94.

454. MacCurdy, J. T. *The structure of morale.* New York: Macmillan, 1943.

455. Mace, C. A. Satisfactions in work. *Occupat. Psychol., London,* 1948, 22, 15–19.

456. McGeoch, J. A. and Irion, A. L. *The psychology of human learning.* New York: Longmans, Green, 1952.

457. McGregor, D. The major determinants of the prediction of social events. *J. abnorm. soc. Psychol.*, 1938, 33, 179–204.

458. MacIver, R. M. *Society.* New York: Rinehart, 1937.

459. McKeachie, W. J. Individual conformity to attitudes of classroom groups. *J. abnorm. soc. Psychol.*, 1954, 49, 282–9.

460. McQuitty, L. L., Wrigley, C., and Gaier, E. L. An approach to isolating dimensions of job success. *J. appl. Psychol.*, 1954, 38, 227–32.

461. Macy, J., Jr., Christie, L. S., and Luce, R. D. Coding noise in a task oriented group. *J. abnorm. soc. Psychol.*, 1953, 48, 401–409.

462. Maier, N. R. F. *Frustration, the study of behavior without a goal.* New York: McGraw-Hill, 1949.

463. Maier, N. R. F. *Principles of human relations.* New York: Wiley, 1952.

464. Maller, J. B. *Cooperation and competition: an experimental study in motivation.* New York: Teachers College Contrib. Educ. No. 384, 1925.

465. Mann, F. C. and Dent, J. K. The supervisor: member of two organizational families. *Harvard bus. Rev.*, 1954, 32 (6), 103–12.

466. Markham, S. H. Incentive wages: a management view point. In *Proceedings of second annual conference on labor at New York University.* Albany: Matthew Bender, 1949.

467. Marks, Rose W. The effect of probability, desirability, and "privilege" on the stated expectations of children. *J. Pers.*, 1951, 19, 332–51.

468. Marriott, R. Size of working group and output. *Occup. Psychol., London,* 1949, 23, 47–57.

469. Martin, N. H. Differential decisions in the management of an industrial plant. *J. Bus. Univ. Chicago,* 1956, 29, 249–60.

470. Martin, W. E., Darley, J. G., and Gross, N. Studies of group behavior: II. Methodological problems in the study of interrelationships of group members. *Educ. psychol. Measmt.*, 1952, *12*, 533–53.

471. Massarik, F., Tannenbaum, R., Kahane, M., and Weschler, I. Sociometric choice and organizational effectiveness: a multi-relational approach. *Sociometry*, 1953, *16*, 211–38.

472. Mathewson, S. B. *Restriction of output among unorganized workers.* New York: Viking Press, 1931.

473. Mausner, B. The effect of one partner's success in a relevant task on the interaction of observer pairs. *J. abnorm. soc. Psychol.*, 1954, *49*, 557–60.

474. Mausner, B. The effect of prior reinforcement on the interaction of observer pairs. *J. abnorm. soc. Psychol.*, 1954, *49*, 65–8.

475. Mausner, B. and Bloch, Barbara L. A study of the additivity of variables affecting social interaction. *J. abnorm. soc. Psychol.*, 1957, *54*, 250–56.

476. May, M. A. and Doob, L. W. *Competition and cooperation.* New York: Social Science Research Council, Bull. No. 25, 1937.

477. Mayo, E. *The human problems of an industrial civilization.* New York: Macmillan, 1933.

478. Mead, G. H. *Mind, self and society.* Chicago: University of Chicago Press, 1934.

479. Mead, Margaret. *Cooperation and competition among primitive peoples.* New York: McGraw-Hill, 1937.

480. Medalia, N. Z. and Miller, D. C. Human relations leadership and the association of morale and efficiency in work groups: a controlled study with small military groups. *Soc. Forces*, 1955, *33*, 348–52.

481. Melman, S. *Dynamic factors in industrial productivity.* New York: Wiley, 1956.

482. Melton, A. W. *Apparatus tests* (AAF Aviation Psychol. Program Res. Report No. 4). Washington: Government Printing Office, 1947.

483. Merton, R. K. Bureaucratic structure and personality. *Soc. Forces,* 1940, *42*, 560–68.

484. Merton, R. K. *Social theory and social structure.* Glencoe: Free Press, 1957.

485. Merton, R. K., Gray, A. P., Hockey, B., and Selvin, H. C. *Reader in bureaucracy.* Glencoe: Free Press, 1952.

486. Merton, R. K. and Kitt, A. S. Contributions to the theory of reference group behavior. In R. K. Merton and P. F. Lazarsfeld, *Studies in the scope and method of "The American Soldier."* Glencoe: Free Press, 1950.

487. Merton, R. K. and Lazarsfeld, P. F. *Studies in the scope and method of "The American Soldier."* Glencoe: Free Press, 1950.

488. Meyer, D. R. The effects of differential rewards on discrimination reversal learning by monkeys. *J. exp. Psychol.,* 1951, *41,* 268–74.

489. Miles, G. H. *The problem of incentives in industry.* London: Pitman, 1932.

490. Miller, D. C. and Form, W. H. *Industrial sociology: an introduction to the sociology of work relations.* New York: Harper, 1951.

491. Miller, J. G. *Experiments in social process: a symposium on social psychology.* New York: McGraw-Hill, 1950.

492. Miller, J. G. Toward a general theory for the behavioral sciences. *Amer. Psychol.,* 1955, *10,* 513–31.

493. Miller, N. E. and Dollard, J. C. *Social learning and imitation* New Haven: Yale University Press, 1941.

494. Mills F. C. *Productivity and economic progress.* New York: National Bureau of Economic Research, 1952.

495. Mills, T. M. Power relations in three-person groups. *Amer. sociol. Rev.,* 1953, *18,* 351–7.

496. Mills, T. M. The coalition pattern in three-person groups. *Amer. sociol. Rev.,* 1954, *19,* 657–67.

497. Mintz, A. Non-adaptive group behavior. *J. abnorm. soc. Psychol.,* 1951, *46,* 150–59.

498. Mooney, J. D. *The principles of organization.* New York: Harper, 1947.

499. Moore, W. E. *Industrial relations and the social order.* New York: Macmillan, 1946.

500. Moore, W. E. Sociology of economic organization. In G. Gurvitch and W. E. Moore, *Twentieth century sociology.* New York: Philosophical Library, 1945.

501. Moreno, J. L. Contributions of sociometry to research methodology in sociology. *Amer. sociol. Rev.,* 1947, *12,* 287–92.

502. Moreno, J. L. *Who shall survive?* Beacon, N.Y.: Beacon House, 1953.

503. Moreno, J. L. and Jennings, Helen H. Sociometric measurement of social configurations. *Sociometry Monogr.,* 1945, No. 3.

504. Morgenstern, O. *Economic activity analysis.* New York: Wiley, 1954.

505. Morse, Nancy C. *Satisfactions in the white collar job.* Ann Arbor: University of Michigan, Institute for Social Research, 1953.

506. Morse, Nancy C. and Reimer, E. The experimental change of a major organizational variable. *J. abnorm. soc. Psychol.,* 1956, *52,* 120–29.

507. Mowrer, O. H. Preparatory set (expectancy) — a determinant in motivation and learning. *Psychol. Rev.*, 1938, *45*, 62–91.

508. Mowrer, O. H. *Learning theory and personality dynamics.* New York: Ronald Press, 1950.

509. Murchison, C. The experimental measurement of a social hierarchy in *Gallus Domesticus:* I. The direct identification and direct measurement of social reflex No. 1 and social reflex No. 2. *J. gen. Psychol.*, 1935, *12*, 3–39.

510. Murphy, G., Murphy, Lois B., and Newcomb, T. M. *Experimental social psychology.* New York: Harper, 1937.

511. Myrdal, G. *An American dilemma.* New York: Harper, 1944.

512. Nadel, S. F. *The theory of social structure.* Glencoe: Free Press, 1957.

513. Nadworthy, M. J. *Scientific management and the labor unions, 1900–1932; an historical analysis.* Cambridge: Harvard University Press, 1955.

514. Nagle, B. F. Productivity, employee attitude and supervisor sensitivity. *Personnel Psychol.*, 1954, *7*, 219–32.

515. National Association of Manufacturers. *Preserving the management function in collective bargaining.* New York: Natl. Assn. Mfgr. Bull. No. 24, 1956.

516. National Industrial Conference Board. *Sharing profits with employees.* New York: NICB Studies in Personnel Policy No. 162, 1957.

517. Neiman, L. J. and Hughes, J. W. The problem of the concept of role — a resurvey of the literature. *Soc. Forces*, 1951, *30*, 141–9.

518. Newcomb, T. M. *Personality and social change.* New York: Dryden Press, 1943.

519. Newcomb, T. M. *Social psychology.* New York: Dryden Press, 1950.

520. Newcomb, T. M. The prediction of interpersonal attraction. *Amer. Psychol.*, 1956, *11*, 575–86.

521. Norfleet, Bobbie. Interpersonal relations and group productivity. *J. soc. Issues*, 1948, *4*(2), 66–9.

522. North, C. and Hatt, P. Jobs and occupations: a popular evaluation. In L. Wilson and W. L. Kolb, *Sociological analysis.* New York: Harcourt, Brace, 1949.

523. Osborn, R. C. *Effects of corporate size on efficiency and profitability.* Urbana: University of Illinois, Bur. Economic and Business Research Bull. No. 72, 1950.

524. Pareto, V. *The mind and society.* New York: Harcourt, Brace, 1935.

525. Parsons, T. *The social system.* Glencoe: Free Press, 1951.

526. Parsons, T. and Shils, E. A. *Toward a general theory of action.* Cambridge: Harvard University Press, 1952.

527. Paterson, T. T. *Morale in war and work.* London: Max Parrish, 1955.

528. Pavlov, I. P. *Conditioned reflexes.* London: Oxford University Press, 1927.

529. Pelz, D. C. Influence: a key to effective leadership in the firstline supervisor. *Personnel,* 1952, 29, 209–17.

530. Pepinsky, H. B., Pepinsky, Pauline N., and Pavlik, W. B. *Motivational factors in individual and group productivity: I. Successful task accomplishment as related to task relevant personal beliefs.* Columbus: Ohio State University, Personnel Research Board, 1956. Mimeo.

531. Pepinsky, H. B., Pepinsky, Pauline N., Minor, F. J., and Robin, S. S. *Team productivity as related to the confirmation or contradiction by management of its committments to an appointed leader.* Columbus: Ohio State University, Personnel Research Board, 1957. Mimeo.

532. Pepinsky, Pauline N. The meaning of "validity" and "reliability" as applied to sociometric tests. *Educ. psychol. Meas.,* 1949, 9, 39–49.

533. Pepinsky, Pauline N., Pepinsky, H. B., and Pavlik, W. B. *Motivational factors in individual and group productivity: III. The effects of task complexity and time pressure upon team productivity.* Columbus: Ohio State University, Personnel Research Board, 1956. Mimeo.

534. Pepinsky, Pauline N., Pepinsky, H. B., Robin, S. S., and Minor, F. J. *The effects of induced orientation and type of task upon group performance and group member morale.* Columbus: Ohio State University, Personnel Research Board, 1957. Mimeo.

535. Pepitone, A. and Kleiner, R. The effects of threat and frustration on group cohesiveness. *J. abnorm. soc. Psychol.,* 1957, 54, 192–9.

536. Pepitone, A. and Reichling, G. Group cohesiveness and the expression of hostility. *Hum. Relat.,* 1955, 8, 327–37.

537. Petersen, J. W. An appraisal of operations research techniques. *Illinois bus. Rev.,* 1956, 13 (11), 6–8.

538. Peterson, R. L. *Building employee productivity.* Urbana: University of Illinois, Bureau of Business Management, 1954.

539. Peterson, R. M. Expected value as a determiner of successive two-choice decisions. *Amer. Psychol.,* 1955, 10, 467.

540. Phares, E. J. Expectancy changes in skill and chance situations. *J. abnorm. soc. Psychol.,* 1957, 54, 339–42.

541. Polansky, N., Lippitt, R., and Redl, F. An investigation of behavioral contagion in groups. *Hum. Relat.*, 1950, 3, 319–48.

542. Postman, L. Toward a general theory of cognition. In J. H. Rohrer and M. Sherif, *Social psychology at the crossroads.* New York: Harper, 1951.

543. Postman, L. The experimental analysis of motivational factors in perception. In *Current theory and research in motivation.* Lincoln: University of Nebraska Press, 1953.

544. Postman, L. and Crutchfield, R. S. The interaction of need, set, and stimulus structure in a cognitive task. *Amer. J. Psychol.*, 1952, 65, 196–217.

545. Precker, J. A. Similarity of valuings as a factor in selection of peers and near-authority figures. *J. abnorm. soc. Psychol.*, 1952, 47, 406–14.

546. Prestridge, Virginia and Wray, D. *Industrial sociology: an annotated bibliography.* Champaign: University of Illinois, Institute of Labor and Industrial Relations, 1953.

547. Price, Mary Alice. *A study of motivational factors associated with leadership behavior of young women in a private school.* Columbus: Ohio State University, Doctoral dissertation, 1948.

548. Proshansky, H. and Murphy, G. The effects of reward and punishment on perception. *J. Psychol.*, 1942, 13, 295–305.

549. Purcell, T. V. Dual allegiance to union and management (a symposium). 2. Dual allegiance to company and union — Packinghouse workers. A Swift-UPWA study in a crisis situation, 1949–1952. *Personnel Psychol.*, 1954, 7, 48–58.

550. Rapoport, A. Forms of output distribution between two individuals motivated by a satisfaction function. *Bull. math. Biophys.*, 1947, 9, 109–22.

551. Rashevsky, N. *A mathematical theory of human relations.* Bloomington, Ind.: Principia Press, 1947.

552. Rashevsky, N. *Mathematical biology of social behavior.* Chicago: University of Chicago Press, 1951.

553. Rasmussen, G. and Zander, A. Group membership and self-evaluation. *Hum. Relat.*, 1954, 7, 239–51.

554. Raube, S. A. *Factors affecting employee morale.* New York: National Industrial Conference Board, 1947.

555. Raven, B. H. *The effect of group pressures on opinion, perception, and communication.* Ann Arbor: University of Michigan, Doctoral dissertation, 1953.

556. Raven, B. H. and French, J. R. P., Jr. An experimental investigation of legitimate and coercive power. *Amer. Psychol.*, 1957, 12, 393.

557. Raven, B. H. and French, J. R. P., Jr. Legitimate power, coercive power, and observability in social influence. *Sociometry*, 1958, *21*, 83–97.

558. Reider, N. Psychodynamics of authority with relation to some psychiatric problems in officers. *Bull. Menninger Clinic*, 1944, *8*, 55–8.

559. Renck, R. Morale in four key groups in industry. In *Conference on employee attitude surveys*. Chicago: University of Chicago, Industrial Relations Center, 1955.

560. Reynolds, L. G. and Taft, C. H. *The evolution of the wage structure*. New Haven: Yale University Press, 1956.

561. Richardson, F. L. W. and Walker, C. R. *Human relations in an expanding company*. New Haven: Yale University, Labor and Management Center, 1948.

562. Ridley, C. E. and Simon, H. A. *Measuring municipal activities*. Chicago: International City Managers' Association, 1943.

563. Riley, Matilda W. and Cohn, R. Control networks in informal groups. *Sociometry*, 1958, *21*, 30–49.

564. Riley, Matilda W., Riley, J. W., and Toby, J. *Sociological studies in scale analysis*. New Brunswick, N. J.: Rutgers University Press, 1954.

565. Robinson, H. A. Job satisfaction researches of 1953. *Personn. Guid. J.*, 1954, *33*, 26–9.

566. Robinson, H. A. Job satisfaction researches of 1955. *Personn. Guid. J.*, 1956, *34*, 565–8.

567. Roby, T. B. and Lanzetta, J. T. Work group structure, communication, and group performance. *Sociometry*, 1956, *19*, 105–13.

568. Roe, Anne. *The psychology of occupations*. New York: Wiley, 1956.

569. Roethlisberger, F. J. The foreman: master and victim of double talk. *Harvard bus. Rev.*, 1945, *23*, 283–98.

570. Roethlisberger, F. J. *Management and morale*. Cambridge: Harvard University Press, 1941.

571. Roethlisberger, F. J. and Dickson, W. J. *Management and the worker*, Cambridge: Harvard University Press, 1941.

572. Rogers, S. The anchoring of absolute judgments. *Arch. Psychol.*, 1941, No. 261.

573. Rohde, K. J. *Variations in group composition with respect to individual task ability as a factor in group behavior*. Columbus: Ohio State University, Personnel Research Board Technical Report No. 18. (RF Project 474), 1954. Mimeo.

574. Rokeach, M. Toward the scientific evaluation of social attitudes and ideologies. *J. Psychol.*, 1951, *31*, 97–104.

575. Rokeach, M. A method for studying individual differences in "narrow-mindedness." *J. Pers.*, 1951, *20*, 219–33.

576. Rokeach, M. "Narrow-mindedness" and personality. *J. Pers.*, 1951, *20*, 234–51.

577. Rokeach, M. and Eglash, A. A scale for measuring intellectual conviction. *J. soc. Psychol.*, 1946, *44*, 135–41.

578. Rokeach, M., McGovney, W. C., and Denny, M. R. A distinction between dogmatic and rigid thinking. *J. abnorm. soc. Psychol.*, 1955, *51*, 87–93.

579. Rommetveit, R. *Social norms and roles.* Minneapolis: University of Minnesota Press, 1955.

580. Ronken, Harriet O. and Lawrence, P. R. *Administering changes; a case study of human relations in a factory.* Boston: Harvard University, Graduate School of Business Administration, 1952.

581. Roseborough, Mary E. Experimental studies of small groups. *Psychol. Bull.*, 1953, *50*, 275–303.

582. Rosen, A. C. Change in perceptual threshold as a protective function of the organism. *J. Pers.*, 1954, *23*, 182–94.

583. Rosen, H. Dual allegiance to union and management (a symposium) 4. Dual allegiance: a critique and a proposed approach. *Personnel Psychol.*, 1954, *7*, 67–71.

584. Rosen, R. A. H. and Rosen, H. A suggested modification in job satisfaction surveys. *Personnel Psychol.*, 1955, *8*, 303–14.

585. Rosenberg, S., Erlick, D. E., and Berkowitz, L. Some effects of varying combinations of group members on group performance measures and leadership behaviors. *J. abnorm. soc. Psychol.*, 1955, *51*, 195–203.

586. Rosenfeld, Eva. Social stratification in a "classless" society. *Amer. sociol. Rev.*, 1951, *16*, 766–74.

587. Rosenthal, D. and Cofer, C. N. The effect on group performance of an indifferent and neglectful attitude shown by one group member. *J. exp. Psychol.*, 1948, *38*, 568–77.

588. Ross, R. B. *Proceedings: The annual fall conference on principles, methods and techniques for increasing productivity, reducing costs and improving human relations.* New York: Society for the Advancement of Management, 1951.

589. Rotter, J. B. *Social learning and clinical psychology.* New York: Prentice-Hall, 1954.

590. Rowntree, B. S. *The human factor in business: experiments in industrial democracy.* London: Longmans, Green, 1921.

591. Roy, D. F. Work satisfaction and social reward in quota achievement: an analysis of piecework incentive. *Amer. sociol. Rev.*, 1953, *18*, 507–14.

592. Roy, D. F. Quota restriction and goldbricking in a machine shop. *Amer. J. Sociol.*, 1952, 57, 427–42.

593. Roy, R. H. Do wage incentives reduce costs? *Indus. lab. relat. Rev.*, 1952, 5, 195–208.

594. Ruch, F. L. *Bibliography on military leadership*. Maxwell Air Force Base, Alabama: Human Resources Institute, 1953.

595. Rudduck, R. T. *An investigation and evaluation of work measurement as an administrative control*. Columbus: Ohio State University, Doctoral dissertation, 1954.

596. Ruesch, J. and Kees, W. *Nonverbal communication: notes on the visual perception of human relations*. Berkeley: University of California Press, 1956.

597. Ryan, T. A. *Work and effort; the psychology of production*. New York: Ronald Press, 1947.

598. Ryan, T. A. and Smith, P. C. *Principles of industrial psychology*. New York: Ronald Press, 1954.

599. Sakoda, J. M. Factor analysis of OSS situational tests. *J. abnorm. soc. Psychol.*, 1952, 47, 843–52.

600. Sarbin, T. R. Role theory. In G. Lindzey, *Handbook of social psychology*. Vol. I. Cambridge: Addison-Wesley, 1954.

601. Sayles, L. R. The impact of incentives on inter-group work relations — a management and union problem. *Personnel*, 1952, 28, 483–90.

602. Scanlon, J. N. Profit sharing under collective bargaining: three case studies. *Indus. lab. relat. Rev.*, 1948, 2, 58–75.

603. Schachter, S. Deviation, rejection, and communication. *J. abnorm. soc. Psychol.*, 1951, 46, 190–207.

604. Schachter, S., Ellertson, N., McBride, Dorothy, and Gregory, Doris. An experimental study of cohesiveness and productivity. *Hum. Relat.*, 1951, 4, 229–38.

605. Schiff, H. Judgmental response sets in the perception of sociometric status. *Sociometry*, 1954, 17, 207–27.

606. Schonbar, Rosalea Ann. The modification of judgments in a group situation. *J. exp. Psychol.*, 1947, 37, 69–80.

607. Schreiber, R. J., Smith, R. G., Jr., and Harrell, T. W. A factor analysis of employee attitudes. *J. appl. Psychol.*, 1952, 36, 247–50.

608. Scodel, A. and Freedman, Maria L. Additional observations on the social perceptions of authoritarians and non-authoritarians. *J. abnorm. soc. Psychol.*, 1956, 52, 92–5.

609. Scodel, A. and Mussen, P. Social perception of authoritarians and nonauthoritarians. *J. abnorm. soc. Psychol.*, 1953, 48, 181–4.

610. Scott, E. L. *Leadership and perceptions of organization*. Colum-

bus: Ohio State University, Bur. Business Research Monogr. No. 82, 1956.

611. Scott, W. A. Factors affecting the learning of personal values through social reinforcement. *Amer. Psychol.*, 1956, *11*, 407–408.

612. Sears, Pauline S. Levels of aspiration in academically successful and unsuccessful children. *J. abnorm. soc. Psychol.*, 1940, *35*, 498–536.

613. Seashore, S. E. *Group cohesiveness in the industrial work group.* Ann Arbor: University of Michigan, Survey Research Center, 1954.

614. Sechrest, L. B. and Hemphill, J. K. Motivational variables in the assuming of combat obligation. *J. consult. Psychol.*, 1954, *18*, 113–18.

615. Seeman, M. Some status correlates of leadership. In A. G. Grace, *Leadership in American education.* Chicago: University of Chicago Press, 1950.

616. Seeman, M. Role conflict and ambivalence in leadership. *Amer. sociol. Rev.*, 1953, *18*, 373–80.

617. Selekman, B. J. and Selekman, Sylvia K. Productivity — and collective bargaining. *Harv. bus. Rev.*, 1950, *28*, 127–44.

618. Selznick, P. Foundations of the theory of organization. *Amer. sociol. Rev.*, 1948, *13*, 25–35.

619. Selznick, P. *The organizational weapon: a study of Bolshevik strategy and tactics.* New York: McGraw-Hill, 1952.

620. Seward, J. P. Reinforcement and expectancy: two theories in search of a controversy. *Psychol. Rev.*, 1956, *63*, 105–13.

621. Shartle, C. L. Organization structure. In W. Dennis, *Current trends in industrial psychology.* Pittsburgh: University of Pittsburgh Press, 1949.

622. Shartle, C. L. *Occupational information: its development and application.* New York: Prentice-Hall, 1952.

623. Shartle, C. L. *Executive performance and leadership.* Englewood Cliffs: Prentice-Hall, 1956.

624. Shartle, C. L. and Stogdill, R. M. *Studies in naval leadership: methods, results and applications.* Columbus: Ohio State University, Personnel Research Board Technical Report, 1953. Unpublished.

625. Shartle, C. L., Stogdill, R. M., and Campbell, D. T. *Studies in naval leadership: technical report.* Columbus: Ohio State University, Personnel Research Board, 1949. Unpublished.

626. Shaw, M. E. Some effects of problem complexity upon problem solution efficiency in different communication nets. *J. exp. Psychol.*, 1954, *48*, 211–17.

627. Shaw, M. E. Some effects of unequal distribution of information upon group performance in various communication nets. *J. abnorm. soc. Psychol.*, 1954, 49, 547–53.

628. Shaw, M. E. and Rothschild, G. H. Some effects of prolonged experience in communication nets. *J. appl. Psychol.*, 1956, 40, 281–6.

629. Shaw, M. E., Rothschild, G. H., and Strickland, J. F. Decision processes in communication nets. *J. abnorm. soc. Psychol.*, 1957, 54, 323–30.

630. Shepherd, C. and Weschler, I. R. The relation between three interpersonal variables and communication effectiveness: a pilot study. *Sociometry*, 1955, 18, 103–10.

631. Sherif, M. *The psychology of social norms.* New York: Harper, 1936.

632. Sherif, M. and Harvey, O. J. A study in ego functioning: elimination of stable anchorages in individual and group situations. *Sociometry*, 1952, 15, 272–305.

633. Sherif, M. and Sherif, Carolyn W. *Groups in harmony and tension; an integration of studies of intergroup relations.* New York: Harper, 1953.

634. Sherif, M., White, B. J., and Harvey, O. J. Status in experimentally created groups. *Amer. J. Sociol.*, 1955, 60, 370–79.

635. Sherif, M. and Wilson, M. O. *Group relations at the crossroads.* New York: Harper, 1953.

636. Shevitz, R. N. *Leadership acts.* IV. *An investigation of the relation between exclusive possession of information and attempts to lead.* Columbus: Ohio State University, Personnel Research Board, 1955. Unpublished.

637. Shibutani, T. Reference groups as perspectives. *Amer. J. Sociol.*, 1955, 60, 562–9.

638. Shils, E. A. Authoritarianism: "Right" and "Left." In R. Christie and M. Jahoda, *Studies in the scope and method of "The Authoritarian Personality."* Glencoe: Free Press, 1954.

639. Shils, E. A. Primary groups in the American army. In R. A. Merton and P. F. Lazarsfeld, *Studies in the scope and method of "The American Soldier."* Glencoe: Free Press, 1950.

640. Siegel, A. E. and Siegel, S. Reference groups, membership groups, and attitude change. *J. abnorm. soc. Psychol.*, 1957, 55, 360–64.

641. Siegel, A. I. Inter-observer consistency for measurements of the intangible products of performance. *J. appl. Psychol.*, 1955, 39, 280–82.

642. Siegel, I. H. *Concepts and measurement of production and pro-*

*ductivity.* Washington: Bureau of Labor Statistics, 1952. Mimeo.

643. Siegel, S. Certain determinants and correlates of authoritarianism. *Genet. psychol. Monog.*, 1954, *49*, 187–229.

644. Simmel, G. *The sociology of Georg Simmel.* (Trans. by K. H. Wolff). Glencoe: Free Press, 1950.

645. Simon, H. A. *Administrative behavior; a study of decision-making processes in administrative organization.* New York: Macmillan, 1947.

646. Simon, H. A. *Models of man: social and rational.* New York: Wiley, 1957.

647. Skinner, B. F. *The behavior of organisms: an experimental analysis.* New York: Appleton-Century-Crofts, 1938.

648. Skinner, B. F. *Verbal behavior.* New York: Appleton-Century-Crofts, 1957.

649. Slater, P. E. Role differentiation in small groups. In A. P. Hare, E. F. Borgatta, and R. F. Bales, *Small groups: studies in social interaction.* New York: Knopf, 1955.

650. Slichter, S. H. *Union policies and industrial management.* Washington: Brookings Institution, 1941.

651. Smith, A. J. Similarity of values and its relation to acceptance and the projection of similarity. *J. Psychol.*, 1957, *43*, 251–60.

652. Smith, E. E. The effects of clear and unclear role expectations on group productivity and defensiveness. *J. abnorm. soc. Psychol.*, 1957, *55*, 213–17.

653. Smith, M. Social situation, social behavior, social group. *Psychol. Rev.*, 1945, *52*, 224–9.

654. Smith, R. G. and Westen, R. J. *Studies of morale methodology and criteria.* (Res. Bull. 51–29). San Antonio: USAF Training Command, Human Resources Research Center, 1951.

655. Smock, C. D. The influence of stress on the perception of incongruity. *J. abnorm. soc. Psychol.*, 1955, *50*, 354–6.

656. Sorokin, P. A. *Man and society in calamity.* New York: Dutton, 1943.

657. Sorokin, P. A. and Berger, C. Q. *Time-budgets of human behavior.* Cambridge: Harvard University Press, 1939.

658. Sorokin, P. A., Tanquist, M., Parten, M., and Zimmerman, C. C. An experimental study of efficiency of work under various specific conditions. *Amer. J. Sociol.*, 1930, *35*, 765–82.

659. South, E. B. Some psychological aspects of committee work. *J. appl. Psychol.*, 1927, *11*, 348–68, 437–64.

660. Spector, A. J. Expectations, fulfillment, and morale. *J. abnorm. soc. Psychol.*, 1956, *52*, 51–6.

661. Spence, D. P. Vigilance and defense as anxiety manifestations. *Amer. Psychol.*, 1955, *10*, 387.

662. Spicer, E. H. *Human problems in technological change*. New York: Russell Sage Foundation, 1952.

663. Stagner, R. Psychological aspects of industrial conflict: I. Perception. *Personnel Psychol.*, 1948, *1*, 131–43.

664. Stagner, R. Attitude toward authority: an exploratory study. *J. soc. Psychol.*, 1954, *40*, 197–210.

665. Stagner, R. Dual allegiance to union and management (a symposium). 1. Dual allegiance as a problem in modern society. *Personnel Psychol.*, 1954, *7*, 41–6.

666. Stagner, R. *Psychology of industrial conflict*. New York: Wiley, 1956.

667. Stagner, R. Motivational aspects of industrial morale. *Personnel Psychol.*, 1958, *11*, 64–70.

668. Steiner, I. D. and Dodge, Joan S. A comparison of two techniques employed in the study of interpersonal perceptions. *Sociometry*, 1957, *20*, 1–7.

669. Steinzor, B. The development and evaluation of a measure of social interaction. *Hum. Relat.*, 1949, *2*, 103–22.

670. Steinzor, B. The spatial factor in face to face discussion groups. *J. abnorm. soc. Psychol.*, 1950, *45*, 552–5.

671. Stewart, B. M. and Couper, W. J. *Profit sharing for wage earners and executives*. New York: Industrial Relations Counselors, 1951.

672. Stockford, L. O. and Kunze, K. R. Psychology and the paycheck. *Personnel*, 1950, *27*, 129–43.

673. Stogdill, R. M. The sociometry of working relationships in formal organizations. *Sociometry*, 1949, *12*, 276–86.

674. Stogdill, R. M. Leadership and morale in organized groups. In J. E. Hulett, Jr. and R. Stagner, *Problems in social psychology*. Urbana: University of Illinois, 1952.

675. Stogdill, R. M. *Leadership and structures of personal interaction*. Columbus: Ohio State University, Bur. of Business Research Monogr. No. 84, 1957.

676. Stogdill, R. M. and Haase, Katheleen K. Structures of working relationships. In R. M. Stogdill, *Leadership and structures of personal interaction*. Columbus: Ohio State University, Bur. Business Research Monogr. No. 84, 1957.

677. Stogdill, R. M. and Jaynes, W. E. Personal versus situational determinants of leadership. Unpublished technical report, 1953.

678. Stogdill, R. M. and Scott, E. L. Responsibility and authority relationships. In R. M. Stogdill, *Leadership and structures of per-*

*sonal interaction.* Columbus: Ohio State University, Bur. Business Research Monogr. No. 84, 1957.

679. Stogdill, R. M., Scott, E. L., and Jaynes, W. E. *Leadership and role expectations.* Columbus: Ohio State University, Bur. Business Research Monogr. No. 86, 1956.

680. Stogdill, R. M. and Shartle, C. L. *Methods in the study of administrative leadership.* Columbus: Ohio State University, Bur. Business Research Monogr. No. 80, 1955.

681. Stogdill, R. M. and Shartle, C. L. *Patterns of administrative performance.* Columbus: Ohio State University, Bur. Business Research Monogr. No. 81, 1956.

682. Stogdill, R. M., Shartle, C. L., Scott, E. L., Coons, A. E., and Jaynes, W. E. *A predictive study of administrative work patterns.* Columbus: Ohio State University, Bur. Business Research Monogr. No. 85, 1956.

683. Stogdill, R. M., Shartle, C. L., Wherry, R. J., and Jaynes, W. E. A factorial study of administrative behavior. *Personnel Psychol.,* 1955, *8,* 165–80.

684. Stone, G. R. The effect of negative incentives in serial learning. II. Incentive intensity and response variability. *J. gen. Psychol.,* 1950, *42,* 179–224.

685. Stotland, E. *Peer groups and reactions to power figures.* Ann Arbor: University of Michigan, Doctoral dissertation, 1953.

686. Stotland, E., Thorley, S., Thomas, E., Cohen, A. R., and Zander, A. The effects of group expectations and self-esteem upon self-evaluation. *J. abnorm. soc. Psychol.,* 1957, *54,* 55–63.

687. Stouffer, S. A. An analysis of conflicting social norms. *Amer. sociol. Rev.,* 1949, *14,* 707–17.

688. Stouffer, S. A., Suchman, E. A., DeVinney, L. C., Star, S. A., and Williams, R. M., Jr. *The American soldier: adjustment during army life.* Princeton: Princeton University Press, 1949.

689. Stouffer, S. A. and Toby, J. Role conflict and personality. *Amer. J. Sociol.,* 1951, *56,* 395–406.

690. Strodtbeck, F. L. and Hare, A. P. Bibliography of small group research — from 1900 through 1953. *Sociometry,* 1954, *17,* 107–78.

691. Strong, E. K., Jr. *Vocational interests of men and women.* Stanford: Stanford University Press, 1943.

692. Suchman, J. R. Social sensitivity in the small task-oriented group. *J. abnorm. soc. Psychol.,* 1956, *52,* 75–83.

693. Sullivan, P. L. and Adelson, J. Ethnocentrism and misanthropy. *J. abnorm. soc. Psychol.,* 1954, *49,* 246–50.

694. Swanson, G. E. A preliminary laboratory study of the acting crowd. *Amer. sociol. Rev.,* 1953, *18,* 522–33.

695. Tagiuri, R. Relational analysis: an extension of sociometric method with emphasis on social perception. *Sociometry*, 1952, *15*, 91–104.

696. Tagiuri, R., Blake, R. R., and Bruner, J. S. Some determinants of the perception of positive and negative feelings in others. *J. abnorm. soc. Psychol.*, 1953, *48*, 585–92.

697. Tannenbaum, A. S. Control structure and union functions. *Amer. J. Sociol.*, 1956, *61*, 536–45.

698. Tannenbaum, A. S. The concept of organizational control. *J. soc. Issues*, 1956, *12* (2), 50–60.

699. Tarde, G. *Social laws: an outline of sociology.* (Trans. by H. C. Warren.) New York: Macmillan, 1899.

700. Tarde, G. *The laws of imitation.* (Trans. by E. C. Parsons.) New York: Holt, 1903.

701. Taylor, F. W. *Shop management.* New York: Harper, 1910.

702. Taylor, F. W. *Principles and methods of scientific management.* New York: Harper, 1911.

703. Teller, L. *Management functions under collective bargaining.* New York: Baker, Voorhis, 1947.

704. Thelen, H. A., et al. *Methods for studying work and emotionality in group operations.* Chicago: University of Chicago, Human Dynamics Laboratory, 1954. Mimeo.

705. Thibaut, J. W. An experimental study of the cohesiveness of underprivileged groups. *Hum. Relat.*, 1950, *3*, 251–78.

706. Thibaut, J. W. and Coules, J. The role of communication in the reduction of interpersonal hostility. *J. abnorm. soc. Psychol.*, 1952, *47*, 770–77.

707. Thibaut, J. W. and Riecken, H. W. Authoritarianism, status and the communication of aggression. *Hum. Relat.*, 1955, *8*, 95–120.

708. Thibaut, J. W. and Strickland, L. H. Psychological set and social conformity. *J. Pers.*, 1956, *25*, 115–29.

709. Thomas, E., Polansky, N., and Kounin, J. The expected behavior of a potentially helpful person. *Hum. Relat.*, 1955, *8*, 165–74.

710. Thorndike, E. L. *The fundamentals of learning.* New York: Teachers College, 1932.

711. Thorndike, E. L. Reward and punishment in animal learning. *Comp. Psychol. Monogr.*, 1932, No. 39.

712. Thrall, R. M., Coombs, C. H., and Davis, R. L. *Decision processes.* New York: Wiley, 1954.

713. Thrasher, J. D. Interpersonal relations and gradations of stimulus structure as factors in judgment variations: an experimental approach. *Sociometry*, 1954, *17*, 228–41.

714. Tiffin, J. *Industrial psychology.* New York: Prentice-Hall, 1944.

715. Tinklepaugh, O. L. An experimental study of representative factors in monkeys. *J. compar. Psychol.*, 1928, 8, 197–236.

716. Titus, H. E. and Hollander, E. P. The California F scale in psychological research: 1950–1955. *Psychol. Bull.*, 1957, 54, 47–64.

717. Tolman, E. C. *Purposive behavior in animals and men.* New York: Appleton-Century, 1932.

718. Tolman, E. C. There is more than one kind of learning. *Psychol. Rev.*, 1949, 56, 144–55.

719. Tolman, E. C. A psychological model. In T. Parsons and E. A. Shils, *Toward a general theory of action.* Cambridge: Harvard University Press, 1952.

720. Tolman, E. C. A cognition motivation model. *Psychol. Rev.*, 1952, 59, 389–400.

721. Tolman, E. C. Principles of performance. *Psychol. Rev.*, 1955, 62, 315–26.

722. Tolman, E. C. and Brunswick, E. The organism and the causal texture of the environment. *Psychol. Rev.*, 1935, 42, 43–77.

723. Tolman, E. C. and Honzik, C. H. Introduction and removal of reward, and maze performance in rats. *Univ. Calif. Publ. Psychol.*, 1930, 4, 257–75.

724. Torrance, E. P. *Some consequences of power differences on decisions in B-26 crews.* (Res. Bull. 54–128). San Antonio: USAF Personnel and Training Research Center, 1954.

725. Torrance, E. P. Some consequences of power differences in permanent and temporary three-man groups. In P. Hare, E. F. Borgatta, and R. F. Bales, *Small groups.* New York: Knopf, 1955.

726. Torrance, E. P. Perception of group functioning as a predictor of group performance. *J. soc. Psychol.*, 1955, 42, 271–81.

727. Trattner, M. H., Fine, S. A., and Kubis, J. F. A comparison of worker requirement ratings made by reading job descriptions and by direct job observation. *Personnel Psychol.*, 1955, 8, 183–94.

728. Tresselt, M. E. The influence of amount of practice upon the formation of a scale of judgment. *J. exper. Psychol.*, 1947, 37, 251–60.

729. Tripp, L. R. *Industrial productivity: a social and economic analysis.* Madison, Wisconsin: Industrial Relations Research Association, 1951.

730. Trow, D. B. Autonomy and job satisfaction in task-oriented groups. *J. abnorm. soc. Psychol.*, 1957, 54, 204–209.

731. Troxell, J. P. Elements in job satisfaction: a study of attitudes among different occupational and status groups. *Personnel,* 1954, *31,* 199–205.

732. Troxell, J. P. *Employee understanding and teamwork for greater productivity.* New York: National Association of Manufacturers, 1954.

733. Tyler, Leona E. *The psychology of human differences.* New York: Appleton-Century, 1947.

734. Uhrbrock, R. S. Attitudes of 4430 employees. *J. soc. Psychol.,* 1934, 5, 365–77.

735. U.S. Department of Labor. *Techniques of preparing major BLS statistical series.* Washington: Bureau of Labor Statistics, 1954.

736. Urwick, L. *The golden book of management.* London: Newman Neame, 1956.

737. Van Zelst, R. H. Worker popularity and job satisfaction. *Personnel Psychol.,* 1951, *4,* 405–12.

738. Vernon, M. D. *Visual perception.* Cambridge: Cambridge University Press, 1944.

739. Veroff, J. Development and validation of a projective measure of power motivation. *J. abnorm. soc. Psychol.,* 1957, *54,* 1–8.

740. Vidulich, R. N. and Rokeach, M. The integration of multiple sets into a new belief system. *Amer. Psychol.,* 1956, *11,* 376–7.

741. Viteles, M. S. *Motivation and morale in industry.* New York: Norton, 1953.

742. von Neumann, J. and Morgenstern, O. *Theory of games and economic behavior.* Princeton: Princeton University Press, 1947.

743. Waddell, H. L. How to make your workers want to become foremen. In *Practical approaches to supervisory and executive development.* New York: American Management Association, 1952.

744. Walker, C. R., Guest, R. H., and Turner, A. N. *The foreman on the assembly line.* Cambridge: Harvard University Press, 1956.

745. Wallace, W. L. and Gallagher, J. V. *Activities and behaviors of production supervisors.* New York: Psychological Corporation, 1952.

746. Walter, N. A study of the effects of conflicting judgments in the autokinetic situation. *Sociometry,* 1955, *18,* 138–46.

747. Warner, W. L. and Low, J. O. *The social system of the modern factory.* New Haven: Yale University Press, 1947.

748. Warner, W. L., Meeker, M., and Eells, K. *Social class in America.* Chicago: Science Research Associates, 1949.

749. Watson, G. *Civilian morale.* Boston: Houghton Mifflin, 1942.

750. Weber, M. *The theory of social and economic organization.*

(Trans. by T. Parsons). New York: Oxford University Press, 1947.

751. Wegner, N. and Zeaman, D. Team and individual performances on a motor learning task. *J. gen. Psychol.*, 1956, *55*, 127–42.

752. Weiner, M. Uncertainty of judgment as a determinant of conformity behavior. *Amer. Psychol.*, 1956, *11*, 407.

753. Weiner, M., Carpenter, J. T., and Carpenter, B. Some determinants of conformity behavior. *J. soc. Psychol.*, 1957, *45*, 289–97.

754. Weiss, R. S. *Processes of organization.* Ann Arbor: University of Michigan, Survey Research Center, 1956.

755. Weitz, J. Job expectancy and survival. *J. abnorm. soc. Psychol.*, 1956, *40*, 245–7.

756. Weitz, J. and Nuckols, R. C. Job satisfaction and job survival. *J. appl. Psychol.*, 1955, *39*, 294–300.

757. Weschler, I. R., Kahane, M., and Tannenbaum, R. Job satisfaction, productivity and morale: a case study. *Occup. Psychol., London*, 1952, *26*, 1–14.

758. Weschler, I. R., Tannenbaum, R., and Talbot, E. A new managerial tool: the multi-relational sociometric survey. *Personnel*, 1952, *29*, 85–94.

759. Westerlund, G. *Behavior in a work situation with functional supervision and with group leaders.* Stockholm: Nordisk Rotogravyr, 1952.

760. Wherry, R. J. *Factor analysis of officer qualification form QCL-2B.* Columbus: Ohio State University, Research Foundation, 1950. Mimeo.

761. Wherry, R. J. An orthogonal re-rotation of the Baehr and Ash studies of the SRA Employee Inventory. *Personnel Psychol.*, 1954, *7*, 365–80.

762. Wherry, R. J. Factor analysis of morale data: reliability and validity. *Personnel Psychol.*, 1958, *11*, 78–89.

763. Whyte, W. F. *Money and motivation: an analysis of incentives in industry.* New York: Harper, 1955.

764. Wickens, D. D. Studies of response generalization in conditioning: I. Stimulus generalization during response generalization. *J. exper. Psychol.*, 1943, *33*, 221–7.

765. Wickens, D. D. Conditioning to complex stimuli. Presidential address before the Midwestern Psychological Association, 1958.

766. Wickert, F. R. Turnover, and employees' feelings of ego-involvement in the day-to-day operations of a company. *Personnel Psychol.*, 1951, *4*, 185–97.

767. Wiener, N. *Cybernetics; or control and communication in the animal and the machine.* New York: Wiley, 1948.

768. Wilensky, H. L. Human relations in the workplace: an appraisal of some recent research. In C. M. Arensberg, et al., *Research in industrial human relations.* New York: Harper, 1957.

769. Willerman, B. The relation of motivation and skill to active and passive participation in the group. *J. appl. Psychol.,* 1953, 37, 387–90.

770. Willerman, B. and Swanson, L. Group prestige in voluntary organizations: a study of college sororities. *Hum. Relat.,* 1953, 6, 57–77.

771. Wilson, L. Sociography of groups. In G. Gurvitch and W. E. Moore, *Twentieth century sociology.* New York: Philosophical Library, 1945.

772. Wilson, R. C., High, W. S., Beem, Helen P., and Comrey, A. L. A factor-analytic study of supervisory and group behavior. *J. appl. Psychol.,* 1954, 38, 89–92.

773. Wilson, R. C., High, W. S., and Comrey, A. L. An iterative analysis of supervisory and group dimensions. *J. appl. Psychol.,* 1955, 39, 85–91.

774. Wispé, L. G. A sociometric analysis of conflicting role-expectancies. *Amer. J. Sociol.,* 1955, 61, 134–7.

775. Wispé, L. G. and Lloyd, K. E. Some situational and psychological determinants of the desire for structured interpersonal relations. *J. abnorm. soc. Psychol.,* 1955, 51, 57–60.

776. Wispé, L. G. and Thayer, P. W. Role ambiguity and anxiety in an occupational group. *J. soc. Psychol.,* 1957, 46, 41–8.

777. Wolf, W. B. *Wage incentives as a managerial tool.* New York: Columbia University Press, 1957.

778. Wolman, B. Leadership and group dynamics. *J. soc. Psychol.,* 1956, 43, 11–25.

779. Woods, W. A. Employee attitudes and their relation to morale. *J. appl. Psychol.,* 1944, 28, 285–301.

780. Woodworth, R. S. Reenforcement of perception. *Amer. J. Psychol.,* 1947, 60, 119–24.

781. Woodworth, R. S. *Dynamics of behavior.* New York: Holt, 1958.

782. Worell, L. The effect of goal value upon expectancy. *J. abnorm. soc. Psychol.,* 1956, 53, 48–53.

783. Worthy, J. C. Organizational structure and employee morale. *Amer. sociol. Rev.,* 1950, 15, 169–79.

784. Wray, D. E. Marginal men of industry: the foremen. *Amer. J. Sociol.,* 1949, 54, 298–301.

785. Wyatt, D. F. and Campbell, D. T. On the liability of stereotype or hypothesis. *J. abnorm. soc. Psychol.,* 1951, 46, 496–500.

786. Wyatt, S. *Incentives in repetitive work.* London: H. M. Stationery Office, 1934.

787. Yoder, D., Heneman, H. G., and Cheit, E. F. *Triple audit of industrial relations.* Minneapolis: University of Minnesota Press, 1951.

788. Zander, A. The effects of prestige on the behavior of group members: an audience demonstration. *Amer. Mgmt. Assn., Personnel Ser.* No. 155, 1953.

789. Zander, A. and Cohen, A. R. Attributed social power and group acceptance: a classroom experimental demonstration. *J. abnorm. soc. Psychol.,* 1955, *51,* 490–92.

790. Zander, A. and Gyr, J. Changing attitudes toward a merit rating system. *Personnel Psychol.,* 1955, *8,* 429–48.

791. Ziller, R. C. Four techniques of group decision making under uncertainty. *J. appl. Psychol.,* 1957, *41,* 384–8.

792. Zipf, G. K. *Human behavior and the principle of least effort.* Cambridge: Addison-Wesley, 1949.

793. Znaniecki, F. Social organization and institutions. In G. Gurvitch and W. E. Moore, *Twentieth century sociology.* New York: Philosophical Library, 1945.

794. Zobel, S. P. On the measurement of the productivity of labor. *J. Amer. Statist. Assn.,* 1950, *45,* 218–24.

# Index of Names

# Index of Subjects

347